Not Alone in My Dancing

Not Alone in My Dancing

Essays and Reviews

David Rigsbee

Black
Lawrence
Press

 Black
Lawrence
Press

www.blacklawrence.com

Executive Editor: Diane Goettel
Book and cover design: Amy Freels
Cover image: Cover image: "Shadow Dance" by Nicholas Carone. Acrylic on
canvas, 2007. Used with permission of the estate of Nicholas Carone.

Published 2016 by Black Lawrence Press.
Printed in the United States.

For Makaiya

Contents

Introduction

A scholar friend once remarked to me that he had talked with James Merrill just before the his death and heard him say that one of his chief regrets was that the poetry, much honored, had in fact received such scant critical attention. By critical attention, Merrill meant the deeper, contemporary engagement with those who were privileged (or cursed) to be reviewed by poet-critics like Jarrell, Dickey, or Bogan, whose praises and maledictions acquired authority from passionate, sensitive, and sustained involvement.

This is a model I find congenial. The late Allen Grossman, who, despite his weakness for gnarly prose, never lacked for these qualities. He found that talking about poetry becomes more suggestively a model of interpersonal experience—for "conversation," in the all-purpose parlance of the moment, than of analysis. In fact, the conversation initiated by philosopher Michael Oakshott in his seminal essay ("The Voice of Poetry in the Conversation of Mankind")—and the conversation to which Grossman's work subscribes—bears little resemblance to the casual give-and-take of daily verbal exchange. As popularized by Richard Rorty and others, this conversation resounds with a serious, implied collaboration that all by itself outpaces the grim requirements for outcomes. Process, in other words, outweighs product; improvisation replaces what is rote. *Conversation* becomes a term reflecting pragmatism's avoidance of absolutes, and it implies one of the chief articles of belief derived from the rise of Theory, namely that words are always in play—there is no end to what we could say. Hence show-stoppers and "totalizing discourses" played a bad support role in either the spread of fabrication or the promotion of actual meaninglessness, aligning themselves on the wrong side not only of history, but of the truth, insofar as the truth was something that could—*contra* Yeats—be known. Conversation about poetry enacts the intersubjective play that poems ideally bring, modeling how people should interact. Thus poetry, with its improvisations arising from form—and by extension, culture—is inherently, if not manifestly, moral. Talk about poetry is an image of the best kind of human life: aware, interested, careful, passionate, generous.

When I began to work in poetry, unproblematic first-person poems had free rein. This was so whether one descended from Eliot and Yeats, by way of Roethke, or by Pound by way of the Beats and the Black Mountain poets. There were exceptions: followers of Olson and Duncan, for instance, struck east-coasters like myself as rather tired of the subjective "I" poetry and as wanting to extend their poetic selves into myth. But we never forgot—and they never denied—the personal origins of their verse. By the time I had my first job in the early 1970s, the grip of this kind of poetry was beginning to give way to newer strains: neo-formalism, narrative poetry, and most threateningly, the "poetics of indeterminacy," in Marjorie Perloff's clinical phrase. It was said that the new poetries had been cleared for takeoff by bearded technicians who knew more about the theoretical underpinnings of poetry than you or I did. I had seen these experts at work, and I had two simultaneous impressions: first, that abstract knowledge had little to do with the feel of poetry, and second, that the theoretical underpinnings were appropriations from the works of philosophers above and beyond the critics who engaged them. I moreover couldn't resist the conviction that technical mastery wasn't the same as real mastery. It took the poem away from the lover and left it at the feet of the lab technician. Couldn't the same be said of those trained during the regime of the New Criticism, where my kind got its education? Of course it could: criticism has frequently slipped into the lab to ball up its muscle and increase its jargon. But such technical savvy as the New Critics developed and passed on retained a sense of poetry's moment, of its centrality in the literary ecosphere, as an image of a multivalent, ideal use of language. When I realized the extent of the implied claim that theory stood on the shoulders of philosophers, I also sensed the implied conspiracy: there was theory and philosophy lined in opposition to the claims of poetry, especially those claims that relied on poetry's musty prestige. It seemed to me, on the contrary, that poets and philosophers—of the wide-ranging, Continental sort especially—had more in common than those same philosophers did with their supposed avatars, the parvenu critics.

It seemed to me then—and to a large extent it still does—that a philosophical mind is more friendly toward poetry than a theoretical mind. Poets as dissimilar as the late Hayden Carruth, John Koethe, Troy Jollimore, Russell Edson, and Jorie Graham lend support to this notion. I began reviewing because of a complaint similar to Merrill's, that there was too little attention devoted to critical engagement with contemporary poetry. Happily, in the years since Merrill's death, the state of poetry reviewing has changed—for the better, and a generation of young, well-trained and ideologically-savvy (and wary) critics has appeared. The appearance coincides roughly with the rapid acceptance of online literary magazines. I myself decided early on that, poetry being finally metaphysical, it mattered little whether it manifested itself as print or pixels. Many of my colleagues evince a bibliophilia that verges on a fetish: they are all about the feel of the manufactured book, and indeed it is just this love grandfathered in from an earlier ethos to recent decades that has helped raise the production values of small presses. This love notwithstanding (and I share it), I long ago assented to the metaphysical tilt of poetry: regardless of its skin and the materiality of its packaging and delivery, it's essentially language at home in the memory and the heart, not just the chilly bed of the page.

With that in mind, I first published poems online in *The Cortland Review*, a virtual lit-mag that featured audio files of poets reading their work. This was back in the '90s, when having a CD accompany a book was a big deal, and nobody seemed to know how or where the internet and literature might converge. One thing was for sure: academics were already busily moving their work to the web, leveraging its ease and ubiquity for projects fertilized by the Age of Theory. Literati were slower to follow, but the last few years has seen a sea-change in acceptance of online literary start-ups and online versions of established printed journals. When I began reviewing poetry for *TCR*, I hoped for the larger audience that the web promised. Now, some years down the road, what began in journeyman fashion has grown by inertial force alone into a survey. It is not in any way comprehensive or sweeping (except in my generalizations). There are poets I wish I had the opportunity to include here but for one reason or another, could not. But despite the more or less random selection, these poets' works do give us a picture of common concerns, both communal and subjective. There is, for instance, in most cases, a sense that the personal is the reversible coat of the social, construed as political, sociological, or mythical. There is the sense that experimentation has a less unsettling role to play than it did for previous generations. Perhaps it is simply that experimentation no longer has quite the *épater les bourgeois* quality. Even hardcore poets of discontinuity, those who used to be lumped together as "language poets" (after the fashioners of the journal *L=A=N=G=U=A=G=E*) make nice with their more conservative compeers, passing out prizes, amiably blogging, sitting on panels and boards. There is the sense too that confession, washed in the blood of materialism, survives as a proud subjectivity that would not be out of place coming from the pen of Tsvetaeva or Akhmatova, poets who fed their nation when the self was made fugitive by the State. And that means that authenticity is making a comeback, as if, having survived the scrutiny of deflationary critics, it made sense for the singular lyric voice to add its testimony to, and for the soul to witness, the mill of history. I consider these essays and reviews to be acknowledgments of that premise, namely that subjectivity enables the real chronicle: the feel of what it is like.

Since I first thought of doing this collection in 2012, seven of the poets, from the some fifty under discussion here, have passed away. Six of these—Kurt Brown, Jane Cooper, Claudia Emerson, Philip Levine, Margaret Raab and C. K. Williams—were aware of the remarks I applied to their work, now published here. Indeed, the initial publication in each case elicited a response or a series of exchanges—of appreciation, gentle correction, and general, always cordial, reply. The sixth, Carolyn Kizer, had already moved into cognitive darkness by the time her death caught up with her in 2014. She was the first person I ever observed draw a blue pencil from her bag and get to work on someone else's poem. The stern eye and faultless ear were the mirror of her love for poetry. She thought that poetry was the greatest achievement in the world, and writing about these poets over the years, living with their words, attending their fashionings, as well as their failures, I know well what she means.

Betty Adcock's *Slantwise*

The title of course directs us to Dickinson's truth, also to the truth that to be slant is somehow to repose, diagonally, in wisdom. There is in fact so much mojo in the title of her latest collection that we are lathered up with poetic goodness before we even venture into the first poem. Betty Adcock has been writing an agreeable brand of poetry for years and has built a fan base that would make a Republican candidate sit up and beg for buttermilk. In *Slantwise*, she doesn't disappoint. Her poetry is accessible and carefully rendered, and that accessibility begins in part with her subjects: family, origins, place—the tangible durables. For Adcock, these are the massy keys that open up the Mystery. I remember something Martin Amis said about Saul Bellow, i.e., that he wrote surpassingly because he quite simply had the talent to see an inch or two below the surface where other writers found their sightlines returning a blank. Permit me to draw this strange comparison between Adcock and Saul Bellow on the same grounds: she works the surfaces to yield another depth, where insight becomes vision. This was Miss Bishop's great talent, and Adcock shares some of that DNA—although not the habit of producing poems as presentation pieces.

Slantwise takes off with a masterful poem (that is indeed not subsequently surpassed). It begins with a pine needle:

one

needle falling through green
shade, through warp and shimmer of
September sometimes,
end over end will

> turn as if marking the passing
> air with form, circumference
> as of time's real motion or
> the approximation of, say,
> a face.

We have all seen this twisting, dancing slow-motion descent in the movies, of leaf or snowflake, the touchdown that accompanies the sudden realism that gravity is a thing. I am reminded of the delicate tracery of A. R. Ammons, who also tried to maneuver space through voice and who also was obsessed with form. That pine needle, of course, is a compass bearing witness to opposite directions it can't bother to overcome or reconcile:

> being only
> a downed, straitened angel,
> pin and linear argument,
> line of prophecy flattened letterless
> whose browning measure
>   beneath notice
> points both ways at once . . .

Even in its ambivalence, it is the "little" text, ancestor of her poem, that "could shine the way / scripture shines." Bloom used to make a big deal of Ammons' poems as operas of Romantic ideas derived from the solicitation of natural fact (and the misprision of ancestral voices). Adcock's poem is no less a performance whose aim is to find prophetic song in natural theology, though elegy, with its old values, is still the mode:

>   barn swallow
> hawk-snatched from the sky, redtail
> gone, gone by.

If you think the poem is headed in another direction, after its nervous reaction before the hourglass, then you've been keeping up. As is the case with many of the poems here concerned with loss, elegy—that *modus operandi* at absence's crater—is always, finally, personal (and hence requires persons). Adcock meanwhile hears another kind of silence waiting to surround "[t]his present chainsaw-battered/ earth." I don't wish to make heavy weather from this or to suggest that Adcock has gone cosmic. The fact is, she rarely strays from the bandwidth that makes up her Muse's comfort zone, and when you think about it, that can be a good thing. In her case it ensures not only compatibility, but consistency. With their classical ears tuned to the plow's drag and their eyes scanning the sky's dignified monotony, southern poets have always been eco-poets *avant le lettre*. The poet who writes, as Adcock does in "Why White Southern Poets Write the Way We Do," that "a mist can sit in a pasture /like a cloud in a basket" requires little retro-fitting with respect to addressing the plight of habitat. In "1932," she returns to personal origins and the issue of identity with a poem that re-members the parents whose convergent relationship she was in no position to observe, being not yet born, and their sad discontinuity, when her mother died young: "There's nothing / I know except that he lost her, and I lost them both." Strange to say, she has the story, but it's all based on rules of plausibility, thanks to a kindly friend, who is part custodian, part interlocutor:

> One of the family that boarded my mother
> has told me this story: all that I have
> of their early knowing one another.

Despite the brevity of the time allotted them, her parents are the dance, and she—the poet—the point of that dance, insofar as dances can be said by means of the human laser-dot to have a point (and the question is by no means academic, as it goes to the heart of identity, as Yeats, Eliot, and busloads of poets will attest).

> The deer have run from a foreign thing.
> There's no automobile out this late.
> The horned owl complains and does not stay
> where they and their lantern are dancing.

Well, for sure, nothing runs like a deer, and the "foreign thing" from which this one bounds is as much the sculpted presentiment of loss, as of the loss itself. Given only clues to which she is, perforce, second-hand in her honoring, a connector of dots, she nonetheless knows and concludes that "it is enough" to know the minimum. Even from the scant hearsay, she is able to construct images that remain forever meaningful, even if they may be false to minute fact. At once the straight-up victim of history and the timeless pair choreographing their roles, they are true to the love whose object she construes, reveling in her own inadvertent complicity in being alive at all:

> I hear them hum

> along with a scratchy saccharine tune
> from that poverty-ridden American year,
> and she turns and turns in the arms of my father...

If such sticks are no bar to the solidity of memory's house, then our truck with time's backward abysm is seriously on a roll. Taking the other tack—that forgetting achieves special provenance in love—becomes the subject of "No Elegy in November," my favorite poem in this collection:

> They will not turn, the dead,
> from their ashen lace or outward-facing
> stone. Having fled along the route
> all planetary matter takes, they race—
> like light for creation—

> invincibly away.

Notice how that editor-unfriendly adverb, "invincibly," steps forward to make the image, and how "turn" almost but doesn't quite remember "return"—as indeed they do neither. Forgetting, too, becomes love's *ne plus ultra* because it takes on the sacrificial nature by which love enables the person to escape the ego's prison. The poem stands precisely in the place of the loved one, and no elegy and elegy are thereby reconciled:

> Unkindling utterly, you will not turn
> nor send your wildfire spirit back to speak.
> You'll not forgive, nor longer wish, nor see
> how you have left the rest of us to burn.

Notice here how the knowing use of the conventional imagery of burning yields "unkind" to hide in plain sight of "unkindling," meanwhile pointing to its assonance partner, "utterly." To leave—to absent oneself through death—feels at first like a special existential unkindness to the survivors, but time will change this too, collapse all into the poem and into the final word "burn." The point, both obvious and mysterious at once, is that only the living "burn," that living is itself burning. The mystery lies with the thought, a thought that follows hard upon the silence gathering after the final period, that only the living know poetry and that poetry itself reconciles the inert symbol with its burning authors.

It is hardly surprising that Adcock takes special care to marshal and deploy just the right words. You sense, reading *Slantwise*, that this is a poet who scans every word like a quality-control expert training a beady eye on the neutral bric-a-brac of parts of speech coming down the conveyor belt, supplied first by literature, then by colloquial conversants. It is of course of the essence of middle-brow conventionality to remark approvingly on the "connoisseurship" of certain wordsmiths, but if verbal connoisseurship were the end-all, it would be no different than any other fetish. In fact, as we know from "1932" and from "Seeing Josephine," about a visit with the poet's childhood "caretaker/playmate"—"Black Josephine, twelve years old when I was five"—words generate their own reality. And although no less a wordsmith than Eliot warned us that words don't stay in place, we see that in some sense we don't want them to. Their very slippage is part and parcel of the reality they describe:

> my grandmother's whispers, fifty years gone,
> overheard once and meaningless then: *Moll's cabin*
> she said, naming *terrible* and *shame*, naming
> my grandfather's nephew *not gone*
> *till after-sun-up.* Those syllables
> rolling away, lodged blue in the morning—
> glory vine around the well, reddening
> on the tomato plants, a dark weave
> in the cock's crow and the lovely trill
> of the peach orchard's mockingbird—,
> all strung now on frailest memory.

One would think it unnecessary to be a charter member of Club *Le Mot Juste* to submit one's own name to doubt. Why, it's practically Cartesian! But Betty Adcock lines up with Randall Jarrell in believing that the greatest, most telling and judicious (and forgiving) phrase in English is "and yet." She begins with "My real name is Elizabeth, so right for a poet." And yet the name doesn't stick (I knew I was an Elizabeth / but nobody listened") but devolves past "Lizzie" to "Betty":

> How awful
> to be *Betty*, all aprons and frosting mix,
> thirties cartoons, fifties pinups,
> boop-boop-be-doops and va-vooms.
> It's a name for a waitress, a bowler, a clerk
> in a store, a housewife, an apple dessert.
>
> It is never, ever, the name of a poet.
>   And yet…and yet,
> doesn't poetry have to be as tough
> as the woman pouring diner coffee?

Betty Adcock can be as delightful in her lamentations as better-known poets are in the full flower of their wit. She knows how to fetch the domestic detail from the clutter and bring it to the front to emphasize contrasts in value. Her skill-set also shows that she can make the ordinary approach poetry by invoking the metaphor implicit when things take up residence in thought. For example, in "House Cats," she observes,

> Think of the way a cat becomes
> another thing: the inside
> of a small dark place, a momentary ribbon
> of wind, a blade of light. All metaphor,
> that body converts into liquid,
> into mist, into wit, into shine!

While cats connect us to our own mythical ancestry from which they first "came to flicker / at temple fires," the magpie habits of the quilt-maker for "an inspired treachery" in "Told by the Madwoman

Who Stopped Making Quilts" connect us to the artistic impulse. In this poem, the paradox of any creation—from the "garbage" (Akhmatova's term) from which poems emerge, to the snippets (often stolen) from which quilts are stitched—lies in its seeming lack of predetermination:

> I gathered figured fabrics and splashes
> of single color, vivid sparks
> the world threw off. I filled my days
> with baskets of the past, small thievings,
> taking part in life by taking part
> of it to make it art.

And in the end, the made thing in the sum of its accidents is like "a flock of winging birds caught fast / in the blinding net of like-ness and these words." That emphasis on the likeness of things, that search for harmony, belies the arbitrary nature of its origins. It is a vision that still moves the imagination, although poems of disaster—of the *un*likeness of things—also must figure their disfigurements (I am thinking here of poems about 9/11 and the Space Shuttle explosion in this volume) into what is still a pattern. Betty Adcock's new volume takes up such issues without showing the sweat marks of heavy lifting. But that is what it means to be graceful, to have an art that speaks to the felt and to the thought that describes the feeling, then to the words that describe the thought. It's what Wittgenstein meant when he said he wanted thought to be a ladder we climbed and then afterward, satisfied that there was no remainder unac-counted for, we would pull the ladder up after us.

David Baker's *Never-Ending Birds*

The title reminded me to keep John Keats at the ready, as I opened and began reading David Baker's *Never-Ending Birds*, for his light-winged dryad and the destiny to which it beckons seems of the moment. Everyone knows the trade-off: you get something by going rogue on humanity, but you lose something too: the fret, the worry, and all that. And we have to be constantly reminded that it was the fret we loved: it sharpened consciousness. It was what made Stephen Crane, for all his bitterness, so much fun and gave us sibling *lecteurs* a kind of clownish dignity, tweaking the nose of the Universe. In David Baker's restatement of Keats' desire, *per impossibile*, for full-throated ease, his last minute psychological repentance, and icy conformity to what the Russians call the "byt," i.e. Fate's everyday wear, the stresses of an old formula for writing literary texts are redistributed to reveal an attraction to borders:

> I hate the world.
> I have come to the edge.

We don't know which line, from this opening to "Posthumous Man," to prefer: do we like the nature of assertion, even if the assertion is negative? Or do we opt for description, even though the brink to which it brings us implies nothing by way of promise? The border between the civilized and the wild is pretty clear in Keats. In Baker, the same distinction reveals that the border itself, like Arizona, is insufficiently policed. A coyote appears, the very image of the outlaw; then the dog, although "I hold the dog / tight on his leash," spins off. That spinning off is both an illustrative action and a *topic*:

that is, it's a "topos" traversed (and versed). Running away—with all its echoes of freedom, irresponsibility, chaos, and renewal—is what Baker is about here:

> He
> trots off at precisely
> one hundred and
> eighty degrees from where
> we emerged from
> the wood, into the woods.

Where we're going is what we're about, after all. It's not the dog; rather, it's not only the dog, not the coyote, the woods dissolving in darkness; it's the fact that borders bring us always into the presence of change. Borders also nudge us into the recognition that brinksmanship, the teetering temptation at the edge, is as much to the point of human nature as we're likely to get without getting all Platonic (and what's wrong with that?):

> Then come to an edge, where the world
> meets the soul, and the soul knows once more
> what it holds.

As Keats taught us, even if that change means that we are stripped of the trappings of the human—its poetry, for instance, its long chain of species memory—we can't help but hold it before us as it recedes into the next meadow. The Keatsian dog goes feral, and in a way that's more than we would do (who return to our "sole self."), without much dubious encouraging, and in the end it doesn't matter that dog and coyote have erased the difference between them:

> He's loping.
> Now he's running through the field towards the woods.
> By the time he is halfway he is gone.

I'm moved by Baker's intertextual riffing between the oblivion-bound Keats and the speaker on his walk, by the sense that tracking—by which the addition of canines supersedes Keats' now-aging,

totemic fixation on birds—is also a haunting, a site where revenants
are as real as bodies. Moreover, rather than let the soul of his poem
be pulled toward an aesthetic star, Baker has us to understand that
metamorphosis is first and foremost violence. Whether the change
is worth the violence that accompanies it is something neither the
realist nor the aesthetician can answer. That it *is* so, that it bears
acknowledging and has borne it for centuries of thought and feeling, I take to be a kind of tacit yes. Starting with Keats you wind up
with Beckett, but then Beckett was a comedian, if for no other reason
than he wrote for clowns whose bitter laughter answers the *byt* and
oblivion alike. Nor did I fail to notice that the two poems preceding
"Posthumous Man" (the very title sounds like an epoch) features the
poet packing a machete, cutting his way through the nonsense of
nature's "clutch" of "hair stuff" to the poetic sense of things laid by:
"You knew all along, didn't you?" he says to himself.

In "The Rumor," the dismembered body of a deer, hauled up
a tree by a mountain lion, lies scattered now in irrelevant, bloody
particulars beneath a new tree of life, but as the monitoring eye and
mind move along, this natural violence, cruel in its casual determination, becomes a hunger that is itself fed. Then, in the imagination's processor, it becomes generalized, a hunger itself desired in
its full paradoxical formula: the lack equals the hunger, which is an
incompleteness. Yet satisfying the hunger can only be pursued by
more separation. Hence is it that we arrive at the fruitful paradox:
oneness-in-separation. Here is the end of "The Rumor":

> Then the body fell, at
> least in little pieces,
> all around the trunk,
> spattered, strews—
> aureole of deer guts, bitten
> skin, bone. The rest went
> on again,
> in the body of the beast.
> And so—we hear—the lovers
> do this, too.

It's a fine formula that Baker hints at throughout *Never-Ending Birds* and that explains, in a sense, why the birds are everlasting. In the sequence of things, the lack precedes the change, "the twisting rough chaotic thing we crave," as he puts it in "Like the Dewclaw." It's what comes in and organizes all the seemingly random components of the biosphere. Finding the tropes for this Darwinian *muss es sein?*, at the DNA level (so to speak), and acknowledging its force without dread amounts to a kind of praise—neither faint, nor cheesy. It is a fit subject for the pen of any serious poet, and I'm glad to see Baker working its emanations, pathways, entailments, and implications. *Never-Ending Birds* has a cumulative force, and the poet's fascination with the evidence of his own paradox invites the participation of readers, who, like birds, are theoretically endless.

> I look at you
> and find—what? Mythology,
> song. Thus slaughter begins,
> among the bullocks,
> when bees are lost
> and must be raised again.
> The nose is stopped
> (who devised an art
> *like this?*) and the body
> beat until its innards fall.
> Then—with marjoram—
> a ferment. Then the offal
> seeds with bees, and up
> they may be gathered.
> Meaning madness
> is its own mythology.

In spite of the violence of this "seeding," it's the spectatorial nature that poetic description shares with the "spring-wild" horses that is really at issue:

> The eyes go everywhere.
> The eyes are orbital, animal;
> they reflect both worlds.

In reflecting "both worlds," Baker underscores the sense that narratives proliferate and mythologies open themselves to multiple interpretations to the point that, not only does veracity itself come under fire, but the spectator can't be sure of a firm footing from which to see. Loose footing notwithstanding, seeing is here a type of tracking and tracking, in turn, a form of mapping, of description, by which the world becomes—in theory—intelligible. Yet in "Ditches for the Poor," Baker avers,

> Language is, in itself,
> already
> skepticism, writes Levinas.

And it may be that attribution, the use of expert witness, is as close to authoritative utterance as we are likely to get. If so, then poetry is less a matter of establishing the basis of true statements and intelligible descriptions, than of faith. Baker is at heart a realist, in the sense that, while he may find his own descriptions problematic, they map states of the world (and of the imagination's imagistic and formal rendering of that world) well enough. So to find the skeptic lurking in one of his poems bespeaks a hard-won acceptance of poetry as a kind of linguistic pragmatism. No doubt that wasn't his original intention, but it wasn't Keats' either.

The way a Baker poem moves down the page, plowing short-line phrase-terraces, reminds me of poetry's ability to reveal anxiety in the rushing mix of the ordinary. Stevens did it in "Domination of Black" and said it was what he feared. Stevens' anxiety was that strands tighten nothingness to make a rope, but for Baker, as for more recent practitioners of this kind of verse, the past and the present are compact. The self is no longer "my sole self" but distributed like the words, tethered to other soils, briefly convergent in the poem, then subsumed by the whatever of the after-poem, by the unintended consequences of soul-making (to bring us back to Keats). Brodsky said that all that was left in the ensuring silence was literary criticism, hinting moreover that the ensuring silence *was* literary criticism. But in the domain of Darwin, which is our world, the silence at the center is just the poet's eye in quiet surveillance, when in fact all poems are surrounded by the cacophony, not only of other words, but of other noises, for which birds make a suitable emblem transitioning us between intelligible and unintelligible noise. This is a book whose often ventilated-looking poems acquire a weight in excess of the sum of parts. Yes, they deal with nature, but David Baker is no Mary Oliver. The benign is a construct, but so is the poem. Meanwhile, it's a jungle out there, and the machete is its own kind of writing. If the animals could talk they would probably say the same about fangs and claws. On the other hand, even if the lion could talk we wouldn't be able to understand it—so goes the adage. And that is why we need serious poets like Baker.

John Balaban's *Crooked Path*

John Balaban is not for the fashion of these times. He would have us believe, in a world characterized by ever-new peaks of cruelty and curtailment, even as the means of cultural custodianship become more and more readily available and sophisticated that—ready for this?—"only poetry lasts." How you feel about the blunt force of such a claim will probably determine how you approach his new collection, *Path, Crooked Path*. I, for one, find it refreshing, even courageous, that one of our most prominent poets would offer humanistic reassurances and suggest that the continuous, "universal" urge to sing in poems and song makes up by itself an alternative, supplemental vision to the way most of our fellows make and prize meaning. It is equivalent to the rope that runs through culture: continuous, but without any one thread going the distance—yet all hemp. And this without the smudge of sentimentality.

Thus Balaban finds himself equally on the old-fashioned side of a number of other issues: poetry is a universal; the upper reaches of poetic culture are linked to the equivalent stratospheres of other languages and literary traditions. No wonder, armed with a belief system like this, that he has moved with such a sure touch in his Englishing of classical Vietnamese poetry. This set of opinions sets him at least (*pace* Auden) still in possession of the idea that poetry, if it does not improve, at least shows that praise and elegy are twinned instruments performing therapeutic and consolatory duty. That this is not a current attitude, now that the care of the art has been overtaken by scholasticism, would be an understatement. Be that as it may, it fits well with the literary mind and moreover seems—not just on Balaban's say-so—to have some international plausibility.

Path, Crooked Path—the title suggests both an inspired errancy, Heideggerian "poetic thinking," which meanders whither it listeth and the jolts, missteps, forward slogging of a life—is constructed around and moves by way of contrasts. In our postmodern moment, he is to be found among the ruins of the classical world, eastern Europe, or Asia. He is the avatar of Ovid, whose misfortunes at Caesar Augustus' hands landed him the hard durance of geographical and linguistic exile, of Akhmatova receiving the terrible charge to remember standing outside the frozen walls of Lefortovo Prison. Often it is the fact of estrangement—especially by war's dislocations, but often by the common discontinuities of death and relocation—that drives these poems.

Balaban begins his new collection in one of the most reverberant of American cultural grooves: Highway 61, extending that mythic route into the post-9/11 era, where, picking up a mugged soldier returning to base and later encountering a crippled man, the speaker observes, "I knew I was on the right road." And yet the road less traveled ("I turned into a less traveled road") turns out to be a variation of this beaten path, as all converge on desiccated flatland, "old haunts of raiding Apaches" and "Home of President and Mrs. George W. Bush." Compared to this scene, the classical ruins of "Looking Out from the Acropolis, 1989" offers a clarified view ("the New World Order the President / praised that winter"). The distance between the stoical gazes and the roiling events on which they look (Yugoslavia, Chernobyl, the West Bank, etc.) and the villains (Pol Pot, Shining Path, German skinheads) deny the comforts of objectivity. And that is the pity of poetry, isn't it? Sweeping moral judgments can look like mere lyric victories, mere words. Balaban's acknowledgment of the fact is one of the strengths of this book.

Elsewhere this political poet queries his lyrical means for their ability to render convincing representations of change. In "On the Death of His Dog, Apples" he bestows—because this ("too," he might add) is what a poet can do—an Elysian Fields for a beloved animal ("I dreamed for you an upland meadow"). Similarly, in "If Only," which also figures a faithful canine presence, he imagines a scene of ordinary peace:

Dinner simmered on the stove.
Pulling weeds in the garden, she smiled,
hearing his tires pop gravel and clamshells
at their rutted land's long winding end.
The dogs leapt up, loped out to greet him.
This is how it should have been.

Lots of animals, especially dogs, inhabit these pages. The creatures take on fuller-than-usual representation (you sometimes feel the attractive pull of the fable), while remaining blessedly free of the sins but full of the virtues that have often characterized them in the pages of literature. In "Some Dogs of the World," mutts enable street-level perspective for cities and inhabitants that have likewise become part of the cultural and historical imagination (for example, Venice, southern California, Transylvania, Hanoi, Paris):

The whole street's shouting
in Magyar and Romanian. And the dogs scatter.
Later, on the road to Bucharest, a bay horse
lies dead in the roadside gravel
where a Gypsy cart got smashed by a car,
a wild dog yanking at its tail and hocks.

In so politically inclined a poet, the lyric and the historical engage in a mating dance in which each is eventually to be seen in terms of the other. Zigging and zagging between the imagined and the factual, Balaban's work suggests how readily the lyric mode offers alternative narratives to what the pedestrian brain registers. In his poems, the image usually trumps the historical fact—indeed, makes peace with the fact possible. The contest further puts us among familiar distinctions: the stolid past versus the ironic present, history versus memory, the personal versus the civic and the national. Meanwhile, things—the nouns of the poem—take leave of their singularity to become comparable to other things. But if this happens, how can the moralist escape from the wildfire of endless significations? The question is not meant for mere academics. Flaubert's way was to give the nod grudgingly to the bourgeois family from which the artist shrank ("They're right, you know..."), and Tolstoy understood that the slippery over-and-under of poetic rendering degraded truth: he argued for straight-ahead, one-to-one correspondences between word and thing. Else morality had no means of defense. But Balaban's poems suggest other approaches.

Many of the poems touch on professional relationships: other poets, living and dead, put in an appearance (Georgi Borisov, Carolyn Kizer, Hayden Carruth, Ovid, Anna Akhmatova, Stanley Kunitz). Presiding over all is the spirit of the late Roland Flint, James Wright's (another champion of dispossessed humanity) chief acolyte—once larger-than life, now sadly smaller than death. These relationships, by the very nature of their origins in love and influence, tend to erode the distinction between the factual and the imagined, just as they span times and geographies, healing separations, suturing wounds. Balaban's premise seems to be that these webs of association reweave the fabric of commonality (they also assume there is a commonality), so that politics, war, and the mill of history are more easily endured. "The Great Fugue," with its titular suggestion of Baroque praise, puts it this way,

> Easter, and I am playing the *Grosse Fugue*, hearing
> the faded voices of those good people
> who did not want to see me falter, but took me in,
> schooling me in an intertwining of spirits
> that like music can fill a room, that is a great fugue
> weaving through us and joining generations
> in charged, exquisite music that we long to hear.

The cities of the world shift the scale from personal to social, but still bear personal meaning—none more so than Miami, Balaban's previous home. This city of towering promise, made suspicious by the shadow of Cuba, by drug violence, environmental degradation, and generally what Sartre put down as "false consciousness," stands as the subject of a series of elegies. The most arresting of these, "The Butter People," tells of tribes of malleable Golems whose survival equates with their shifting, a quality like butter. In the Miami context, they are sex offenders, the lowest of the low, who melt into the poet's neighborhood in a parody of successful assimilation.

In "Eddie," the poet discloses that a crippled homeless man of the poet's acquaintance has been run over by a red-light-running truck. The poet wonders in a surmise that resets the poem in compassionate recompense, answering the objection that he might be better off dead:

> His legs were a mess
> and he had to be lonely. But spending days
> in the bright fanfare of traffic and
> those nights on his bench, with the moon
> huge in the palm trees, the highway quiet,
> some good dreams must have come to him.

"Remembering Miami" registers the last word: "The damn place never made any sense." The final poem of this section, "Anna Akhmatova Spends the Night on Miami Beach" suggests in spite of— and yet through—the incongruity of the title, a means for poetry to re-achieve the honor of work, by means of the work of a poet as far removed from Miami Beach as is imaginable. But imagination takes it in nonetheless: it is her book (in Kunitz' translation) lying on the beach. She is "she," made palpable beside "these trivial hungers /at the end of the American century."

The note of elegy struck in "The Miami Suite" continues in the final section. The lovely "Varna Snow" recounts Ovid's exile. The poem ends,

> But, now, acacias
> fragrance our evening as poplar fluff drifts
> through imperial rubble. Only poetry lasts.

The last sentence quotes, not Ovid, but a classical Vietnamese poet. The sentiment is not incontestable, as the poet knows, but remembering such a line increases the possibility that art's redemptive claims will be recognized and numbered among humanity's other deeds of power. "Driving Back East with My Dad," his biological (but estranged) connection to Romania, puts the same point in Eliotian terms:

How I wish for a lyric ending to this prose tale:
a moment when the travelers, going in the direction
they faced, found they had already arrived.

Would it be impertinent to note that *Path, Crooked Path* is well written? Balaban's charm is to be at one with his occasions: there is no reaching after effect, although the distances of time and place involved are often considerable. The poems benefit from their sense of incarnate devices and leave the cumulative impression of a life lived and grown into, without the poet's succumbing to the belletristic. Having said that, I will point out that very occasionally he sounds a hortatory note that undermines the textual integrity of the poem. The long, already-mentioned "Looking Out from the Acropolis, 1989," an otherwise engaging poem, seems to tip its hand to find the poet replaced by the stump speaker ("It was snowing in Chicago, snowing on the cardboard huts /of the homeless in the land of the free."). That and the rare whiff of clubby professional familiarity deflate slightly the poet's alternative honor roll of admirable poets. But these are caveats to the final impression of a poet assuming his place on a larger stage, one for whom artistic and moral are aspects of the same *Übertext*. The marginal, the despised, and the low lyrically engage his vision in ways that the mighty, who also always lay claim to forced enlargements of vision, come up short.

The persistent urge still to get it right in the hum of late capitalism is another form of irony, but the poet knows that irony is always, without exception, in the secondary position. Balaban's poems include not only modern and recent wars and atrocities, but American banalities of all sorts, as well as our mounting reacquaintance with the environment, to go along with the seemingly unswerving fate of the dispossessed. In the face of this he brings a consolatory and therapeutic faith in the power of poetry to clarify and unite. God knows it is easy to decry the efforts brought on poetry's behalf when the art is itself under constant siege, not only from censors and ideologues abroad, but from levelers and taste-makers at home. Balaban's poems take cognizance of these, and then resume the effort to push the rope through, which is why he may be our most astute and compassionate disillusionist.

The Geography of Love
Ron Bayes and the Life of Poetry

Does anyone care about the life of the poet? The *death* of the poet: now *there's* a phrase that fits the tongue nicely and that offers a subject worthy of criticism. So Joseph Brodsky, my mentor and friend, observed. As I move into my seventh decade, I begin more and more to raise my hand to answer the first question this way: *I* do. After all, the first phrase comes to take on more resonance than the second, which seems to me a detail, a marker that merely ensures that the elegy, unlike its subjects, will never die.

I am rather interested in lives (few though they be—and even less fit, usually) lived in the light of poetry, lived as if they were themselves poems. Oscar Wilde asserted that he was his own best work, that the quality of his life—his friendships, loves, interests—constituted a *magnum opus* to be put at the head of his works. Indeed, it is one of the interesting features of the literary life that if you construe *corpus* as metaphysical body, the career of the other—social and existential—body becomes its contrasting term. Nor is it unthinkable to turn the telescope the other way around and suggest that the person was the first work of art, the poetry—the made things—arriving to corroborate evidence, as it were, to this fact. At one end of the spectrum we have Mallarmé, who famously opined that everything existed to wind up in a book. At the other end, we have his contemporary and comparable aesthete, the Divine Oscar, cheerfully inverting Mallarmé and finding that the book—every book—winds up in a life. In other words, the body of work includes the body of the poet. In the standard Western view, corpse gives way to corpus: the latter takes over, a deputized marker for the departed person. But Ron Bayes follows another influential strain of discourse that springs from Eastern traditions (by way of Pound, among others), in preferring celebrations of friendship among the living, to elegies for the dead. The emphasis is on the lived, rather then the mourned: presence over absence. In this respect, Bayes' aesthetic coincides with that of his old Northwest friend, poet Carolyn Kizer, who similarly had little truck with the worship of the past, feeling that the elegiac imperative, so prevalent in English poetry, even took on a tinge of necrophilia, if looked at, squintingly, at the end of a hard day.

This west coast aesthetic corrective, in addition to looking beyond what its practitioners understood to be the day-to-day assumptions of the eastern Establishment and its merely made-over Euro-principles, could also claim a salutary entailment is representing a healthier outlook. It was just such an outlook that came to bloom in the San Francisco Renaissance and established a considerable foothold in that artistic, east-coast set-aside, Black Mountain College. Thus Bayes and Kizer, two poets transplanted diagonally from Northwest to Southeast at critical times in their lives, participated in an extension of Emerson's switch from peering through the lens of time to looking through the lens of space. The benefits spoke for themselves. A young(ish) country needed to consider its present, for it had no (or scant) deep past with which to underwrite its national aesthetic project—with exceptions noted for that of non-English-speaking indigenous peoples (a special linguistic case we are just coming to terms with) and the prehistoric, pre-linguistic past—the province of naturalism(s) common to westerners like Gary Snyder and William Stafford (another Oregonian). Hence is it that we wind up with a way for poets who spring from small towns to self-create, inscribing their anonymity on the face of the land and thereby rendering both the land and themselves known and knowable, felt, and subject to experience.

In spite of its emphasis on the present and a desire to find there the surprise of the new and fresh (Creeley) the metaphor that we are ourselves a work, toiling in tandem with our productions, is an old one, and I will not rehearse its history here. But I wish to bring this to the forefront because it is certainly germane to the career, at once rich and elusive, of Ron Bayes.

While he has as undoubtedly set his imprimatur on the face of North Carolina poetry through the *St. Andrews Review*, The St. Andrews Press, and *Cairn*, his poetry is as hard to find as it subjects, which are often pins on a map of the less-travelled: Umapine, Laurinburg, Iceland, Port-au-Prince. Others—Philadelphia, Tokyo, Montreal—need not justify their registry, but they belong to the same personal archipelago of meaning, places that by virtue of their associations participate in the same kind of personal mapping, of punctuating vacancy—of space, of meaning.

These places are not simply the lot of any poet in motion across both landscapes and timescapes, for place, in Bayes' economy, also acquires an emotional dimension, a metaphysical perspective, an historical rooting and routing. In the context of Modernist poetics—and context is ever important with a poet as allusive and wide-ranging as Ron Bayes—place suggests locations resonate with more than their pasts. To the first-time reader, some of the places may present only the credentials of their unfamiliarity (Umapine), but the poet plays a trump card that Stevens made famous in "Anecdote of the Jar," namely, the *invention* of significance—literally the placing of a jar, itself resonant as a container, urn, reliquary of valuables, of memorial contents or of general provisions. Around this dual-action invention—one relating to the past (memory), one to the future (providing), the new is mapped, and a net is cast. When one place becomes two, a real map begins to take place, is drawn, and before you know it, a world itself comes into view. As with place, so with time. The places of the imagination show what it was like to be alive on this date, with those memories, these particular acts. They merge into the larger time of history and event, so that the intersection of times in the continuum—not unlike Olson's field of composition—is like the intersection of things in space.

Meaning is a made thing, and the significance of meaning (if you will) is that it not only reaches into two dimensions simultaneously, it also mediates between public and private. Moreover, meaningful speech has the effect of truing public discourse at the same time that it gives private utterance equal footing, so that it doesn't require the sugar-rush of sentimentality or the misplaced application of sincerity to get underway. If our poets are anything, they are about a celebration of the subjective, a way for private discourse to shed its obscurities and join with language users in mutual testimony, which is also, I might as well add, an act of communion.

Bayes is a meaning-maker, tying together disparate locations and persons, anecdotes that time would have otherwise blown away like paper cups, snippets of commercial verbiage as easily as stony riddles, with the zeal of a Talmudic scholar who relishes the lacunae of a sacred text—even one that deprives him of the immediate gratification of received meaning—as surely as the surety of the sacred words actually before his gaze. Take a look at the concluding section of "Not as a Foolish Man":

> But oh the Places I love now. And how I
> would return to you, to you
>
> With the absolute same passions,
> the desires somewhat clearer,
> & the great hopes still, and still
> not as a foolish man.
>
> One of you (colder even than Montreal)
> I feel as a sudden lover to;
> old Reykjavik. Then, quick, hot
> Old San Juan and wild Tokyo.
>
> Why,
> why cling to the geography of love?
> I do not know, Dear Friends—
> or why I'll hang before I quit.

Bayes' method of poetic documentation takes its cue, of course, from the *Cantos*, but also from Olson's *Maximus*, Dorn's *Gunslinger*, and, to my ear, the poems of Paul Blackburn. Bayes' lovely sense of how a poem takes up residence on the pages through collages and quotations add the sense—worthy of Picasso, Duchamp, and Cor-

nell—of contemporaneity. They do so without failing to give the
sense that incidents, meetings, and events constitute the exterior
phenomena of our lives, and oftentimes these verge on a phantasmagoria that is at once history and fairy tale—which as soon as the
word hits the page, it is. The epic *Umapine Tetralogy* is rife with the
documentary evidence of its own coming into being, and it feels, in
retrospect, a dream of the quick and faithful mind surveying landforms from some perspective high in the air, before plunging into
savory—or asinine or humorous—particulars. But as geography,
the tetralogy and many, if not most, of Bayes' works take note of
where they are in a way that bespeaks the self-exile's desire to seed
numerous locations, irrespective of history or reputation, to see what
will take root. That is, they seek to take root within the imaginative
space of the poem, just as it has presumably already moved beyond
intimation in the imagination of the poet.

The Poudian-Stevensian-Emersonian charge (if such can be
imagined) to push back the darkness by both shoring ruins and
naming places goes, for Bayes, under the name of "the geography of
love." By this pesky and careworn-sounding term, we should understand what Richard Rorty, quoting Paul Tillich, called "the symbol
of ultimate concern," an auspice at all times available to poets, who,
while they may share little in terms of tradition (indeed, they may
be members of incompatible or warring tribes) nevertheless partake
of the craftsman's knowledge that "[a]ll human relations untouched
by love take place in the dark." In this observation, Rorty saw love
as compatible with his neo-pragmatism, in that love and (his) philosophy were both manifestations of the will to progress. While it
is debatable that poetry is progressive, it is certainly beyond debate
that love is as much a motive as it is a theme.

Love signals the primacy of the subjective, and "geography of love"
indicates a world both refashioned and renewed. It is like proposing
an idea that has recognizable cognates: the idea is original by virtue
of its singularity, but it comes from pieces that we know (and we
know that the poet knows that we know). Bayes' "geography of love"
is in another sense, his constellation of poems, and yet by specifying geo-graphy, he locates his points of ultimate concern, not in the

heavens, but on the surface of the earth. The heavens can take care of themselves, while we must find our way about. Bayes suggests that we *make* it more than we find it, but it is no less to be revered for that. More than any other poet I know, Bayes gives the uncanny sense of posthumous utterance: he walks among the artifacts of a serviceable everyday world he has imagined and invited us to imagine with him. He is one of those poets whose work enlarges you by getting you to speak in a vocabulary you didn't know you would use until, trying it, you found it to be both fitting and true. He is one of the geographers who has shown us how maps are made, how they overlap, how they trace memories, and propose destinations, all under the sign of the "ultimate concern." It doesn't matter whether it was Philadelphia or Laurinburg; what matters is that one loved it there, in that delicacy of intention that every artist feels and that Bayes brings to the point of exquisite revelation. Bishop, a poet of quite a different temperament than Bayes, had it right when she wrote, "More delicate than the historians' are the map-makers' colors."

Laure-Anne Bosselaar's
A New Hunger

It is no unkindness to say that irony is the compliment poetry pays to history. When the impulse to sincerity is pickled in experience, it becomes ripe for equivocations, puns, rhymes: all devices of ambivalence. *A New Hunger,* Laure-Anne Bosselaar's third collection, gets under way with the long-ago family catastrophe readers will recall from her first English collection, *The Hour Between Dog and Wolf:* her banishment, as a young girl, to a nunnery. That parents connived in such an unpleasant deed is something that has been the object of a life's contemplation. It is not entirely unlike the situation of political writers who find the tragic suddenly fallen within their grasps long before the maturation dates that await all. Thanks to swift injustice, careers are unlocked, enabled.

The poet of *A New Hunger* tracks the continual aftershocks of that seismic event in brimming speech ("you went about your life without me"), ambivalent recollections ("that is all he needs—to remember the same"), and plain old wordplay:

> that's what I sold my mother's
> bed for. The one she died in. Sold it
> for a song.
> > ("Garage Sale")

Yet her intelligence is such that she is in fact ambivalent about ambivalence, conflicted about multivalence, and hesitant about repetition, so often outed as mere sameness. After all, love makes us rethink the drag of duplications, for acts of love are, more often than not, acts of repetition. To step away from love's rituals is to become, in a sense, a willing participant in time, which, like a mighty river, swirls into history. Yet, just as the impulse to tame the clock doesn't stop, neither does the act of making poems. Considering that painstaking craft invites the very pain it seeks to control, Bosselaar registers the distance between her abandonment and the present with consistency and patience. Hers is a wound that figures in the gap between Europe and the U.S. All the same, way more time passes than does space, but since neither is finite, this passing is like a great treasury expenditure, not something petty, and not easily dispensed.

The 14-page opening poem, "Against Again," is a backwards-looking memoir, in places reminiscent of the open-ended journalings of Charles Wright, but as willing to ride on the back of narrative moments as lyric ones. There are no under-clued surmises here, but queries of origin that grow less solicitous over the course of the collection. The narrative marches even-shouldered with the lyric, often overtaking it. Finding a sustaining love is like locating a narrative, an unfolding where ironies are subject to supervision, if not control.

A Proustian, Bosselaar keys on smells and tastes: "The only thing that clung to me was her perfume / the first time she left me at a nunnery." Food is highly allusive. The atmospheric change from Chanel to cabbage provides the equivalent of a Fall, and the journey from swallowing to digestion becomes a grim, ironic pilgrimage. The European's preferences also run to trains—trains and buses, not cars. "Against Again" begins not at the nunnery, but on a New Jersey commuter train, on which she is aware of a man whose presence offers "transitory intimacy"—a thought not easy to defer or dispel. Indeed, it raises the question: can adult relationships replace what the parents took away? It's a question that trails many of the poems in this book. Working the Old World/New World contrast, she puts us in mind of an older (and therefore literary) mindset that poets of my generation—with notable exceptions—had moved away from. And forget that we benefited from the Emersonian bargain, whereby what we lose in time's depths we gain in driving around space's exterior vastness.

The feeling of sumptuous attention of Bosselaar's poems derives in part from this familiarity with discarded perspectives that for her calls up a non-disposable world accessible at all points as literature. This is what Robert Calasso speaks of when he writes of the gods that go into hiding in poems. And yet, the presence of the Old World and the old gods does more than haunt the contents of Bosselaar's poems. It is, in Linda Gregg's great phrase, "like being alive twice" to be able to ride the Jersey trains and speak of wimpled nuns, linden tea, and "barrenness." For her, riding and reading ("I don't open the book I hold in my lap: I'm reading faces / around me"), the face and "facing" register as both reading and, later, "counting" (how near we also get to *countenance*).

Not surprisingly, children prompt her attention and wake the ombudsman within, to say nothing of the present mother and forsaken child. Thus she moves from casually observing children to the thought of *her* mother. The move is both cinematic and, once reset, memoiristic. The mother's curls are "seductively set," a snare. The nun's faces, by dour contrast, are "without curls." "I spent my childhood clinging to an image of her face." This admission piles disillusionment on top of abandonment, and at a moment when "illusions" are favored because they "serve" (just as, ironically, handkerchiefs are one of the few personal items permitted by the good sisters because they also "serve").

As for the child, its value is that it stands to be fully vested—a presupposition her own parents denied in orphaning her. So in extending this status to other children, she does so to herself, retroactively, in acts of tentative (at first) and thoughtful (later) self-investment. It is auto-restitution, late justice, and Keatsian poetic healing all in one. Questions remain. Would one really want the work of a life, an artistic work, to be set in light of such abandonment? Presumably not, but the stone that troubles the living stream also bends the water, giving access to its deeps. The Sibyl's voice is indistinguishable from that of the inner girl. The small child's presence puts us in mind of the pressures under which innocence operates:

all she can see are legs. For her,

this train is packed with pants, belts, zippers, and shoes—

and look at her face: already courageous, defeated,
and old with it.

We are reminded here of Bishop's "In the Waiting Room," a poem
about discovering that the very self is one of *them*. In a larger sense, it
is about belonging and finding one's place in a world become Dick-
ensian by virtue of denying us more conventional ways and means.
Something of Miss Bishop's sensibility also haunts these poems in
their questioning of origins (home), their Jack-and-the-Beanstalk
kids among adult knees, and in the bravado—the reverse of the
lament—of losing. Although Antwerp's streetcars become New
York's and New Jersey's commuter trains, the title itself ("Against
Again") indicates both against one more time and against repetition altogether.

Cycling through narcissistic parental indifference, the poem
moves to the default mercy of nuns: "The only thing that clung to
me was her perfume / the first time she left me at a nunnery." When
this admission sounds, it's clear we're not on home turf anymore,
what with the "thick-soled sandals," the beatings on the backs of
heads ("they didn't leave bruises"). Although—

> Nun's faces replaced mother's: thickset in wimples
> so tight the wrinkles and jowls were pushed forward
> like the skin of old fruit—
> she survives in the wool-gathering of time and the crooked halo of
> memory:
> some nights, I kissed myself in a mirror. I swear,
> once, the mirror breathed Chanel No. 5
> back into my mouth.

It's curious that Bosselaar figures identity by way of first taste and
smell, then of swallowing, which is to say ingestion and incorporation, parodies of the Catholic's transubstantiation of the Host. The
nuns' cuisine ("Boiled fish and rutabaga. Stewed horsemeat.") provides the fare, but it's by swallowing that we get to the reality principle: you swallow, even incorporate, even perhaps transubstantiate,
but you are not nourished. The fact is foreshadowed by the "sixty
four / pairs of ravenous eyes" that greet her at her first arrival.

"She was beautiful, violently beautiful and blonde," she remarks with great distance, greater injured love at this narcissistic diva. Ironically, her mother's laughter is remembered as "a child's." A moment of accidental awkwardness has the effect of canceling the mother's decorum and of foreshadowing the child's own future career:

> and hours later, I had spilled ink on her rug.
> *Ink.*

> *

> And it comes back to me: how *adoringly* I'd
> breathe—

> in sync with her—

> the few times she held me.

The complicity of the priests and nuns with the mother (and father) extends to the regard for their apparel: "Mother wore a Brussels lace veil and elbow-length gloves / closed by long rows of tiny black pearls like glimmering rosaries." The mother's emphasis on decorum and refinement is echoed by the father's indifference: cologne and Chesterfields are more his style. When they send postcards from distant places, they don't bother to write a message, just signing,

> with only Father's four, spiked, green-inked letters
> "*Papa*" under her blue "*Maman*"—

At her father's funeral, the mother whispers how adoringly the priest's alb had been embroidered, how delicately refined it was. Following the episode of the spilled ink, the poet mills the year through its mitigations: charity work ("knitting socks / for prisoners and the poor"), outdoor laundry and the intimation of some great cleansing. At this point—summer—the poet returns us (or rather, we are pitched back) to the train, the man still sitting next to her:

> and I suddenly
> long for that hand, yet just as suddenly need it to close,
> to flip back, palm down, and stop being so intimately
>
> open there, vulnerable and foreign.

The desire for "transitory intimacy" to reassert itself is interrupted
by the present, for this moment carries with it all of travel's instability, even a degree of vagrancy. At the same time, in coming back to
the present, a contradiction looms, as the transitory and intimate
are naturally opposed too ("I'm sick of this train, the fleeting faces").
The lack of sustained intimacy has elevated the transitory variety
beyond its value—so she recoils in protest to her own emotional
pragmatism in countenancing such an "unavailable" intimacy in the
first place. The poems ends with the equivocations of desire:

> A transitory nearness,
> a transit story.
>
> And always this hunger,
> an exhausted longing—
>
> the wait and the weight.

One of the great questions for poets is precisely *how* can we forgive
our parents? It was a key question for poets of the previous generation (Schwartz, Lowell, Plath, Kunitz, Roethke). Must one somehow
accept their neglect as a kind of negative empowerment, something
like the family version of a negative theology?

The middle piece to *A New Hunger* is a crown of sonnets ("The
River's Mouth, the Boat, the Undertow"), the mirroring form of
which connects the child's truth (the suddenness and finality of
loss) with the adult version, which, unlike the child's, gives way to
rationalization.

Each sonnet is both mirrored within (tercet-quartet mirroring
tercet-quartet—often taking the form of before/after, proposition/
fact) and linked without, the last line providing the first of the suc-

ceeding poem. The linkages are therefore associational: a blizzard leads to a lover dead in a skiing accident, the sounds of birds to actual birds, clouds to *les merveilleux nuages* of Baudelaire, and from there to a series of poems on poets and writers: Baudelaire, Crane, Lorca, Gide, Goethe. And as the garland is traditionally circular, this one begins and ends with the phrase "letting go." Considering the instances of clinging in the preceding narrative of "Against Again," letting go is indeed the imperative that hangs over the whole collection. Whether it can be accomplished is another matter. There is some reason to believe that there is progress not in letting go but in the ambivalence that such an imperative creates and that is represented by the divergent aims of the first two sections. At least we don't succumb to the lure of false "closure" (a notion that finally seems to be reaching the status of a cliché).

The first sonnet concerns losing (a balloon). Readers will be reminded of Bishop's "One Art" in these lines:

> Too soon you're the one saying: It's *only* a glove,
> dog, lover or job—as you move on, just one of the many
> bending over another job, dog, love. But the balloon:
> how suddenly it was gone.

Loss is in some sense a vagueness placed on fact, a lack of specificity, in need of correction. Thus we learn "The Czechs have a word . . . for what hurts exactly ('litost')." In a moment of deflationary candor she muses, "Would a word make such pain more tolerable? / As if language could help." But it is after all one of the broad premises of *A New Hunger,* that poetry helps control pain. Allen Grossman says it contributes to the management of violence, which is to leverage a new proposition out of an old. Bosselaar's version stands with the older perspective.

Standing in the shade of these big production pieces, the third section of lyric and occasional poems might seem slight, but chalk that up to the power of contrast. With their humbler scale, these poems, some formally inclined, work their way through the needful particulars with commendable understatement and graceful implication. Picking up what we might call the carryover value of Bos-

selaar's aesthetic—the strength derived from the wound—we find
ourselves immediately in familiar, if wistful, territory. "Stillbirth"
finds the speaker overhearing—and turning as if in answer to—the
name of an unborn child ("I was told not to look"). In "Elegy," she
recalls the special gap that figures her exile where, "crossing a summer meadow in Belgium...I found nothing there I wanted to bring
back." The forced incorporation of the central poem "Swallowing"
picks up a thread begun in "Against Again":

>   *Swallow that,* the mother orders, *swallow that*
> *now.* Child begging, *don't leave again, don't go.*

>   And the mother: *Swallow that.*

> From swallowing she proceeds to swallowing's inverse: singing.

>   *Sing child. Sing louder.*

>   And the child does. Becomes good at it.

>   Bellows hymns, swallows more....

That singing and poetry come from the place of forced hosannas
is but one of the ironies this poem is meant to underscore. The don't-
leave-me theme that is her starting point becomes but tinny bathos
in the "torch songs..." blasted on "the radio...deaf now to sirens."
Yet this theme that sits at the source of her song finds over the years
that it is in no position to emphasize its own exceptionalism. The
plea not to be left behind (she references Jacques Brel's "*ne me quitte
pas*" in "The River's Mouth, the Boat, the Undertow") is cancelled
out of existential exhaustion.

The trenchant "Garage Sale" examines another facet of poetic
origins related to "Swallowing." Here the suspicion that the mother's
bed was a sexual, specifically, luxurious one—for which the poet/
child was abandoned—finds the poet engaging in lyric payback.
Poetry is, after all, a song—with a pun on the idea of both a saving
song and of a worthless one (by the bye smuggling in a swipe at com-

modity thinking). Beyond these, the song is one "of yearning like an orphan," who is rewarded, if she *is* rewarded, in exchange for her music. The book as a whole is suffused with an orphan's yearning, which is both powerful, aggrieved, and inexplicable.

A place of dissolution and transmutation, combining her chief metaphors is the theme of "On a Bench by the Hudson." Far from succumbing to the spectator's passivity, this poet finds her objective correlative ("my pulse a swirl"), which is both her transformed experience and the image of "my journey away from my country." It even—in its sweeping abandon—carries her into the perilous present, as we recall that part of Ground Zero, presumably within eyesight of this, was bounded and held by the Hudson. As illuminations go, this is supreme: that smallness, evanescence, ambivalence warring with affirmation, that understanding of the *lacrimae rerum*, is present in the taste of "sweet salt." Such a Wilburian moment, always the realist's *desideratum*, exists in subjectivity as well as in nature, but it is seldom that one can corner its mercury, but the phrase "that wide-hipped mother of a river" from the next poem shows the poet closing in.

Forced praise gives way to real praise in "Awe," a poem whose title will remind some of Emerson's teaching that the disposition to awe ("surprise") was the American trope *par excellence*. In "The River's Mouth, the Boat, the Undertow," she had reminded us that what we fear most is "not death, but to lose wonder". The capacity for awe is thus generative, another version of the capacity for self-renewal:

> rocking I loved in the Scheldt river
> a half century ago
>
> —how I needed that river too—
>
> already then longing to be taken away,
> taken along, yearning for
>
> a mother, a place, anything to belong to...

Again, Bosselaar locates desire with belonging, which also entails recognition, much in the way that Bishop does in sober affirmation, but lightly edged with cautions.

In "Night," she has moved many spaces beyond the events that make up her life and, *mutatis mutandis*, her career. Poised in the darkness, the questions come down to the one we always present to the darkness: *What are you?* While this night brings on its ritual solemnities, its sounds and memories, her own prayer for her children contains the directive to "Wrap a wing around the orphan."

On Edgar Bowers

Born in Georgia, educated at Stanford (where he studied with Yvor Winters), Edgar Bowers brought a severe classicism to his poems. His verbal compression, allusive surfaces, and learned demeanor all contributed to the impression that his difficulties were, broadly speaking, those of a literary culture, not of an individual poet. At the same time, one senses that the layered artifice provided the buffer against a chaos not necessarily or only tied to culture. His poems are hard-won gains—or perhaps stand-offs—in which the discipline of poetry as much constrained the poet's freedom as it did subdue intractable subject matter. But as Bowers knew, the poet's freedom is illusory, and in catering to it, he runs the risk of entertaining the very chaos he would elsewhere avoid.

A soldier in Germany in World War II, Bowers drew upon European settings and characters for some of his most important poems. Typically, the locales and the characters who appear are chosen because they are associated with historical themes. For instance, in "The Prince," a German Junker faces the consequences of his own militaristic milieu ("I come to tell you that my son is dead. / Americans have shot him as a spy"), while in "From William Tyndale to John Frith," the English religious reformer Tyndale, awaiting his auto-da-fé in Holland, writes to his most loyal disciple, who is himself in prison in England awaiting execution by fire. In "Aix-la-Chapelle, 1945," a soldier observes the ironic conjunction of the French south's "sensual calm and beauty" with "the dragon's gore / From off the torn cathedral floor," which "Forces [the] mind's dark cavity." At the moment when such ironies reveal reality's dual face, Bowers' poems remind the reader that, imperfect and provisional as it is, culture enables the making of a poetry replete with layers to track and constrain, in the accents of literary device, the force of events where no special pleading can hide the layers of bones from the layers of history. All the same, Bowers was aware of the "Orphic futility" of arresting evil with a name, as if, in that futility, he must always be seen to measure his own complicit participation. At the same time, it is probable that casting the problem of culture's futility in terms of good and evil fails to do justice to the nuances involved. A dysfunction suddenly perceived as systemic (the modern intellectual's typical stance toward the question of culture and history) signals less something that had been previously overlooked than ongoing rhetorical maneuvers designed to serve power rather than truth. Since the poet shares the same tools as the rhetorician, indeed, of the tyrant, his only recourse is to declare his faith in the provisional nature of truth, even as he holds objectivity as a virtue.

In Bowers' work, objectivity is manifest in a position taken relative to issues of style, and thus style—and with it prosody, form, and tone—becomes equivalent to staking out a moral position. This was the argument Bowers' teacher Yvor Winters used to excoriate insufficiently formalized poets. At all points, the poet's work stands upon matters of moral import, so this argument runs, extending all the way down to the last philological or philosophical implication of a word. Otherwise, not only is chaos come again, but language is an unfit instrument of belief (Eliot, for one, wrote passionately for its fitness but accepted its unfit condition as our portion of incompleteness). Otherwise, the sophisticate, already managing with glozing words to accommodate violence, cannot distinguish between moral actions and "behaviors" and, hence, cannot apply the Orphic name to his humanity since that humanity is indistinguishable from the bestial—not edified by discernment, but sunk by cleverness.

Clearly, such burdens harry poets and in so doing find out their weaknesses. In Bowers' case, sheer compression sometimes drove the poet into the sort of obscurities that arise when one attempts to reduce many things to one thing, a side-effect of which is to render the poet sonorous and long-robed. But a poet of Bowers' accomplishment was, of course, as aware of his own dangers as he was of the contents of his wallet, and the impasse that stood to block his poem's ascent of Parnassus sometimes became its own theme ("O for that madness again / Where illusion spoke Truth's divine dialect!"). Not for Bowers the naive identifications of a Whitman or the enticements of free verse. His "classicism" consisted not only in self-restraint, but in self-awareness, a mode of consciousness with respect to itself with which Baudelaire opined the death of poetry. For Bowers, poetry was, in that sense, already "dead," but as in recent negative theologies, its death was all the more reason to keep the writing hand in trim. After all, words' emergence across the steppe of the page enacts history ritualistically, and although they can never pull off the big tricks:—to end death, to expose all of cruelty's disguises, to edify beyond the patron's reach—they can give more than a momentary stay since their highly wrought productions (i.e., poems) also exist to bear the traces of incarnations—in suitably secular garb, of course—that translate the old notion of a "passion" into the modular twists and turns of language. These let passion go—just as metaphor itself does—by other names.

The Day Brodsky Died

I was walking across the creaky floor of Root Hall at Hamilton when a colleague stopped me and said, "I just heard that Brodsky died. That was the poet you translated, wasn't it?" The question itself betrayed both the fault line between academic and literary domains and the solicitude we all feel at the palpable loss of another. I had seen Joseph at a reading the previous fall in New York. He looked at me, scanning the changes he saw and declared, "What an improvement!" It was the first time I had seen him in years. Following an intense period from the moment of his arrival on these shores in 1972, until the summer of 1977, we had been in constant touch with visitings, enthusiastic dinners, road trips in his AMC Matador with Gucci interior, epigrammatic correspondence, lengthy phone calls. But three times that number of years had passed, since a falling out over a woman: I had presumed to date one of his exes. In those years, his Roman-candle fame had spread unstoppably, as had his heart condition.

It was a day like the day I lost my brother to suicide: snow everywhere. The sun, as the Prince in *Romeo and Juliet* said, "for sorrow, [would] not show his head." Unlike that day, I knew this one was coming. We all did, even the Nobel Prize committee, which hinted at the precariousness of his health, awarded him the prize at 47. And which he was no doubt destined to win at some point, had the Fates not warned all who were listening that such a future was very possibly subject to denial. Looked at another way, he was eight years younger at his death than I am now writing this.

That date—January 28—divides time for all who knew him well, into before and after. Joseph had himself remarked how apt the phrase "death of the poet" seem contrasted with the less vivid "life of the poet." He knew he would die early, and he gave much thought to his only handy defense: elegy. And so, in his quick-witted way, he knew to make posthumous speech in all its forms his study. One of these forms was translation, as he reminded us in an important essay on Cavafy that appeared in *The New York Review of Books*. Cavafy's straight-faced words, a kind of writing-degree-zero, he argued, could hardly conceal the fact that they wanted first and foremost to be translated, that in fact translation—the posthumous voice—was their destiny. At the same time, he was quick to point out that the dead were best described by the dash in their life dates, not the numbers with which they are bookended. As he put it another time, "nobody lives for the sake of his obituary."

Everyone knew that smoking would kill a man whose heart, like a paper shack, could do little to lessen the coming storm's severity, let alone prevent it. He told me that when he lay hooked to tubes in the hospital after his first heart attack all he could remember was being intoxicated by the smell of tobacco then on the breath of Edith Gross, an editor at *Vogue*, who had bent down to kiss him when she visited. And after our parting of ways and not long before his death, his friend Derek Walcott visited Hamilton, and I asked him, whose own habit was way past addictive, if Joseph was still puffing, and his response was instant: "He smokes in church."

What a pity then that his own translations—mine included— fell short of a Cavafyesque standard, and yet how could they not? I know of no Russian translations that match the complex, interior and intramural graces that the language affords. The inferred lack, indeed the very fact of it, was achingly apparent when Pasternak's poems of Zhivago first appeared in 1958, as it was when Kunitz applied his Prospero's wand to the resistant, personal texture of Akhmatova's poems in 1973, and as it was when Merwin offered up his controlled take on Mandelstam, also in 1973. Good as these were, they also left readers wondering what the fuss was all about. Thus the language that guards against foreign takeover or taint, also guards against the obvious posthumous option (i.e., transla- tion). And yet, in insisting on that option all his life, Brodsky called into question whether the posthumous voice wasn't another variety of the attempt to attain an Absolute—what poetry really looks like in the mind of God, as it were. And that is both beyond words and beyond the irony that two dimensions could, in God's inscrutable wisdom, be somehow greater than three. This noble, but impossible ambition, which he also identified and admired in Tsvetaeva, is what drew many of us to him.

The day Brodsky died, I still smoked myself. Later that very day, after class, I opened a window in my office and lit a cigarette, blowing smoke into the dark north—though the dark north, being itself, blew it right back. It was a day not unlike the day a few years before when I got the call that my brother had blown his brains out in Ohio, as an early winter storm moved in, and roads got hard fast in the suburbs. In both cases, I remember there were stars where I was—"salt on an axe-blade," in Mandelstam's (and Merwin's) description—but where my brother's were when they died, there were only clouds. Unlike my brother, Joseph had died in his sleep, but neither, being indoors, perceived the last of starlight before taking the last breath.

The first time it was borne home to me that Joseph was actually mortal (though young), he had taken me to spend the day with Anthony Hecht in Rochester. On the way back, as snow lay all around the black ribbon of the New York Thruway, he suddenly sprang up and clutched his chest, which he pounded three times hard with his fist, then slumped back, silent. Given, as he was not, to any hint of self-pity, he looked out the window as we sped on our way, and said enigmatically but simply—as if he were talking about the fate of poems: "the houses are dark, but the people are darker, the houses would say, if they could."

Kurt Brown's *No Other Paradise*

What becomes a poem most: nouns or verbs? The legacy of Modernism, from whose dream we have still not fully emerged, suggests that when a poem looks in the mirror, what it sees is a creature for whom verbs hold pride of place. This opinion belongs to the greatly under-examined fealty of this part of speech to the lure of dynamism. On this view, the verb is the dynamo of the poem, and the whole unfolds at the behest of these energetic facilitators. But there is another tradition. Brodsky, in an early poem, tried to tie it to John Donne ("Big Elegy for John Donne"), in which the dream of Donne is a dream of things raining down and rolling in, like Frost's apples. Brodsky's poem was self-serving, to the extent that John Donne's poems, as Camille Paglia's title *Break, Blow, Burn* suggests, aligns the Metaphysical maestro more easily in the verb camp. Brodsky would have made a better case had he invoked Whitman, that Homeric-sized cataloger of things, for whom things were the stuff of the poem, and democracy itself sat atop and astride this stuff, this *res republica*, like a kindly dragon guarding his horde. But he didn't like Whitman's feral allegiances, and thereby hangs a tale. The poetry that sets about, not directly to interpret, but to acquire real estate in the phenomenal world seeks to take a census in the hopes of conferring citizenship, of mapping zones of commonality. The strongest poems of Kurt Brown's *No Other Paradise,* including the long title poem, belong to this tradition.

At bottom, this mode, which prefers the thing to the action, also hopes that patterns will emerge that support the notion—more of a wish—that in spite of the lateness of the day and the knowingness of our colleagues, the world as we live it stands capable of hanging together in some meaningful way, that it isn't just rampantly insignificant all the way down—which would make us day laborers in Babel. However, it occurs to the poet that it may be that this hanging together, if it indeed is seen to come about, comes about courtesy of the poem itself. That is, the poem is that by which the world hangs together, and the very thought is as fright-inspiring as it is embarrassing. Poets have tried to avoid the conclusion, so dear to postmodernists, that it's all a construction. But when their very means start to point to that conclusion, to the point where (as Brodsky reappears to drolly remark in another poem) "the sea, madam, is someone's speech," the thing is to declare that Babel is Rome—and we know what to do when we're there. Mallarmé, who never to my knowledge traveled to Rome, did; likewise Robert Lowell, who did (and left the characteristic powder burn of his poems as proof). Kurt Brown, who has Fortune to thank that he has another game, does not naturally emerge from this tradition, but he winds up there, and he is poet enough and *Mensch* enough to embrace what his art turned up and to accept its implications:

> not the realm of spirit but the meta-physical
> Plato's world of imperfections the cracked and worn
> and misbegotten heaven's junk but where we
> breathe and love the body's fractured paradise
> not the shadow but the rock not the image
> but the bone when the dead long this is what they long
> for thronging to the known like flies
> not our dreams but the destination of our dreams
> not the word but the implication of the word

("The Known World")

Quite right. Brown doesn't get tripped up in the verbal fetishism that awaits poets keen on word acquisition because it's the metaphysical, not the physical, wherein the mojo resides. We may make a big fuss about the materiality of it all, including the alphabet, but if you think that you have done a day's work expending your expressive treasure in pointing up the fact, then Nadezhda Mandelstam, who committed the whole of her husband's work to memory, would like to have a word with you.

In "Fire Sermon, 1950," the speaker remembers the rote consolations and credos of a Lutheran upbringing, and perhaps it's the time, so near the end of the War, that widens the always-in-play nature of irony between the intended divinity of the words and nature's quizzical contrasts:

> *This is the Lord's house* he said
> and suddenly a synod of crows collected in the tree outside
> gabbling louder than our prayers.

The surprising "synod" substitutes for, without replacing, the standard and, as everybody knows, wonderfully poetic "murder" of crows, which in its turn puts us in mind of the bishops—wherever they are—who congregate in the name of this noun. In other words, the poem goes about its own testifying by coöpting the expected sacred and switching it with the deflationary mundane. Even their "gabbling" discourse seems, as it swells, to exceed the reach of prayers. Which is not to say that the poet has been unhappy with his spiritual training, but this poem, even as it whets the knife, finds a connection between what Luther might have done had he been alive in 1950 and what is traditionally beyond the pale of Protestantism—and by extension, human gestures in the direction of the holy:

> Luther wrote by the small flame of a candle.
> For us, the holocaust had just ended, though we'd heard
> about those prophets sauntering through a furnace unscathed.
> *Glory in excelsis!* we sang. *Halleluiah!*

The problem for the modern is the increasing inability to specify the "sacred" in the increasing face of the profane—and its sometime deputy, the mundane. Is the profane, then, to be somehow incorporated within the fabric of the holy? Does the inability to specify and commit, to lapse into a standoff, mean that in time one will come to resemble the other, to wear the look of the other? The poem thus ends,

and we sang *halleluiah! halleluiah!*
while around us real mountains filled with crows
black as ministers in their robes.

The doubling in the fine poem "Fire Sermon, 1950" is not surprising. It's not that Brown is some kind of conscious stylistic dualist. It's rather that his poems frequently draw attention to contrasting poles. For instance, in "Knowledge and Ignorance," he works the difference between presence and absence as a function of time in a way that skirts hackneyed attempts at this old dichotomy:

language circles itself looking for a way out
a way of expressing what it can't
after the passing of a jet silence can also be heard
that only the jet's passing makes evident
and knowledge stands forth out of ignorance
like a soft cliff which the blue waves at its base eat away . . .

Since these comings and goings approach, draw even, and supersede each other in the temporal continuum, what earlier eggheads would have called, simply, duration—and understood as a medium, Brown also understands as a stress test, in the old-fashioned sense of *durance*. Hence to live is to live in durance, to endure. There is a literary consequence too. Instead of the starting and stopping of sentences with their conventions of caps and periods, Brown prefers the less over-determined eddy of phrases, and many of the poems in the collection are a matter of phrasing, as the excerpt above suggests.

Likewise, in "Baloney," a meditation on authenticity, the poem proceeds as a flow that contrasts artificiality, perhaps a gloss on our belief in artifice, with the incessant stream of what bears us away. The representation of these ice floes (or are they more like particles in a cloud chamber?), seem to be headed toward some objective reality, only to be found wanting in offices of realism against the indifferent *whatever*:

things do work out   though not in the way we planned
and illusion is a shore towards which we drift

> abandoning the real   our little boats made of aluminum
> and plastic   breasting the dark uncompromising waves...

Several poems here seem to take this test ("Mortal Message," "Counting the Faces," "Somebody Else," "River") and bear a stylistic similarity. It may be said that Brown understands drifting to describe our situation better than setting out or driving toward. This fact alone would align him with the naturalism that haunts many contemporary poets, except that his is happy to resolve itself in the music of the poem, at least to resolve itself in the détente of forces, the little (us) and the big (it) through the maintenance of linguistic balancing, of language's ability equally to "map" wayward thoughts as well as catastrophic closures (and disclosures).

Behind all this, of course, is a meditation on mortality and what we might call mortality's career—the discontinuity of form that forces us to become relational. Which immediately makes one wonder: is there anything left to be said on this subject? To which an answer begins to insinuate itself: what occasion is freed of it? The closure of the mortal works within the realm of duration, the medium in which it finds itself (and finding itself equals finding itself mortal). Thus the question of identity takes hold:

> the mill workers see it hands bleached with chemicals
> heads humming like precise machines
> the scholar the fireman the ex-con
> we all know what's going to happen it's so plain
> and yet we rush past

("Secrets")

For a poet of Kurt Brown's distinction, identity is about the fullness of the noun, and in that sense, he is an Adamic poet for whom naming is a poet's "work":

> To lift the tongue, to shape the vowels
> the way a mason shapes a brick
> *gasket, nozzle, spindle, plate*

to grasp each word, then stack it
end to end with other words
using grammar as our grout
to weld our thoughts and bind them into place;
to rise each morning
numb with sleep, and climb the scaffold,
coffee streaming from a mug—
O this is work, bloody work
mainspring, chisel, turnbuckle, bolt...

Attempts to elevate the "nominal" are widespread among versifi-
ers, as if poems were improved by channeling Rilke's "house, bridge,
fountain, gate" mantra. Brown, however, betrays no indebtedness
so nakedly, which suggests that his thoughts have marinated in a
private blend a long time and therefore bear something of his mark
(to mix a metaphor). They are meditative without the *largo* of classical meditation. Indeed, one of the things that marks these poems
as original is the sense of motion, of oscillation and vibration, that
accompanies the meditative unfolding.

The poem that will mark the memories of most readers, I suspect,
is the title poem. Weighing in at 16 thick blocks of text, it is a poem
that combines the inventory duty of Whitman with the picture compression of Crane, by way of Lorca's picaresque. The journey through
the city, which becomes a pilgrimage in ordinary, also can't escape
side-swiping Milton and Eliot (poets reconciled in another paradise)
to say nothing of the expansive O'Hara and his polar opposite, the
Dante of the closed system. If God is your Best Idea, then Paradise is
your Best Place. Hence we know before our eye even lands on the first
line that every paradise to which we are capable is lost. And yet!—as
Jarrell would interject—it is precisely *ours* and so we would have *No
Other Paradise*. In Brown's terms,

we wake to our own reality
purely imagined the ghost-life of money war
history's fractured narrative we had a paradise
it was around here somewhere

The poem builds by amassing the things of the city, and these blocks begin to resemble, beyond Crane and O'Hara, beyond Kinnell's Avenue C, the musical blocks of a John Adams, discrete chromatic wholes held together by a single vision—or ear:

> o sigh-flanked city crux of origins locus of souls
> we wake to our own reality *just now and always again*
> train wreck widow's cry the murderous indictment
> banks of light-shot ineffable turrets rise the tide whelms...

There is something of a postmodern heroism here in the attempt to make the quotidian stand in place of what used to be the eternal. Whitman showed the way, but his register is not Brown's. Instead, there is the love of affiliation, invulnerable to irony, and no other magic than the here-and-now need be considered:

> who can tell his life from this rabble of announcements
> from Sin City "Open for Lunch" Kotz Bros. Welding
> Raju & Sons 24-hour Tow Hair Health Inc. Nic's Locks
> and Hindleman's Smoke Shop from no other paradise but here...

It's a terrific poem, rigorously posed, but lovingly and deftly executed. *No Other Paradise* takes the measure of, and bests, Jack Gilbert's similarly titled *Refusing Heaven* in sweep and feeling. This book widens and rewards with each re-reading and will, it is fair to say, move Kurt Brown more than a few steps up the Parnassian slope.

Kurt Brown

An Appreciation

Readers of Kurt Brown's last volume, *Time-Bound*, will note how many poems ride along boundaries dividing what we already have and what we have already made familiar from what we have no access to. The poem knows, so to speak, what follows the last line and the last period. It is where that poem didn't reach, whether that was a matter of formally declining to disturb the silence or simply conceding its mystery. Kurt Brown's poems are "liminal," a word I learned in graduate school (and wish I could have left it there), and because they are so, they are aware of what they are not saying (and some take the opportunity to point this out) or cannot say, and in the course of hinting of this awareness, in effect say it—or something to the effect. It is, as Frederic in *The Pirates of Penzance* would say, a most intriguing paradox. As Brown puts it in "The Hierophant of Hartford," his encomium to Wallace Stevens, "The objective world and the mind are separate, but one. / On points of paradox his poems danced." That Brown was drawn to boundaries and to the paradoxes that seem to destablilize fate seems all the more prescient in light of his sudden death last summer: "language circles itself looking for a way out / a way of expressing what it can't." ("Knowledge and Ignorance")

Now with the posthumous compendium that is *I've Come This Far to Say Hello: Poems Selected and New*, we see the lifelong themes that rolled into place, the topoi and threaded interests, the islanded satisfactions of love, the delights that are proper to any man. The handsome, valedictory volume opens with "Cartology," a relatively

straightforward but nevertheless telling piece that signals Brown's
bias for a system of sense-making borders and grids, figures that
seem, in their inevitable distortions, to leave geographic reference
behind, in favor of imaginary destinations that have their own
beauty as symbol:

> I love to run
> my fingers over blank provinces,
> those white quadrants the mind cannot
> enter, waiting for the birth of the first
> animal and the new flowers...

One is reminded right away of Bishop's "The Map," where a
more painterly eye is drawn to the cartographer's colors than to the
boundary lines (he was looking for intelligibility, which is to say,
circumscribed knowledge; she was looking for home). Poets are so
much more intelligent than we give them credit for. I would hope
that Kurt Brown's passing would not encourage a too-hasty summa-
tion of his accomplishments, as his seemingly late publications would
suggest might be the case. In our moment, poets are punished with
indifference or condescension for the congeniality of their verses,
as if the equilibrium of the poem—where that occurs—bespoke
a talent insufficiently hooked up with the negativity of the poet's
time. That negativity provided much of the contrastive mood in his
penultimate book, *No Other Paradise*, what I take to be the high-water
mark of his career. And yet it was, as he put it, "Such a bright thing
/ to come from that dark water, that cold sea."

Kurt Brown was rather one of those poets who come along so
perfectly attuned to the bias and feeling of the time (including the
time of poetry) that his poems seem to be a kind of bellwether. Jane
Kenyon was such a poet, as was, as is, in a more self-conscious way,
Stephen Dunn—who wrote an insightful and affectionate preface to
Brown's *Selected*. Thomas Lux and Dorianne Laux are two more from
the same cloth (he offers an homage to Lux in his spot-on impersonations of poet-friends in *Sincerest Flatteries* [2007]). His very American-
ness, you might say, set him apart, though you would be hard put to
find a poem that merely traveled on the charm of its cowlick.

In my review of *No Other Paradise*, I called attention to Brown's bias for naming and then for holding nouns to account. It was, I said, his version of elevating the nominal over the agency of verbs, as if verbs were not the linguistic darlings we know they are, animating and ordering the page, telling nouns how high to jump. But first there must be stuff, and also at the end of the day, as Whitman knew. And so it is understandable that inventory precedes consciousness, in a sense, and also of its finer version, *awareness*, followed by its more mammalian cousin, *acknowledgment*.

While Brown trades on the Boomer vibe, and his poems reflect both a realistic and attractively authentic discourse filled with the things, events, and telling personal stories from a representative life, he was also a seeker, encountering—yet skirting—death, including the dead-ends distributed impartially throughout the field of our endeavors:

> All poems say one thing: *death is coming.*
> Why else do they spruce you up,
> pale disheveled corpse—wizened, shy?

> ("What Poems Say")

As he says in "Knowledge and Ignorance," "language circles itself looking for a way out / of expressing what it can't." It was Robert Creeley who remarked that he didn't write about what he knew, but rather wrote about what he *didn't* know. Brown comes up from the same muddle, where the life-and-death questions—the issues of time and feeling, of wonder and disappointment—unfurl and meet even the accommodated man, be he ambling along in his tennis shoes or feeling mortality's breath rising and falling in unison with intimacy:

> How often have you made love to someone
> because the Angel of Death passed by your door
> throwing an icy shadow over your life—
> just to let you know He's still there
> in case you forgot...

("Return of the Prodigals")

In Isaiah Berlin's familiar distinction, Brown was a hedgehog, that is, a creature who hugged to the One Big Thing he knew, but at the same time, he was a poet who was capable, in fact driven, to develop a dissident relationship, a push-back, to that knowledge:

> why not speak of what we know
> instead of dangling   always   above the ineffable
>
> on the opposite side   no address   no message
>
> *what matters is that we have been here at all*
>
> so they say   but what does the wind say
> after the men are gone   blowing through those empty cables

("Snapshot")

The ineffable, that staple of Romantic ideology, is offered to us in a number of flavors. For ages, it was unreconstituted nature, the physical makeup unreasoning and more often than not, unreasonable to our growing sense of purpose. In Protestant culture, it came to seem a way of designating, perhaps rationalizing, the silence of God. For Wittgenstein, it was that which cannot be said (and as Frank Ramsey remarked, "If you can't say it you can't whistle it, either"). For Rorty, following Marx, its unsayableness was so much the case, that he dismissed it as not worth the effort to try. Or for that matter, whistle. But Simon Critchley, by way of introducing a new generation to Jacob Bronowski's '70s TV series *Civilization*, sees the same ineffable as "uncertainty," a moment that enjoins us to acknowledge our humility before the fact that certainty isn't ours. Following up this roll of questers is Charles Wright, who approaches the verbally inexpressible this way: "Vision [...] is a mystic concept. Vision is close to wordlessness. One uses certain kinds of images to escape or transcend language. Like pointing a finger." And this is where Brown comes in.

> But soon
> even he falls silent, until silence itself resounds

more durable than any word.

("At the Retirement Home for Slang")

He is being wise who calls it merely practical. The mystery of the ordinary is the genius of the American poet: that old-time ineffable—about which the poet always writes (or points a finger) discloses not only itself, but the nouns that give it such shape as we can encounter it. You can call it knock-down, *démodé*, discount, hackneyed, whatever, but I'm talking not only about all the stuff that extends into space, but also what's invisible: memories, fantasies, dreams, the past, subjectivity itself. Considering the nesting rituals of bluebirds, he comes close to referencing James Wright's bluebird jumping up and down, for whom the branch did not break, but unlike Wright, he demurs. Sister Bernetta Quinn, the Modernist scholar and poet, once told me vis-à-vis the poem, that "the branch was *Christ*. Jim didn't know that—but it was." You wonder what Brown would have made of such an assertion. Just as in Wright's poem, the circumstance refuses to exaggerate the hangover (call it the drag of the quotidian) just to curry favor with what Wittgenstein forbade us to speak. The fact is, life itself inclines us not to go on suicide missions in search of certainty, but to settle. The fact doesn't make the poet any less the seeker:

> I wouldn't call it the tree of Paradise,
> but it looks pretty good to her. I wouldn't say
> she was practical, or wise.
> I'm only telling you this to let you know
> what happens, sometimes,
> in a world we often look down on.
> And they're not fools. They know
> what they want, gathering what they can
> to fly into the face of their longing.

("Bluebirds")

We can go deeper into Brown's poems than you might imagine at first read because the familiarity of place and personnel quickly impresses us as fitting material for a poem. But Brown doesn't stick the reader with one perspective, one party line, nor does he push insight, without finding that the edges come curling back:

> A man spends his whole life fishing in himself
> for something grand. It's like some lost lunker, big enough
> to break all records. But he's only heard rumors, myths,
> vague promises of wonder. He's only felt the shadow
> of something enormous darken his life. Or has he?

("Fisherman")

It would be a fallacy to read the poet's own death into his poems in any way other than his thematic discontinuities. Still, we read *I've Come This Far to Say Hello: Poems Selected and New* with intimations of prescience. Perhaps that's just the thing, after all, that can't be said, for not always, but in so many ways in poems peculiar to the most national of our bards (and I'm thinking here of poets as different as Stevens and Dickinson—both of whom are referenced here), death is that ineffable—not the silence of God, but the silence of the human: "All poems say the same thing: *kiss your loved ones; say goodbye*." ("What Poems Say")

And yet discontinuity dreams itself into being—or nonbeing. It's a good lesson for the American inside the living person; it takes the exceptionalism down a notch. But not without the dusty, nostalgic poof when absence directs its conductor's wand to presence and plays presence in all the registers of that word.

Only an American poet, I think, could have found in the antics of our homegrown Miles Gloriosus, the TV wrestler, such a celestial pantomime (in Stevens' phrase) as this:

> For God
> has found them, sister, unannounced,
> and wrenched their bodies from
> their souls. And he has thrown them
> for a loop, knocked the breath
> out of their lungs, left them flattened
> and amazed.

("The Sitters")

I have omitted all that is specific and concrete in what I had hoped
is a real, but what I fear is merely a glancing, appreciation of Kurt
Brown's work. Let me sum up by saying I would like to read him in
fifty years, to see how well he carried forward the truth about us.
But by then, we will have joined him and settled once and for all
the questions regarding the significance of that *terra incognita* that
loomed where he was headed and into the face of that longing we
seemed never to be without.

Michael Burkard's *Lucky Coat Anywhere*

You know what they used to say about prepositions, rabbits, and logs. It's about all the words available to describe how the first gets around the second. Of course, there are both finite and unlimited ways of doing this. The finite are attached to the prepositions that give us the GPS information: they are about precision. But we also know there are other ways. We are taught (if we are taught) to approach art the first way—prepositionally, and the methods that inhere in this approach become crochets over time. For what art teaches, if it teaches anything, is not to trust the prepositions to have the whole truth about those wily rabbits. Michael Burkard's poems make the same point, but because there seems no way around the impasse created by poems so resistant to paraphrase, his has often been confused with other kinds of poetry. Nowadays, poetry readers are old hands at reading "discontinuous" or "indeterminate" poetry. We are taught that the cloud-chamber effect of the mind's sloppy unspooling chimes nicely with reality: it is, in effect, the new realism. However, it would be misleading to lump all paraphrase-resistant poets together, if for no other reason than the fact that lineages matter.

I have been reading Michael Burkard's poems since the 1970s when they were received with much more chin-stroking than now. Back then he was variously thought to be a) an imitator of Ashbery, b) a language poet, or c) the loopiest avatar of Iowa expressionist aesthetics—with perhaps an overlay of French and/or Eastern European surrealism, perhaps with a sprinkling of Russian, à la Pasternak or Chekhov. I remember going to hear him read with a poet who has since surpassed both Burkard and me, certainly in name recognition. After the reading she turned to me and said, "I think he may be more important than any of us." She meant, presumably, poets of our generation. The remark struck home: we were all in our ways ambitious. What she heard in that reading was not the puzzling loose ends and obsessively picked-over curlicues, which often boiled down to merely a fascination with words in their naked strangeness. Rather, she heard beneath the language-y heaving of the surface the ease that Burkard felt with that language. It was all the more impressive in that language was, to us, so problematic, and would continue to be so, as the subsequent years forced us to confront the bad news of endless theorists punching holes in our vaunted subjectivity and demanding that we justify our endeavors in ways we had never contemplated before. Burkard seemed to write blissfully apart from those concerns. He seemed to feel comfortable coming and going among his chosen registers, pausing here and there to linger over a bit of language, not alienated in its triviality (or, for that matter, its majesty, if such were still possible), but it was masterful, and that same quality has been on display throughout Burkard's career.

A quick look, by way of contrast, with the poet to whom he is most often compared—Ashbery—shows that the latter, whose alienated language and ironic stance are pro forma postmodernist yoga poses—often embarks upon poetic projects, true experiments of language, and just as often with experiments, with results that are sometimes puzzling (think *The Tennis Court Oath* or *Flowchart*), although the hits are as triumphant as the misses are palpably bummers. Burkard's career doesn't chart the same kinds of peaks and valleys, nor does it exhibit the kind of progression we recognize and look for in other poets, thanks to our training. Nor does Burkard subscribe to the school of proven ways. In fact, his disinclination to do so could lead you to surmise that here is a poet whose ambition, because it doesn't arc into a familiar career, also doesn't take the shape of an *oeuvre*. Yet, you would be wrong, and as if to preempt that thought, NightBoat Books also recently published *Envelope of Night: Selected and Uncollected Poems, 1966-1990*, a black, square stepping-stone of a book.

The new work bears out the suspicion that he is a fine, if odd, poet. One of the many dimensions of his fineness is the possibility that he is something more than fine and that it is we who are odd. *Lucky Coat Anywhere* is all by itself an ample volume. If no traditional progression marks the distance from there to here, still one finds what the Burkardian universe has always been comprised of: dreams, travel, streams (of water, of conversations), geographical nodes and depots, friends, family. The poems record what it's like just to go down the stream, but they also want you to feel that stream too, both of consciousness and subconsciousness: the boats and secrets, the distances and voices, the devices and accessories of transport are all here. I suspect that Burkard's work is in some way an extended essay on transport, particularly in that secondary sense of ecstatic movement where consciousness doubles back and looks in on itself (though closer to what the French after Baudelaire meant than to the blossoming of conscience in the act of auto-surveillance, which is the province of moralists, not aesthetes like him).

The question of discontinuous or indeterminate form notwithstanding, Burkard's poems provide an example of limited aesthetic wholes, although—and here is the rub—they also do the contrary thing: they don't meet up with familiar integrity and closure standards. The ambivalence is not a posture. As a result, readers and reviews have had a hard time pigeon-holing his work. None of the identities mentioned above seems to fit just right. He is far from the theoretical poetry left, whose diffidence toward significance and the benighted disciples of transcendence are the hallmarks of American *poetomachia*. I remember a former colleague of Burkard's once losing his tolerance for too much of that spiritualist talk—which must have reminded professors of his generation of the table-thumpers in Yeats, Madame Blavatsky, the '6os, and all that—and responding with a rousing, "You can take your transcendence and stick it up your ass!" While casting a Gioconda smile at the material side of words, Burkard is fond of stories and self-mythology. The narrative or submerged narrative of the poem often straddles the line between reality and dream for its source: the poet doesn't seem to find the distinctions all that meaningful. He's also fond of language's ability to become dream-like and haunting when it becomes quotational, and

he often will pause to rehearse a word or phrase in quotation, as if
considering a rare specimen or revisiting a phrase for its dreamlike
quality. Here is a passage from the poem "anger" that shows many
of Burkard's felicities on display: the theme-and-variation, the ease
of subjective discourse, the after-Kafka feeling of menace mixed
with absurd humor, the use of quotational inspection, and the final,
emergent tone of tenderness:

> the next day and the day after that I was forced to read an inter-
> view in which
> > I said I loved myself—I was talking in the interview about
> > myself by
> > name—in the third person—my voice was described by
> > investigators as
> > "pinned to the gills of a fish"
> "if you must know" they said—"don't stop reading aloud until
> we tell
> > you to" was another thing said as a reminder
> my voice wanted to see you darling but you were nowhere to be
> found
> i was glad for that—I would not have wanted you to be found
> still I missed you like today—and I tried to hear you in the words
> > between the words I had to read—sometimes I pretended
> > you must
> > have written these words for me—as a major joke
> > I would eventually get

While the distance between them is not inconsiderable, Burkard
does sometimes favor Ashbery, but without the elder poet's tony
urban eclecticism and in-the-knowness. Where Ashbery is centrifugal, Burkard is centripetal. It is closer to the truth to see Burkard's
styleset as rooted in Iowa (where Middle America, also, hatches its
avant garde) and its aesthetic reach, with a dose of Tate and Knott
to raise the decibel level. Yet Burkard is not everyone's cup of tea. In
truth, in spite of my friend's prediction, Burkard has, over the years,
turned into something of a coterie act, although his readers were
and are devoted. The times have caught up with him, and while his
poetry may not have brought him the sober attention of a Harold

Bloom, it doesn't inspire the puzzlement of editors or reviewers anymore, either. And yet my friend was right in sensing something about Burkard's importance, although it has taken me several decades to realize what that is.

Words are public tools. Their application in matters of privacy (the matter of lyric poetry, for instance) has always been problematic and, so to speak, unnatural. Poets have ever resorted to tricks to force language to cohere as closely as possible to experience and called it authenticity. More recently, poets have noted the widening distance between the plane of language and that of experience, with the result that the tools of language become ironic, and language itself in the course of its descriptions and expressions, becomes eventually—sometimes completely—quarantined within quotation marks. Burkard's work seeks neither the license for authenticity, nor the estrangements of form. His great talent is to write as if he thought words, thoughts, and feelings were interchangeable, and thus he almost exhibits a sense of serenity with his linguistic circumstance. For others making (or writing) poems is at best a game of approximations and educated guesses, in spite of endless workshops and the flogging of craft. Because ease is omnipresent, you can point your finger anywhere in Burkard's poems and find the poet signifying there as truly as the conventional poet does when forced, in escalating stages of suspense, to show you the reveal, as magicians say. Burkard's work is a kind of *sortes virgilianae*, the old practice of opening to a random passage in Virgil to find one's fortune. For instance:

> 6.
> When talking about black horses
> in white envelopes we are obviously
> talking about very small horses.
> It is important to tell just how,
> if at all, the horses died, and to
> be precise as to whether the horses
> are figuratively dead or really dead.
> The envelopes become less and less
> important.

7.
But days later the envelopes
become more important in unexpected
ways. You realize very deeply
they are white, not off-white
or almost-white or anything-else-
white but white. They are also
small, not much larger
than the small black horses.

("Black Horses in White Envelopes")

As is evident here, Burkard also flattens the emotional range,
ledge-walking next to a drop into yadda-yadda that he consistently
avoids. It is an impressive performance. It is as if he were comparing
himself to a parody of himself, but showing that imagined parody to
be untrue to the nature of conversation's aims, which are to have no
aim, other than the to-ing and fro-ing of existence itself.

Several of the longer sectioned poems here remind me of the
cadenza-filled jazz compositions of someone like Tim Berne, whose
improvisational spaces add up to a cacophony of energetic vibra-
tions, to theme-and-variations with a vengeance, as if to suggest that
no theme can stand without its variation—often escalating variations, and no semblance can emerge without a resemblance. After a
while, you may be led to feel that the original formula has been lost,
but it hasn't. It just takes its position as a seeding mechanism from
which other versions arise as the mind works forward, as the emotions move through their metamorphoses. The whole then coalesces
around the guiding voice to form a larger aesthetic whole, though
without the falsely reassuring click of closure, such as characterizes—or should I say besets—more conventional lyric set pieces.

"A Retreat of Chairs" is such a set of poems (there are four). The
first poem begins with the kind of noodling familiar to musicians:

some of my favorite handwriting isn't there
—that should be no surprise
you want to be a shore to a wounded boy

in one sketchbook some pages are kept there
to keep the safe and flat—how can i talk about this?—

and on/within one early page is a piece of writing,
and a piece of drawing—the drawing is very heavy ink—

And so forth. The second poem still seems unwilling to reveal the meaning of the cryptic title ("old wood, an eater late at night when (where?) no one /can watch what his mouth swallows—"). The third poem, however, introduces a Kafkaesque note that approaches this eponymous chair:

at one university you can request, on your birthday,
and you have to provide proof it is your birthday
beyond the records that university currently keeps,
and you may be called upon to do this in front of
a strange panel, and then you will exchange places
with one member of the panel, for a few minutes, to
see what you yourself would have thought of this
additional birthday "evidence,"...

("retreat of chairs (3)")

Notice how Burkard moves in and out of quotational space, dandling the word "evidence," which takes on all the believability of a John Boehner tan when uttered by the "strange panel." The fourth poem finally delivers the goods, as if no delay or alternative had been in the way:

at this one university you can request to go on
a retreat of chairs, you have to be a chair, you
cannot be the chair of a suicide, nor can there be
a suicide's chair within three generations of your
family or any of your last family.

With their recursive images and rhetorical loops, Burkard's poems reload all the old questions that cluster around the problem of a private language. Is it desirable or even possible to write in such a way that you privatize discourse and so deprive it of its conventional job of communicating content? The answer, in a nutshell, is no. A so-called private language presents a contradiction on its face: it loses its "privacy" by virtue of the premise of communication itself, which is its social nature. Yet how does one experience the most intimate, profound, or for that matter, ordinary dreams of others? How does one escape the lyric poem's endless demonstrations of solipsism? Burkard's poems answer by not paying you back for coming at them by conventional readings. And that, reader, is a good thing.

Because language is also omnidirectional, it lends itself to perspectives, and the only bird's-eye view is the imagined one. It's also Stevensian, and a number of the poems in *Lucky Coat Anywhere* seem riffs on "Thirteen Ways of Looking at a Blackbird," which is, you might say, the ultimate poem because it concedes everything while refusing to give up giving up. I have been reading Burkard's poetry for a long time, and his work has been important to me: in my own instance, my friend's pronouncement on hearing him read has proved true. He is one of the poets I turn to when I need to be reminded how poetry improves upon reality, and I always find there that trope of surprise that Emerson promised us, if only we would cleave to the homemade, not the handed-down. For surprise calls upon our capacity for wonder, which is the stance of the lover, not the manipulator, the analyst, nor the power-freak.

Jane Cooper

The Flashboat: Poems Collected and Reclaimed

Poetry of a higher order courts two kinds of difficulty. The first is formal, connected with the degrees of ellipsis, or leaving out, that a poem can sustain and still be subject to understanding. This sort has been long thought—wrongly—applicable to some early New York School poetry (and *all* language poetry) but is most rightly applied to poems with submerged narratives, poems whose effects are conspicuous even as their occasions are more or less invisible. The second sort of difficulty is encountered in poems registering deep struggles that by and by the poems come to embody as well. When this happens, such a poem becomes emblematic of the value (for the poem) and dignity (for the poet) that may accrue in the struggle for significance—even if insignificance is the result. The assumed "depth" implies hidden forces by which one may posit anything from God to history to psychic wrestling. The struggle takes place below the urge, and the resulting poem is both a description of the struggle and one of its forms. Its victories are not mere lyric victories: they may also be real gains. As a result, the poem collapses the contested ground between imagination and reality. It is therefore the kind of difficulty often associated with wonder, the flip side, you might say, of bafflement.

Jane Cooper's poems are of the second, more metaphysical sort. *The Flashboats: Poems Collected and Reclaimed* maps 50 years of shrewd reflection and dogged engagement. While descending into fields of struggle may run counter to post-modernity's infinite regressions, where no buck stops, Jane Cooper's poems incorporate encounters. And that's not all: they acknowledge the force of the question whether the lived world is a) atoms all the way down or b) may be conceived somehow free of the dictatorship of matter—as with history, God, traditions, Zeitgeists, or mindsets.

Cooper's first poems are hyper-alert to historical context. As she puts it in a speech, "Poetry is a way of giving people more life, a more vivid awareness of the exact moment they are living through—first a sensuous [sic] awareness, then a historical one." While it may be the province of the "I" to have experiences in the here and now, it is only part of a sequence, the end of which is judgment. While her early poems hash through the difficulties of relationships (a recurring theme), they never have to do so without keeping one eye on the times. The poet knows better than to give sexuality, friendship, domesticity, or the artist's quandaries stand-alone billing. A World War II poem ("The Faithful") suggests this inescapable doubling:

> *What if last night I was the one who lay dead*
> *While the dead burned beside me*
> *Trembling with passionate pity*
> *At my blameless life and shaking its flamelike head*

It is revealing to contrast Cooper's response to the Second World War with the famous responses of her male poet colleagues, whose publishable psychic scars helped form a new personal discourse seemingly unavailable in the 1930s. Cooper's reaction was an attempt to triangulate a different set of problems: non-participation, guilt, and responsibility. For instance, her feminism would be partly colored by the grim absorption of the war years and the idealistic aftermath when the Marshal Plan seemed, among other things, a metaphor for the American renewal of Euro-culture. Clustering around cultural centers herself—Vassar, New York, Princeton, Oxford—Cooper had imbibed the prevailing notion of a Noble Cause, a nostalgia not uncommon for a girl reared in the South, but now sanctified with the halo of Einstein's hair. In "After the Bomb Tests," scientific saintliness becomes the object of artistic query, just as the scientist's object (or fetish)—the atom—has become a source of study and means to a higher end. Here, with Kepler standing in for Einstein, the crossover between artistic and scientific inquiry suggests that their opposing alchemies are often complicit in their desire for power:

> The atom bellies like a cauliflower
> Expands, expands, shoots up again, expands
> Into ecclesiastical curves and towers
> We pray to with our cupped and empty hands.
>
> Could one harmony hold
> The sum of private freedom like a cup?
>   Kepler, curious, rose
> Started to cross himself—then like a lover
> Or virgin artist gave himself to his power.

As *The Flashboat* makes plain, running parallel with the poet's attempts to come to grips with history are her attempts to measure private trials—the disillusionments at ten o'clock, in Stevens's phrase. These include not only the artist's dilemma between work and private life, but also the prior matter of health (Cooper has all her life suffered from a reduced immune system):

> My body knows it will never have children
> What can I say to my body now, this used violin?
> Every night it cries out strenuously from its secret cave.

("Waiting")

Not only the body's pilgrimage but also its rhetorical representation becomes an issue. Cooper speaks of an artistic affinity for theme-and-variation approaches to writing about experience, and over time these have acquired sufficient irony to pack, in their turn, abundant cautions when needed to constrain occasional excesses:

> Yes, I'm the lady he wrote the sonnets to.
> I can tell you how it was
> And where the books lie, biographies and his
> Famous later versions now collected
> In one volume for lovers. (You

Can never really analyze his method
If you only read those.)

("Long View From the Suburbs")

By mid-career Cooper had made the cartographer's sense of intelligible distortions a part of her own artistic awareness. Accuracy is not the only compliment fidelity pays to art: Mercator's projections make coordinates too, although they occur in no existential realms other than ones we may be said to imagine. In Cooper's rhetoric, the distance between what was necessary to endure then, as opposed to now, is equivalent to the difference between Mercator's gigantic Greenland and the much more modest island offered by Planet Earth. Therefore, because perspectives vary, the possibility of human acknowledgment-across-time (and its emanation, forgiveness) looms large. In one of several pieces devoted to the modalities and endurance of disability, benediction becomes benefaction in lines that recall Whitman:

*Mercy on Maryanne who through a hole beneath her collarbone drinks the
life-preserving fluid,
while in her arm
another IV tube drips something green. "It never affects me," she says,
"I'm fortunate."
She has Crohn's and rheumatoid arthritis and now osteoporosis, as well as
no gamma globulin,
as we all have no gamma globulin, or at least not enough. Mercy on Aaron,
her son, who at fifteen has Hodgkins and arthritis and no gamma globulin,
who is
out of school
just for the moment. "He's so bright," the doctor says, "He'll make it up."
But of course you never (As I remember) quite make it up.*

("The Infusion Room")

The world mapped by desire is also a world where distinctions between safety and participation do not arise. But witness—the taking-in—replaces projection—the thrusting out; not surprisingly, the poet comes to question the tools of her art, as in "A Room with Picassos":

> I can stand and stand
> In front of canvas and artistic paraphernalia
> But nothing there will answer me with pride:
> I am the exact shade of shame and desire.
> Your justification in the face of his
> Simple indifference to simple fire.
> I am the offering which always moves
> Anyone, no matter how far away he is from love.

Cooper is admirable in the degree to which she accepts resistance of people and things to reductive meanings, even when these might only provide gentle rubrics and consolations. Unconsoled, she can say, as in the speak of "My friend" {sic}, "But I don't know, she broke off, / whether I'm making myself clear..." The hesitation here clears more ground than a legion of necessary fictions. It is not clear, in one of several poems involving historical personages (Emily Dickinson, Georgia O'Keeffe, Willa Cather) what led Rosa Luxemburg to extol, on the one hand, the glories of war, and on the other to tender beauties of the natural world. But these contraries stand for the poet's capacity to accept the spectrum that begins with mere inconsistencies and ends with solid contradictions as saying something worthwhile about the world:

> *It's no use telling myself I am not responsible for all the hungry little larks*
> *in the world. Logic does not help*
> > *Never mind, we shall live... shall live*
> > > *through grand events*
> > > *Have patience*
> *Thus passing out of my cell in all directions*
> *are fine threads connecting me*
> *with thousands of birds and beasts*

("Threads: Rosa Luxemburg from Prison")

The poet knows that often contradiction favors truth more closely than logic, and this knowledge situates her poems with a familiarity among paradoxes that the mind rejects, although the body never stops squirming through their medium.

Beyond these frank and wise poems of acknowledgment—poems one feels the result of infinite winnowing—she has chosen to include several prose narratives, the last of which is a memoir of, and meditation on, a serious childhood illness. Here is a world where contingency, like original sin, preconditions all subsequent states and consciousness. But what kind of mooring is contingency when we must both set out from it and abide by it? Cooper's poems—trusty, spare, hopeful, yet beautifully deflationary—log the rigor of this ultimate paradox.

Mary Cornish's *Red Studio*

Mary Cornish's moving, meticulously composed *Red Studio* joins Tess Gallagher's *Moon Crossing Bridge* and Carol Muske's *Sparrow* as a volume occasioned by spousal loss that becomes noteworthy as it deepens into meditations on the role of poetry, not just in the management of grief and the rites of mourning—important as these things may be—but as examinations of poetry's debt to the occasion of our mortality. For method, her style looks to Louise Glück's *Descending Figure,* which set, for a generation, the gnomic tenor through which classical myths reveal their continued ability to mediate between what we might roughly call the Here and the Beyond.

Having made note of these immediate predecessors, I should add that, as a genre, the modern elegy holds its own against other genres in making sufficiently capable poetic signifiers. These days, finding "what will suffice" is likely to fall to the elegist before any other poet can brandish her alternative genre. This is for several reasons, not the least of which is our species' 24/7 awareness of biological death and its effects—mass discontinuities and what we once called "alienation," the sense of exile—especially self-exile—and the creepy prevalence of death as a cultural commodity. At the same time, the ability of the elegist to address loss and to convene the rites of mourning are, and have been, the object of a war of attrition since the dawn of modernity because the consolations traditionally assigned to elegy—religious, emotional, psychological, political—have been gradually eroded, demoted, demystified, and not replaced, stripping the poet down to her final elements, and leaving Lycidas and Adonais standing in their moccasins.

With the franchise for mourning extended to all whom we loved in life and thought, the occasions for elegy have never, it seems, been greater; yet the means have never fallen so much under suspicion. But while giving personal loss its existential due, Cornish is led to consider the "gifts" of death, and whether these gifts—in fact, the poems under review—constitute what we think of as late modern consolation. This is one of the key questions that the book raises. Traditionally, the elegy made solemn gestures to things outside itself as having the power to console, redirect, and motivate. Now the question is whether something like what consolation once was can be found "inside"; that is, whether there is anything extra-linguistic at all about the elegy anymore, or whether it isn't all just learning to accept the artifice—the poem, the symbol—as "sufficient." Cornish is aware that the power to re-member has something of a palliative quality that is eventually followed by forgetting anyway. The trick, you night say, is to naturalize forgetting, but entertaining that thought makes you wonder if forgetting, the putting-away of representation, isn't somehow also chock-a-block with that very death that gave rise to all these artistic escape hatches and linguistic heavens in the first place.

A number of poems take on the subject of building artifice directly, in terms of performance ("The Art of Misdirection," "Performance," "Hand Shadows," "Saigon Water-Puppet Show"); other poems are themselves "performances," that is, poems in which the subject provides an evolving artifice, commenting on itself as it does so ("Fifteen Moving Parts"). The preponderance of work in *Red Studio* has artistic transformation as its project, for grieving itself is well handled by art and by classicism—including classical myths—that manage to put grief by. This the classical can do by virtue of its long prestige, if only to hide grief behind the stiff upper lip of a mask. Desires and longings in Cornish's poems are often tied to ancient antecedents and forms:

> As if they were strangers arriving at the gates of a city,
> an arch defined the proscenium.
> The traveler was lost, or he was not—
> *omnia mutantur*: all is transfigured.

("Incarnate")

It may be one of the great paradoxes of expression that the private, personal, and intimate can scarcely make their way into intelligibility without first being constrained by form and then morphing into symbol. The public then stands for the private and personal that it relinquishes. In this way, the poem tracks, indeed often reenacts, the career of its subject. Such is *a fortiori* the case with elegy. But the elegy adds a special supplement in that this progress makes an arc bridging the contingent world, from which the subject of the elegy has been subtracted, with that immutable world Yeats found so attractive, though it often threatened to sink under the tinkling weight of its own irrelevance. Cornish subscribes to this school of alchemical transfiguration and continually gives us the bridge as image of the short voyage into the art, a bridge that poets of another age would have built to wed earth with heaven, but for her purposes is made to change memory into a more stable, often metonymic or symbolic, image:

> There's an arc
> between the living and the dead, as when
> a crow rises from a field, sun on its back.
> Below, the shadow moving.

("Legato")

And this:

> I'm crossing a bridge
> to the Lantern Festival
> in a poem by Li Ch'ing-chao.
>
> My lips are red,
> my jacket gold-threaded,
> my hair-ornament winged.
>
> All night, paired dragonflies dart
> between the large-leafed mulberries.
> Grief cannot find me.

("Carnal Prayer Mat")

Finding an appropriate image waiting on the other side of the arc has another benefit, for one of the problems of the elegy is the burden of significance that attaches to grief. The poem from which the preceding excerpt was taken addresses this problem and in so doing redefines the elegy's mission by denying consolation's claim on our attention. Consolation, so to say, is what keeps us from being natural in a world of still-natural things, and in Cornish's poems, while there is a push to build artifice, there is a counter-pull to naturalize. The push-pull feature situates many of her poems in a seeming paradox, though the final feeling is that the paradox itself is no matter (though it is a form). For the poet building artifice, even the most common rituals are a part of acquired (or received) knowledge. They may imitate natural "rituals" (for example, seasonal ones), but they are fundamentally different:

> Slowly Latin names begin to lift
> off tree limbs, off the backs of bugs.
> Even my own three names rise up
> and disappear over a hill.

About this world of bridges and arcs there are also other recognizable staples from the repertoire of transformation: protected gardens ("how little it takes to suggest a garden: /a chestnut leaf on a wooden bench") vines and bindings that reveal hidden links ("You tied back vines, I held the twine between us. It was good"), and aviaries of birds, each capable of flashing into symbolism. One of the fullest statements of the kind of transfigurations you are likely to find in these poems occurs in "Lotus Feet," a poem in which the speaker binds her feet to transform them into something incapable of maintaining allegiance with the earth on which they would otherwise travel, so that she may join her lover in spirit:

> Although a powdered fragrance fills my shoes,
> the odor of decay seeps through.
> In this way, I join him.

*

In this way, I am steadfast.
If I could lift my feet around his waist—
again, two swallows, flying.

Cornish divides *Red Studio* into the requisite three sections, the
first two of which comprise series of linked elegiac lyrics, with a last
section of more occasional—though still, at the DNA-level—elegiac
poems. These sections do not, as students are fond of saying, "flow."
They're not meant to. Rather, they have the cumulative, deliberately
"oriental" feeling of something that could be judged frozen in place
if looked at from a certain vantage, where *tableaux vivants* and *nature
mortes* are the rule, but people and what they do as social creatures—
i.e. the whoosh of plot—not so much. Here language itself is in suspension: the passive voice, the contradictions gelled in parentheses,
deny progress, once the symbol is set. There is also a certain sense of
repetition here, not unwelcome, a triptych, rather than a concession
to narrative's drive, which is to say fiction's influence.

I should say that the opening poems, though seeking refuge, as it
were, in art, are among the most naked and flat-out heart-rending
descriptions of loss I know of. See how in "The Lane" she begins
quietly appropriating her subject:

Left alone with his dead body,
I took off my husband's socks,
put my face on his feet.
Unbuttoned his shirt, pulled down
his pants, stroked and kissed his legs, chest,
penis. There was nothing I did not want
to hold...

Let's be frank. If this doesn't destabilize your composure, even as
it hints at many of the problems with untranslated grief, then you
haven't been taking your B vitamins. Mary Cornish knows, too, that
this level of deliberate immediacy is problematic, for nowhere else
does she reach such a pitch, although several poems of thwarted or
remembered eroticism ("Body Ornament," "We're in the Kitchen,"
"One of the Shapes") run a close second. The libidinal energies that

inform this collection are considerable, but they are rarely without harness, as they would be antithetical to art, as she conceives of it here—that is, passion is closer to pain, not its ritualized control.

While *Red Studio,* as a text, is haunted by the dead husband, even his infrequent appearances are often figured as parts (e.g., hands) that signify both the presence of the person but the absence of the partner. Imagistic and linguistic equivocations abound in this volume, often leaving the reader with the reverb of ambivalences—negatives and positives in each other's faces—with which to deal. Brodsky felt that ambivalence was a "necessary" response to our times, and he meant, for starters, that there is no way to adjudicate between mutually opposed beliefs, what I'm calling the push-pull of wanting to love, yet feeling love itself beginning to enable forgetting—with the House of Art somehow the lair of traitors.

Remember when poets were praised in reviews for "taking risks"? Did anybody but a sophomore think these risks were anything other than lyrical "risks"? The poems of this first collection take what seems to me a *bona fide* risk, and what is at risk is not just a lapse in taste. Wittgenstein said we know zilch about death, and the gentleman had a point, you have to admit. But the poet knows a good deal about loss, and grief, and discontinuance, and emotional and sexual deficit. So what's poetry's debt? This book more or less defines poetry as words having something to do with death. The interplay between nature and art is that between death and words, their subsets. Rituals throughout ride maintenance, and the elegy, knocked down, is still capable of siding with the figural over the literal. It is the literal we grieve for, but it is the symbols that redeem us. Or if the idea of redemption is not your cup of tea, then note how talismans cover the viscera, and you will be on your way to believing that aesthetics was behind the moral imagination all along—and not the other way around.

Stephen Dobyns' *Winter's Journey*

I once attended a dinner at which I explained that Stephen
Dobyns' poems typically took the form of a bolero. By that I meant
to say that they start off modestly but build to a climactic moment
that owes less to thematic coming-together, than to formal necessity.
It happened that Dobyns was present at this dinner, and hearing
my description, screwed up his eyes and said, "You mean my poems
remind you of Ravel's *Bolero*?" Years later, Dobyns, I maintain, is still
wool-gathering, but I can tell you it is high-level wool-gathering, and
the result, *Winter's Journey,* his fourteenth collection, is as engaging
in the fling of reference as it is fitting in the warp and woof.

Midway through the fifth poem in *Winter's Journey,* Dobyns surmises, "Maybe I'm straying from what's said to be said in a poem."
It is not an idle surmise. Dobyns' poems wander all over the place,
and his meandering meditations may well strike readers as more
closely resembling prose than poetry. At the same time, he also wonders, "but where does such an opinion come from?" In one sense,
it's no matter, in that he knows that he stands at the end of a long
line of peripatetic poets, Whitman and the Romantics included,
for whom the poetry of epiphany is a reflection of timelessness that
looks nostalgic as it recedes in the rearview mirror. Such poets prefer
tramping the soils of history to penning immortal lines. For them,
writing verse suggests either the tracing of the mind's journeys or
the creation of inventories that present themselves to those same
minds. Socrates recommended *peripateia*; so did Heidegger. The
latter even suggests that "meandering" is the form that constitutes
poetic thinking as such, unlike straight lines (and tidy forms), which
presumably fall under the category of rationality, Blake's Urizen and

his avatar Isaac Newton, who, with a compass, obsessively tries to survey the floor of Hell. For Dobyns, the same wandering is accomplished with his dog. In fact, readers are likely to hear the theme song from "Lassie" when Dobyns picks up the leash and heads out to walk and ruminate.

And what engages him these days is the mess the country has been in since 9/11. What poet hasn't been moved to record the change of heartbeat after that date? Dobyns is not interested in prophecy. In fact, although he is a poet who stands by the motivational effects of wonder, it's the other ironic and disabused side that often drives these poems.

"Napatree Point" is a good example of the kind of meander Dobyns is good for, and he wastes no time getting down to tacks. While a couple of poems in *Winter's Journey* tend to the windy side, "Napatree Point" moves coherently, if despairingly, into its subject— the lure of nihilism which wars against the duty of engagement. The dog trotting amiably by his side both circumscribes the poet's ramblings and brings him back to a reality for which the storms of war, the questions of national destiny, and the underlying questions about who owns the soul of America are just noise. In a sense, Dobyns answers the question that vexed Freud in *Civilization and Its Discontents,* namely, how to reconcile the claims of the family with the claims of civic and national purpose. The dog's implicit answer is simple: it's the family, stupid. And with the family comes the personal and idiosyncratic, and with it comes also lyricism, the stuff of poetry. Not for nothing are the poems in *Winter's Journey* bookended with traditional lyric poems. Not for nothing does the poet present himself as a person in need of political and metaphysical relief, his companion mutt like the mascot in a Dutch Master's painting.

If the answer is simple, arriving there is not. Indeed, Dobyns never quite accepts, intellectually or ethically, the dog's unequaled delight in the here-and-now. Qualification is the mind's defensive cross-hatching; its lack of complexity leads it either to parse trouble into intelligible and manageable bits, or to erect a screen. The dog would argue the latter and bark (meaning, "why bother?") for good measure. But that's the thing about accepting the responsibility of citizenship: the dog is either a reminder that privacy has primacy, or he is an ideal being invulnerable to the beyond, whether you construe that as political, philosophical, or temporal (the future and with it, mortal anxiety).

In "Mourning Doves," when he wonders if he isn't "straying" from poetry's domain, he is also led to ask, "but where does such an opinion come from?" It is a question he comes back to more than once, as in "Possum":

> Maybe that's why I've been writing poems on subjects
> mostly found in prose. I feel guilty pursuing the usual
> material when the world hovers at the brink of collapse.

It is the possibility that there might be an extra-poetic set of topics that a good poet avoids, presumably in favor of some more mannered—even genteel—set of topics ("flowers and sex"). Yet the genteel is not satisfying, and sex, however tamed by lyricism, remains a wildness that typifies all of nature, as we have heard. The real subject of "Mourning Doves" is human credulity, made acute in a democracy, having been presumably less so in the autocratic past:

> Back then fake prophets were as thick
> as leaves on an oak, as they had visions, preached
> salvation, and urged their followers to kill the Jews
> to ensure redemption. In time they would be hanged
> or burned at the stake; then a new prophet would
> arrive in town and new visions would get people
> marching again, eager victims of bogus information
> and ruthless ignorance.

Such examples of mass gullibility have ties to more recent examples. I quote this next at length, as it gives a feel for much of the state of acid bemusement in which Dobyns finds himself:

> The trouble with having a mind that includes
> an imagination, a sense of possibility, and a flexible
> grasp of cause and effect is that it can lead to astonishing
> pinnacles of human achievement and incredible lows,
> like the woman who found the Virgin Mary in a grilled

cheese sandwich, saying: "I went to take a bite and saw
this lady looking back." Ten years later she sold it
for twenty-eight thousand bucks to an online casino
that wants to take the sandwich on a world tour. This
is not uncommon. A couple in Nebraska have a pretzel
showing the Virgin holding the baby Jesus; a fellow
in Nashville displayed a cinnamon bun with the face
of Mother Teresa and a woman in L.A. found the face
of Jesus on the furry ass of a terrier mix named Angus.

Through his cloud of high dudgeon, Dobyns keeps his eye on
the natural and the personal. It's that desire for balance where the
outside world is so conspicuously haywire that keeps Dobyns' lute in
tune. He wonders, too, about questions of generic fit in "Possum":

A lyric poem can be a burst of emotion in one moment
of time and a narrative poem can employ its story line
to set up a lyric moment, but a meditative poem can be
a fretful thing, with dark musings coming and going
like crows weaving through winter trees.

But all these critical noodlings have a common denominator. It is
the old debate between knowing and believing, thinking and feeling. In "Rabbits," he puts it this way:

For years I've tried to balance
cynicism and wonder, like balancing a brick and a feather,
and I'm sorry to say that often I've fallen on the side
of the former.

Winter's Journey presents a variant, at once intelligent, amusing,
outrageous, and deeply humane, of the tug-of-war between what
we might call "instrumental knowledge" and felt experience. The
Enlightenment set knowledge on a pedestal as the model for what
the interior life of serious humans concern itself with, the prerogatives of knowledge outspending the prerogatives of felt experience
by a considerable margin. In other words, the life of the mind has
recently been held in higher esteem than the life of the spirit, holis-

tically construed. Spirit has been on the defensive, its trappings hijacked by charlatans and power freaks. For all his misgivings about the poet's ability to take on the endless horrors and absurdities, at the end of the day, his views are compact with Chekhov, of whom he relates:

> In a letter, Chekhov wrote
> that he didn't need to say stealing horses was wrong,
> he only had to describe a horse thief exactly.

("Napatree Point")

Wonder may invite the dangers of naïveté, and naïveté may prove wonder's Achilles' heel in the face of the onslaught of every kind of badness—especially the conniving, in-the-know kind, but Dobyns may claim more than the moral high ground, as he knows that figures of speech exceed numerical figures, and stanzas are better ways to talk about ourselves, be we ever so fallen, than decades and epochs. Entertaining, sardonic, troubled, and pissed, in no particular order, Dobyns' *Winter's Journey* allows this poet, long a fixture of American letters, to show what his work looks like at maximum extension.

Stephen Dunn

Here and Now

Dunn has made a career of Dunn telling it like it is. How, you ask, in this day and age can that be? Who has the leveling eye that is not shaded and consequently changed irreparably by the frame of its own report? Well, consider his approach:

> I've had wives and lovers—
> trust that I know a little about trying
> to remain whole while living
> a divided life. I don't easily open up.
> If you come to me, come to me
> so warned. I am smooth and grayish.
> It's possible my soul is made of schist.

The speaker here is a stone. But no matter: it's also all of us and him. And here is the fallout:

> Life itself is promiscuous. It feels right
> to place a few renegade details together,
> let them cavort. A moment later,
> it feels right to discipline them,
> smack them into shape...

Dunn offers in place of an aesthetic a push to be truthful in the service of a higher good, which turns out to be no "good" at all, no higher auspice, just a naturalism that would have pleased Johns Keats and Lennon:

> For you and me
> it's here and now from here on in.
> Nothing can save us, nor do we wish
> to be saved.
> Let night come
> with its austere grandeur,
> ancient superstitions and fears.
> It can do us no harm.
> We'll put some music on,
> open the curtains, let things darken
> as they will.

The thing is, the refusal of mystery in light of the "austere grandeur" of the indifferent world, is itself an elegiac response to mystery. It says, in effect: this is the equivalent of that, although with some unavoidable hesitation. As a stance, or final position, it is reactive, since it only makes a big deal out of our unsponsored solitude in view of a world-perspective that is no more—but which still provides a powerful ghosting effect—by presupposing its importance. Before it heads to the deep end, it is the poetry of the stiff upper lip, but with a drink on the patio. Dunn's downsizing of ego, expectation, hopes, etc., are of a piece with much of the demystifying of lyric intimation in recent years (see Ira Sadoff and others) and of art generally (see Dawkins' *Unweaving the Rainbow*). Dunn is okay with the loss of spirituality, that heart's mirage, and this new collection is not the first place we learn it. Indeed, it has been one of Dunn's themes to confront the New Man in himself, the one who appears without pre-approval, since his early collections. So, no Rock-n-Roll heaven for poets, no Tradition of the lyrically saved, no Yeatsian *Vision*. In sum, no Golgonooza, and yet, in another sense, with the falling away of all these struts of spirituality that used to prop up the poet's tower, there can be nothing left *but* Golgonooza.

Stephen Dunn's rise to prominence in the '70s coincided with issues surrounding poetry's accessibility. How to retain readers, and after the rise of MFA programs, how to "build audience"? Much contemporary poetry left readers perplexed (not that this impression has been alleviated with the years), and after the '70s poets branched off into schools whose mission was, in part, to stay relevant either dumping pronoun-centric lyrics or by looking for extra-literary models. Dunn was one of several emerging poets who knew that accessibility has a lot, way beyond matters of prosody, to do with timing of phrases, and that the model for that was stand-up. Today, our exemplars of that—Billy Collins, Tony Hoagland, David Kirby—could exchange the 92nd Street Y for The Comedy Club. Dunn looked to be a member of that tribe, but having his own concerns and following the bent of a different kind of talent, went his own way.

His superb new collection, *Here and Now,* breaks no new ground, and yet Dunn's advances are as hard to pin down as his breaks. In it you will find the hard-boiled realist behind whom stretches a romantic shadow, in whose silhouette the poet stands, figure to ground, drink in hand, eyeing the party. Dunn is smart on his feet, and loves to track a thought or feeling to its lair; this is a result of his poetics of ambivalence. That is, each subject automatically introduces its opposite. Reality arrives with theme and variation already in place, ready to be experienced. He is one of the smartest poets around, and I don't mean in terms of marshaling ideas. I mean in terms of mental footwork and the timing of movement, things more central to poetry's success than theoretical, religious, or political philosophies underpinning the Muse's hairdo.

> The world thought
> I didn't understand it,
> but I did, knew that to parse
> was to narrow
> and to narrow was to live
> one good way.
> Awash with desire
> I also knew a little was plenty
> and more than I deserved.
> And because I was guilty
> long before any verdict,
> my dreams unspeakable,
> I hunkered down

and buttoned up,
ready to give the world,
if I had to give it anything,
no more than
a closed-mouth kiss.

("The Puritan and the World")

"One good way" reminds one of Flaubert's startling remark about the bourgeois family, namely that their conformity placed them on the side of the angels. Dunn glosses this sentiment, or something like it, throughout *Here and Now*. In "Ars Poetica," a poem about Fred Astaire and the sense of *sprezzatura*, he puts it this way, "I could tell he was feeling / for limits, and what he could bear." Dunn expends a lot of energy on limits in this collection, especially when you consider his real quarry is not limiting, but spilling over. His theme, as in previous collections, concerns the push-pull of relationships and self-description, and how we reconcile the difference between spilling and limiting.

One of the more vivid poems to emerge from this collection is "If a Clown," which begins with a nod to most people's ambivalence about this representative of the comic species. But Dunn uses the hypothetical opportunity to make yet another *ars poetica* (there are several in this book).

If a clown came out of the woods,
a standard looking clown with oversized
polkadot clothes, floppy shoes,
a red, bulbous nose, and you saw him
on the edge of your property,
there'd be nothing funny about that,
would there?

As with clowns, so morals: context is all. A context-less clown makes no more laughter than a context-less moral rule makes approbation. Art, too, requires a minimum of outline, although as Impressionist painters were fond of pointing out, no "outline" occurs in nature:

> And if you were the clown, and my friend
> hesitated, as he did, would you make
> a sad face, and with an enormous finger
> wipe away an imaginary tear? How far
> would you trust your art?

At the same time that he is imaging contexts for clowns, he imagines quite literally going to the dogs in "Don't Do That," a bad-boy poem that has become something of a Dunn specialty, although as I say, his real fare is not the provocation as such, but recognizing something like justice the moment when it must be reined in:

> My hosts greeted me,
> but did not ask about my soul, which was when
> I was invited by Johnnie Walker Red
> to find the right kind of glass, and pour.
> I toasted the air. I said hello to the wall,
> then walked past a group of women
> dressed to be seen, undressing them
> one by one, and went up the stairs to where
> the Rottweilers were...

That moment comes when it is the dogs themselves, the presumed comrades in misrule, belong to the same system of constraints as the poet:

> They licked the face I offered them,
> and I proceeded to slick back my hair
> with their saliva, and before long
> I felt like a wild thing, ready to mess up
> the party, scarf the hors d'oeuvres.
> But the dogs said, No, don't do that...

In "Shatterings," Dunn moves into poet schtick imagining a class taught in "Whatever I Feel Like Talking About," where a few students have "mastered the boredom they think conceals them," a few hungry students remain, seeing through the poet-teacher's impromptu account of Trotsky and Rimbaud. Because the account reeks of self-aggrandizement, two exits follow, one by an excitable student who exclaims,

> let's tear up
> all our notes from this class-ridden class,
> let's caress the world with leaflets.

But a second student, an *ephebe* version of the True Poet, himself trues the poem with his exit:

> But there, isolated among them, is that boy,
> my Rimbaudian, all testosterone and refusal,
> the one I always teach to, look how
> he shrugs and heads toward the exit
> as if the future already had assured him
> it has openings for someone so unafraid of it…

Dunn has always hinted that a sense of estrangement tags most interpersonal dealings (the word "interpersonal" would be evidence of such). It goes hand-in-hand with other kinds of doubleness—ambivalence, secrets, duplicity that provide his subjects. In "The Melancholy of the Extraterrestrials," he steps into the Stepford/Conehead world of simulacra who weary of their mission:

> At night I'd bring home a weariness,
> and when I'd look in the mirror I'd see a creature
> made of smoke and pretense, losing desire
> to please the mother ship…

If blending is a burden, how much more is it to maintain the pretenses of duty? But pretense is another version of Astaire's burden, and if we are to endure being squeezed by our contradictions, we only have to wait. In the fine, accepting "Evenings like This," fury is not a meal that nourishes forever, for

> here comes Barbara with the shameless

store-bought cheesecake called Strawberry Swirl,
which, for a while, tends to end all arguments,
though there was a time we'd have renounced it—
back then when evenings like this were emblems
of excess and vapidity and a life that made us furious.

With Dunn, there is no acceptance without attitude, no provocation without its supporting rhetoric. And all that adds to energy and pictures of middle-class American life captured using the Vivid filter. Dunn's poems, as they accumulate in the mind, finally rise to an almost novelistic status: I put him not only with Dobyns, Kumin, and Collins, but with Updike, Cheever, and Ford, narrative bards of leafy developments in disturbia, with their affairs and stubborn self-begettings, mutts that won't learn, promiscuities, and old, biting memories.

The Despoiled and Radiant Now
Ambivalence in the Poetry of Stephen Dunn

For Stephen Dunn, seeing double poses no obstacle on the way to clarity. Double-seeing is what we do, and he has carved a much-admired career out of exploring what makes us ambivalent and of how ambivalence typifies something in our moment. Brodsky, a poet so superficially different from Dunn that it is hard to imagine an overlap, asserted that for a poet, ambivalence was a necessity. Of course, he was largely referring to imagination's survival mode when in Orwellian political (and consequently linguistic) circumstances, and for him the strategies and tactics obtaining in these circumstances were always in play. Dunn goes him one better in finding the necessity for ambivalence inherent *a fortiori* in daily life, without the heroism implicit in the expatriate's utterances, and his poems describe how that necessity plays itself out in the world of human relationships. In its regularity and dynamism, Dunn's fondness for counter-thesis would make a Hegel smile. It's an ability to appear synoptic when reflecting upon the mind's tendency to experience a thing and almost immediately to entertain its opposite. This opposite can take the form of a rejected alternative, a road not taken, an unchosen career, a personal secret, or, in its rare, expanded version, a whole secret life. Novelists' careers have been founded on less.

The secret, that privatized country of imagination, comes into play trailing a long literary pedigree. Like scarcity and prayer, secrets create value. One value they create for sure, whether as the result of a revelation harbored or the *Pater Noster*, is a more robust accommodation of the imagination to, as we would say, interiority. So in one sense we may allow ourselves to think that the ambivalence poets feel and write about has a positive component. It is the counter-alternative in the ambivalence that is at issue in Dunn, the one he seems interested in setting to theme. It's the imagination's equivalent of the road not taken, and it is none the worse for that, as far as Dunn is concerned: "Still I can't be sure, as you were, that what's hidden is any more mysterious /than the palpable immensity that isn't." ("Loosestrife")

The sense of ambivalent encounter that so often appears in Dunn's poems reminds me of something else the Russian said about ambivalence, namely that it stood to be a saving trait in a poet. In postponing commitment, the poet maintains a freedom that appears when ambivalence shades into equilibrium—a sort of discount freedom, based on a *détente* toward positions usually already compromised. This is not magical thinking. Indeed, freedom like this shades also into anomie:

> It was the hour of simply nothing,
> not a single desire in my western heart,
> and no ancient system
> of breathing and postures,
> no big idea justifying what I felt.

("Zero Hour")

As strategies go, the relinquishment of any "big idea" becomes itself the ghost, or trace, or elegy, of a big idea. Even lassitude has its poetry, but you won't get it by flying the flag of a traditional theme. As everyone knows, the Russians and French were onto the heaviness of anomie. It's a testimony to American exceptionalism that Whitman's sunny disposition pulled our poetry in toward imagism and mysticism. Anomie's lack of grasp allows the hand to dangle down into the lower depths. As he showed so adroitly in early poems, boundaries are enablers, as his more than passing acquaintance with formalism also shows. In interviews, he says things like, "The Commandments rose out of somebody's understanding of human nature; given who we are, we need a lot of Thou shalt not's."

When we go in this direction, we discover, not only that wish (and that need) to expand our interiority, but we find the not-chosen rife with imagination's fruits. It is not a stone's throw from the not-chosen to a fantasy land of counter-facts that tap the brake pedal of conformist behavior. It's not fantasy so much that matters anyway, but the psychological or human predisposition to imagine alternatives and to have lived with both those chosen and those not. This latter can become a kind of shadow life:

> It's why when we speak of truth
> some of us instantly feel foolish
> as if a deck inside us has been shuffled
> and there it is—the opposite
> of what we said.

("The Reverse Side")

Dunn is of the school of Chekhov, one of whose characters remarked (or rather thought) that it's the secret life that chiefly bears our significance. He also reminded us that we should be shadowed by a man with a hammer, who would be there to whack us, by way of reminder, every time we thought fit to avoid the pain of others, or by extension, to deny the secret life, with its sorrows and impossible desires. And Dunn knows, like Chekhov, why that life is secret:

> But by the middle years this other life
> had become his life. That was Odysseus's secret,
> kept even from himself. When he talked about return,
> he thought he meant what he said.

("Odysseus's Secret")

On this Chekhovian view, secrets are also a locked part of human interiority, and it is such interiority that has a purchase on a significant portion of modern personhood, just as deeds did in bygone epics, if the poets are to be believed. And the difference between

secrets and other sorts of interiority, is the difference between a
memory and a prayer. I would even venture to say that this Chekhovian view constitutes the tenor and atmospherics of much of Dunn's
poetry. Now it may be, and I think this may be Dunn's suspicion,
that the carrying of secrets and the need to divulge or confess them
enables us to consider ourselves in a new light of consequential-
ity, dignified by the knowledge of imperfection, inspired by those
same imperfections, to move away from faultless dreams, allowing
us something denied the gods, what we grandly call a tragic vision. I
mean, it is all intramural, is it not? Neither gods nor animals understand our weeping, our inconsistencies, our need for rhetoric, to say
that which is not, as well as that which is.

Usually, we don't know people's secret lives until there is a rupture
or an unlocking. The subsequent release paints us as even more
partial—even more mortal (i.e., discontinuous)—creatures than
we had feared. This is tragic in the classical sense: things are not
meant to work out. Its revelation as a secret also ruins it as a secret:
it is under wraps no longer. Meanwhile there is something usable in
discontinuity, in what doesn't finish (even in secrets). Dostoyevsky
knew it and nailed incompletion to tragedy's porch. Dunn mentions
elsewhere that as a young writer it was Dostoyevsky who turned his
head around. After that, he was good to go: the seeming inconsis-
tency in Raskolnikov's opposition to animal cruelty would pose no
problem for Dunn:

> So next week why not admit
> that what Raskolnikov did
> has always made you dream?
> The more you expose yourself
> the more you become unrecognizable.

("The Soul's Agents")

The secret not only creates the value of interiority, it gets another
project going. An awareness of the value of secrecy kindles an awareness of mystery, and from that flows all manner (but not all) of
art. Writing one's life in public is both anathema to that sense of

the sacred and unaesthetic, insofar as poems are concerned. But emerging from the high water mark of confessionalism, Dunn is unafraid of the potential insult that follows from revelation. Take his well-known "The Routine Things Around the House," where the speaker both elegizes and thanks his mother for revealing to him her breasts, a bounded moment of tender instruction that left him, he argues, a regular guy without hangups.

> this poem
> is dedicated to where
> we stopped, to the incompleteness
>   that was sufficient
>   and to how you buttoned up,
>   began doing the routine things
> around the house.

Now no one should be under the illusion that the boundaries of behavior reflected in the boundaries of form or any other aesthetic approach do more than offer the "momentary stay against confusion" which the poem proposes as its contribution to human solidarity. I note that the "stay" is just as mortal as the sayer; only the confusion seems to have a purchase on the long run. In an interview, Dunn puts it this way: "I do think that in our poems and in our stories we can offer those momentary stays against confusion. We can create coherencies out of the raw stuff of life, the chaos of it, the fraughtness of it. Credible fictions that for a while seduce us and others into acceptance of them. Versions of a life, not a life. Yes, if we do them well enough they may well indeed constitute a life, especially after we're gone."

There is also the presumption that goes with necessary fictions. Consider the ending to Dunn's well known "At The Smithville Methodist Church":

> Evolution is magical but devoid of heroes.
> You can't say to your child
> "Evolution loves you." The story stinks
> of extinction and nothing

> exciting happens for centuries. I didn't have
> a wonderful story for my child
> and she was beaming. All the way home in the car
> she sang the songs,
> occasionally standing up for Jesus.
> There was nothing to do
> but drive, ride it out, sing along
> in silence.

Human relationships and dealings are of course layered, as are the ambivalences they foster. It is one of Dunn's strengths to find these layers and write the narratives that are appropriate to them. As travel writer David Downie once wrote, "Time can render true what began in falsehood." The thing about authenticity (or inauthenticity) of feelings goes back to poets like James Wright and John Logan. The fact of authenticity began to lose force when lyric poetry began to undergo a destabilization in the 1970s—and for the same reason: things like subjectivity itself were put under a microscope and revealed their parts. This shift notwithstanding, Dunn acquitted himself well by building a sense of knowingness in the poems he made, and he went right on writing poems about men and women. Part of what he knew was that authenticity is not to be confused with the likes of sincerity: the latter was always self-divided. What better way to say this than to first look in the bedroom? To have a partner is to enact an ambivalence; it is inherently unstable, as the title, "Sleeping with Others," attests:

> I am unreachable.
> If I were standing next to you
> you'd see for yourself
> how far away I was.

Dunn is one of the great poets of domestic mystery, and that mystery is in turn founded on yet another division: the satisfaction and the outrage of solitude. Rilke went so far as to declare that love was the mutual protection of solitude, and insight that would have quite sobered the woozy rhapsodists of Plato's *Symposium*. The ambivalence, the combining power of many viewpoints, in married life is nowhere more apparent (nor so well hidden in plain sight) than in speech.

Dunn is also perhaps our preeminent poet at clarifying what's intractable. It is no small feat. Where other poets are content to gesture or skirt the difficulties of description altogether, Dunn jumps right in and sheepdogs wandering meaning through the gate. Keeping discourse between such navigational guidelines would seem to suggest that Dunn is a realist, by which I mean a poet who steers his way between desire and nothing in a dialectic that has profound stylistic implications. His own poems, for example, owe something to the *sprezzatura* of a James Tate, while also seeking the aesthetic oneness of closure. Not for him the discontinuous, the merely textual, the fodder of irony. Although his demotic ease might be mistaken for the work of a poet who likes to spin language, his work comes from older stock and his persistent explorations of the Id's agenda and the power associated with that, in contrast to redemptive or illuminative moments (secular division), mark him as a poet who has not moved far beyond the gravitational field of the Verities:

> You've faked so many feelings
> in your time you wonder
> if it could have been
> the ghost of faked feelings
> offering you an authentic sadness

("The Song")

Secrets and lies are often paired. The linguistic ramifications are similar: both secrets and lies are exceptions to a general rule. Just as secrets require a presumption that revelation would be bad, a lie requires general truthfulness in language as normative. This is the reason, among other things, that Satan's mission in *Paradise Lost* was doomed from the get-go and that there is no honor among thieves. For Dunn, the subject of secrets and lies, of ambivalent suspensions of allegiance, suggests an acquiescence to boundaries, even as it requires boundaries to be manifest at all. And therein lies a paradox, the kind that a resourceful poet can hang a hat on. Dunn also knows the incentive power of temptation:

> the soul on its own
> is helpless, asleep in the hollows
> of its rigging, waiting to be stirred.

("And So")

The individual, particularized soul—the poet's, say, becomes the general "the soul," as if to demonstrate a principle, rather than render a confession. It is the principle he is after, almost as if he had discovered an elemental force previously unnoticed by literature. At bottom, the truths to be discovered in the relationships of ordinary people are every bit as significant to the individuals as approved motives or larger, tectonic forces like history—a region American poets have had to struggle to claim in lyric poetry. It is the prison of days that is at issue. At issue too, is how to render the personal moment, leaving the poet unsure at times whether to claim the privilege of singularity (authenticity), and further, whether that singularity may best be experienced as shaped by relationships, moral development, or a new historical epoch: "our solitudes are so populated / that sometimes after sex / we know it's best to be quiet." ("Sleeping with Others"). At times in his poems you sense something like Stoicism:

> The truth is,
> I learned to live without hope
> as well as I could, almost happily,
> in the despoiled and radiant now.

("A Postmortem Guide")

At others we experience situational conformity and at still others, desire for what it can't have, as if imagination were a skyhook. And behind all is the ticking.

Claudia Emerson's
Secure the Shadow

Claudia Emerson's follow-up to her celebrated *Late Wife* opens with two fires, one visible, one invisible. Like all fires, they manifest contrasting qualities: the prospect of utility, but also the more (and aesthetically interesting) danger of immolation (and of auto-da-fé). The visible fire is a house fire seen from the highway; the invisible one is underground, mineral, nuclear, the realm of Pluto rising. Hence to begin a book of this one's somber colors is like lighting a match on entering a catacomb.

Formal, meticulously wrought, Emerson's poems have a thing for (unrhymed) couplets and alternating indentations. It's the way to go if you're dealing with the kind of subject matter Emerson is dealing with, for this is a book about death. And yet, putting it this way fails to suggest either the poet's nuanced approach, or the muffled and sublimated outrage at the facts of our discontinuity. Wittgenstein's Zen-like apothegm—"death is not a part of life"—alerts us to the fact, otherwise passed over, that talk about death tends to be either glib or naïve: it's something about which we can't develop an informed opinion. There is, from this perspective, nothing to be said about death. At the same time, that border is also where language learns the steps to its song-and-dance, including the verbal "gestures" that point us toward whole regions utterly resistant to articulation. But articulation is not all of (or for that matter, the top of) expression, and while precise capture may be denied, it does not follow that intimation likewise fails. What is *no* for Ludwig, is *yes* for Stevens. To be fair, Professor Wittgenstein professed not to understand poetry, and you can see why: he thought it was an instrument that only worked within a rational framework. It was therefore flummoxed by the irrational. That was the young Wittgenstein. The more mature man conceded a place for the unsayable—at least as a possible component of what needs to go on in our minds in order for the rational to gather force and do *its* thing.

Emerson frames her collection between two mortal events: the early death of her brother and the late and presumably "natural" death of her father, who has aged out, and whose departure could not be subject to the sense (and the critique) of untimeliness— except that it is. Even the most "natural" of demises is strange and sets in motion customs and responses that are inexplicable in the face of rationality. All the more so is she weirded out by the deaths of the nameless in nature, from animals to vegetable life, whose annual demise really does spell the significance of seasons. It is, after all, the prerogative of poetry to assert how it is with subjectivity. For its part, subjectivity only acquires its thematic halo with the acknowledgment of a subject's peculiarity and consciousness of that peculiarity—not only what it has in common with others of its kind, but what it has only in its own case. And death fits that bill better than any other feature. As Everyman knew, you can't die another's death.

You can observe it, though. And you can say how it makes you feel whether this is a description (including self-) or a memory. In this regard, she has much in common with death-fascinated and yet resistantly documentary photographers specializing in the aesthetic glow, glamor and pity of mortality: I am thinking of E. J. Bellocq, Diane Arbus, and Sally Mann. And with Emerson, there is the additional sense, so deeply human, that to lay poetry at the feet of oblivion implies a kind of moral victory, although "victory" is perhaps too grandiose a word here. It should come as no surprise that she mounts a considerable formal engine to accomplish these offerings, and her formal courtesies embed her work within a matrix of southern figures, not the least of whom is Faulkner, but also include Robert Penn Warren, Eleanor Ross Taylor, and Betty Adcock.

The opening poem, "Late April House Fire along Interstate 81," sounds like a landscape painting, and this, in turn, puts us in mind of aesthetic responses. A poet like Dickey would allow for such a response (as with "Firebombing") on the theory that denying the possibility—on moral grounds—that violence and beauty like to hook up puts us in denial about something human in us, something that satisfies but doesn't improve. And the question is, which is the more perverse, the secret fascination or its denial? Perhaps all curiosity is like that. Emerson, however, allows herself to be drawn to this fire, but keeps her distance. Her verse, too, both draws and distances, as does the ambivalence of her recurring images: bodies, fires, smoke, blades, and flowers, vegetative weavings, interlacings, even old lace itself, all formally secure and distant, while hinting at some still-to-be-had intimacy.

> I had wondered for some time about its source,
> The smoke a fixed-roiling column visible
>
> For miles, unchanged by the wind...

The poem is, in a sense, a narrative of self-notation. While the poems in *Secure the Shadow* deal with family death and with death generally, it is also a book that examines the credal role of artistic creation in history and memory. The epigraph from Faulkner clues us in: "Memory believes before knowing remembers." Now if memory does anything of the sort, it must be added that memory precedes history and so enjoys a precedent status. It is not only what befalls us, courtesy of the mortal coil, it's also how our feels give us push-back, and because we can set the time of the poem in our image, form (Emerson is a formalist) gives us a little wriggle-room against necessity:

> The flame's straight rush—contained, bright-rising
>   Enravishment...

———

> But this was
> Anguish, not yet grief. And so I slowed

But did not stop to watch someone else's
    Tragedy burn past this brief, nearly

Beautiful suspension that changes nothing.

The anguishing experience is *after*, the grief is after, as is the tragedy. So the poet declines to stop—it would be the equivalent of aestheticizing violence ("the *nearly beautiful* suspension"). The *suspension* changes nothing, and yet the whole is about the violence of change.

In "Half-Life: Pittsylvania County, Virginia," Emerson writes of an invisible fire, a vein of uranium, evidently the largest in the country, that smolders directly beneath the town in which she grew up. In a part of the country that imagines Hell a fiery enclosure underground, the arrival of the atomic age, indifferently meting out cancers, starts to accumulate some of the fear and trembling associated with Old Time Religion. The poet remarks on the irony of naming an element after a frozen planet: it is at once wildly arbitrary and yet somehow deeply relevant to the indifferent ground of her childhood.

That some slow, cold distant planet formed
    With a core of ice and stone and named
For the embodiment of sky and heaven
    Should have anything to do with it seemed wrong...

That she will set up a poem by front-loading it with *that* clauses (both anchored and administers by the key verb "seemed") gives the reader the sense that this cosmic creepiness takes place in a wonderful cabinet, a Joseph Cornell box of carefully selected descriptive items that, by virtue of their selection, become talismans:

The percussive, intermittent tick

Of their Geiger counters has escalated
    To something measureless—the place itself
a worse genetic element, the very land
    guilty.

Time and again, Emerson nails this kind of description—it's just-
so observation and jeweler's precision. It might be that the formal
distancing holds the frequently odd and random nature of things
at bay, along with their predisposition to supplant art with the grotesque—a predisposition that has all too often come to characterize southern literature as a whole. In this poem, the language of a
trial is appropriate because the land itself holds a "secret" and won't
"confess" in recognizable ways (its language is cancer). It is by articu-
lating the slow violence of radiation that she supplies the plausible
"evidence" that results in the "guilty" verdict:

> The houses on the street where I grew up
> Marked with its slow plague...insatiable—
>
> The chimney ciphering
> like the church organ-pipe, one long note
>
> unplayed, the sound unaccounted for. She would have been
>   bound inside herself to a stake—burning at it,
> the rope around her wrists giving way a little
>   every day to the stronger bonds of invisible fire;
> what if it were in the walls, the brick laced with it,
>   the water, the melons and eggs, the milk; what if
>
> she sifted it with the salt into the flour and fried it
>   in the pan, telling her daughter to run away
> from her, to go you go, every day,
>   as far as you can. But what if it were
> in her apron with her little knife:
>   she could see clearly herself in its blade.

Of course the what-ifs tilt heavily toward the truth. They are
alternative descriptions, plausibilities, that narrate what is otherwise a "cipher." By the last section we come to a choral "we ("We had
already memorized the three-bladed / black fan, symbol for the
fallout shelter"), and this parting of ways between memory-as-belief
and Faulkner's memory-as-knowledge:

>   I never saw that shelter, never met
>   anyone who had, but believed in deep shelves
>   of syrupy pears and peaches as I had been taught
>   to believe in heaven, safe, dreaded
>   place I was told I would go...

That safe place "I was told I would go" is now the unsafe place, both the "guilty" land of undeserved cancers and the hell of Sunday school. Knowledge moves on, notwithstanding the fact that belief was ever the poet's original stance. Craft, meanwhile, so often bought at the expense of freshness and spontaneity, is not a situation for Emerson. Her crafted lines and judge's eye are not merely associated: they are the same thing. Sometimes the difference between the poetry we want and the poet we get comes down to a poet's ability to pull off surprises within constraints both of form and of realism. That is, we are most pleased, most transported, by the unfolding of what we know, as if realism itself were a miracle. In "Elegy in July for the Hotel Astra," we read of the revenant structures— themselves self-elegies—after the Interstate has rendered US 1 obsolete:

>   The desolation without season, summer
>   somehow heightens it...

Right now you are asking, what is "the desolation without season"? The poem about an aftermath begins with the assumption that there is something we know that must correspond to such a description. In *Jerusalem*, Blake says "they became what we beheld." I have said elsewhere that *pushed* description becomes *vision*. Emerson's motel elegy is a case in point.

>   July, long
>   month that had meant their greatest thriving,
>   offers itself again to the decades' abandonment.

>   But most have fallen beyond use,
>   windows paneless, still numbered doors ajar,
>   anything worth salvage hauled out piecemeal,

the only inhabitants small birds, black snakes,
     wasps and vines, cavity-seekers, their shadows.

The eye whose vision penetrates surfaces where the gaze of others
stops; the ear that hears a distant music no on else can make out; the
touch that registers what lives within textures: these are the qualities
we find so desirable. They make the poetry we want. Unfortunately,
they are also rare enough in what we get, which rareness adds fuel to
the elegiac engine, supplying the reader's imagination with poetry's
equivalent to the painter's negative space:

The road took with it

     the unreachable looking, the mirage's
          vivid shimmering above fresh blacktop
     a shining unattainable refraction,
          a vision disappearing quick as the light
     sweet crude we used to chase it—irresistible
          that fleet mirror of what was sky.

Emerson's poems sometimes seem a working out of causal chains:
the *X* did something to *Y*, which is a kind of *1*, *2*, and *3*—the visionary result, and, let's face it: this visionary result is where we wanted
to be anyway. The act of reading makes manifest the movements it
takes to get there. In "It,"

     My cousin liked to dangle me upside down
          by the ankles, my aunt's crossed in thick disapproval

     at eye level, the world gone wrong, blood fallen
          in a dizzy rush to my ears until, almost

     made afraid, I heard his familiar laughter
          as though from some sealed depth beneath me.

Until he is called up…

When her cousin is called up, he is simultaneously called down, in this formula. The "world gone wrong" is "the very land guilty" of "Half-Life: Pittsylvania County, Virginia." Images of Vietnam, where this cousin served, begin with stock images (water buffalo, rice paddy), but the destined-for-hackneyed quality does not extend to several images—the immolation of Buddhist monks, for instance, or the iconic screaming girl, both of which follow. Now ubiquitous, these images have only one benefit: they resist being commodified. Emerson imagines "the self as fire." In contrast with such burning is the cool image of a doll that her soldier cousin sends her as a gift ("her face visible beneath a pale caul / of tissue paper"):

> But I could imagine
> no part of her in the plots of my other dolls,
>
> no dream house or car, no man. She was sewn
> tight into her only dress, her form,
>
> a full grown woman's, rigid, inside it, posture
> strict, unbending, her gaze untranslatable.
>
> She had traveled across the ocean in the belly
> of a plane, in dark storage with letters, packages,
>
> those flagged caskets...

The doll brings her to realize how ill-fitting the images are, except for the one iconic image of the burning girl (the doll might have found place in her childhood):

> the scorched disfigurement
>
> of her back unseen, inescapable
> as what had been the road
>
> behind her, its vanishing point
> consumed inside an earthbound

cloud, her scream—seared
        aperture to something

the image cannot document.

The girl is a victim of Napalm, but the cousin is a casualty of Agent
Orange, the defoliant used to deny the enemy vegetative cover:

                    He would be
            matter of fact, telling me about

        the Agent Orange he'd breathed, believed revenant
                in a tumor, the cancer in his throat...

The memory itself metastasizes into something new: voice, body,
the existential memory of which history offers its crude, approxi-
mate narratives mixing common images and generalization:

            his voice I would hear burning with

    a knowing beyond memory—wordless,
            imageless—the body's own account.

That body is also subject to the volume's title poem, where the
common (southern) ritual photography of dead children suggests
how far into denial we are willing to travel, brandishing aesthetics to impose on our extremity of grief and nostalgia. The poem,
both in subject matter and control, reminded me of the work of
photographer Sally Mann—another Virginian—who is also drawn
to children as access to other worlds and to the mystery of material
death. Emerson sets down examples of this practice as evidence of
its acceptance, which she declines to brand as grotesque or acutely
morbid, even though, on the face of it, the practice can't entirely
escape its dark, exotic, ultimately abject cast:

    The photograph contains the whole if it:
            he wears a white gown that might have been
    for the christening, no shoes, his plump hands

> posed, folded, dimpled, the hands
> of a healthy child, the face still round with baby fat.
> Whatever took him, then, took him quickly—
>
> whooping cough, pneumonia, a fever,
> something that left no mark…

That ominous "left no mark" seems to echo the language of the pervy coach in Gary Gildner's "First Practice," who tells his football charges, after inciting them to antagonistic aggression, not to leave any marks. Surely not leaving a mark, in some sense both increases the bona fides of death, but also of the family, whose mourning includes the wish for representations of the dead child who, on this side of *vita brevis*, may well have had no other images made. Of another baby, dead nine days, we learn,

> the mother refusing to part with her only daughter—
> the rigor having come and gone, the body
> posed seated, posture flawless—head turned
> so that she gazes away slightly to her left.
> at something just beyond the gold-embossed
> frame in thoughtful enthrallment…

The word "enthrallment" is tied to a narrative of colossal posthumous irony because it is not just sight, but *enthralled* sight, for what could be more enthralling than death? Emerson recognizes here a kind of postmortem decorum that these photographs reflect, a southern emphasis on morals and manners, now askew. But every child of a southern mother acknowledges that the accent on manners follows one throughout life: why not beyond? It would have been easy to leave such oddities on the porch of the bizarre and leave it at that, but Emerson provides them with a degree of meticulous attention that tends both to suppress and subvert irony. She is of the school that had just as well leave irony behind when ultimates loom. Kafka himself had assured us that no irony was to be had there, and so the strangeness of the custom is, as it were, washed clean of its taint.

In "Animal Funerals, 1964," Emerson recounts another way into
the fascination with death, this time not the death *of* children but
through them to the feckless land where children must first make
sense of the senseless:

> Roles were cast: preacher, undertaker—
>
> the rest of us a straggling congregation
>   reciting what we could of the psalm
>
> about green pastures as we lowered the shoebox
>   and its wilted pall of dandelions
>
> into the shallow grave one of us had dug
>   with a serving spoon...

These poems not only associate death with children, animals,
dolls, and weeds, but with qualities. In "First Death," a great aunt's
demise proposes the burden of speechlessness, not only as a corol-
lary to mortality, but as a commentary on poetic utterance:

> and from the threshold, I could see
>
> my great-aunt's face abstracted in half-light,
>   her mouth a deeper shadow closing—
>
> what she might have understood
>   of my labor already vanished on her tongue.

Her mouth has become a "shadow"—the niece's instructed care
does not return as acknowledgment or thanks. She has done the
needful, which amounts, we might say, to abandoning the need
for acknowledgment, for thanks. Does the *needful*, therefore, leave
poetry behind? Is there a further implication that forgetting might
be a necessary part of felt language, including poetry? If so, the poet
is on her own; the poem is on its own. But isn't this the case anyway?
One is on a ledge, and in important ways, justice lies in that. Emerson's image of this ledge is the porch ("Variations from the Porch"):

I don't know

what felt safe about that bleak
        reclusion, out where anyone

could have seen me; but I
        understand now that when

a bird sleeps under its own wing,
        it is the world that ceases to see.

The sleeping bird, self-covered, ties the poet to the unknown, and
the confidence with which she launches her words into space (the
space of the page, as well as of consciousness), must come to terms
with its ambivalence between embrace and objectification. When
she watches the unseasonable rose,

        slightly out of place and season
                intricately entwined and in full flower,

        I thought first how beautiful
                it was, and then how wrong.

The ambivalence itself seems to blossom as well,

                . . . it bloomed in quiet fury

        as though to please me,
                or again, fully taken with itself

Our connections to, and departures from, the natural world—in
short, our interactions—tell us something about the anxiety with
which we approach our own place. Gardening becomes subject to
ritual: it is ritualism that is at the heart of the interactions. Emerson's poems lie on the page as orderly as a garden—and as anxiety-
inducing: she matches the "frozen slurry" with patterning of her
own, as a kind of objective correlative to nature in the form of the
poem. Her *cultivation* reprises and replaces the natural abundance

with verbal abundance and replaces the self-binding of weeds and
flowers with the bindings of formal poetry. In a memorable aside,
Peter Ackroyd notes how the interlacing of word and vine in medieval illuminated manuscripts suggests a fencing in of the darkness
of the forest, so poorly defended against, so much the domain of
the unknown. Emerson's poems have that quality—tight weavings
to keep something at bay—the kind of something her brother felt
in "Old Elementary,"

> Terrified or furious, he would call me:
> *it's in there,* he'd swear, *in the old elementary*—
>
> desperate to blame something—asbestos,
>   radiation, unhappiness itself—
>
> to place, displace the cancer onto the first school
>   he despised...

This "displacement" is also the mechanism behind "Half Life:
Pittsylvania County, Virginia," where danger lies hidden and strikes
in ways that seem to escape rational inquiry. The elemental feelings
of grief and blame, subdued and reformed by ritual, bleed over into
other areas. Two poems about animal deaths ("Animal Killings" and
"Documentary") link up to the deaths of her brother and father.
Both deal with our recourse to myth and legend as a way of imposing form on kindred, but ultimately unknown, lifeforms. The latter
involves a legendary giant boar—once a domestic pig—captured
in a swamp:

> The narrative, already virile,
>   the town nearby embellished—
>
> how he heard before he saw it,
>   killed it with a single shot
>
> or sure it would have killed him—
>   how the creature had all the features

of a wild boar in its sheer size,
    the coat mud-rimed wire, tusks thick

as a man's forearm, but also how
    it bore sure signs that someone had once

owned it, claimed it in the docked tail,
    in the ear...

Something claimed "in the ear"—a phrase with a Rilkean echo—
returns us to the fine way Emerson's poems deliver fidelity and exac-
titude of detail, the image, often nested or interwoven, of things
passing from one state to another. It is a hallmark of her work, and it
has the feel of *work*, as if she were offering up something real to the
unreal and uncanny situations that are the occasions of the strongest
poems here. I think of no less a dynamic duo than James Dickey,
whose comrade POW performs a dance upside down before he is
beheaded, and the radical Christian Leo Tolstoy, whose stricken
anti-hero Ivan Ilych cannot die until he has suffered every pain
and humiliation, undone every illusion and moved outside himself
(there is, in fact, no "self" in the usual sense left), making his confession to the Void. Emerson's poems belong with this company; they
exemplify such offerings as characteristic of the poet at her most
human, by offering the subjective *as* human, its freakiness intact,
and by making us believe that this offering is the most poetic of
documentary rituals.

On Katie Ford

In the short space of two collections, Katie Ford has emerged as one of the most recognizably thoughtful poets of her talented generation. Manifesting a rigorous aesthetic combining allusiveness with inwardness, her poems mark the multivalent ways by which the moral conscience registers dailiness with history (also myth) and how consciousness itself perceives the relationship of the small to the overwhelming, the weak to the deadly, the remote to the pressing moment, the insignificant to the topical. A graduate of Harvard Divinity School and of the University of Iowa School of Letters, she has made an impressive readership for herself in less than a decade with her collections (which also include a chapbook) and appearances in such periodicals as *The American Poetry Review, The New Yorker, Partisan Review, Ploughshares,* and *Poetry.*

Prepared, therefore, by talent, temperament, intelligence, and training to write with a mature hand that belies her debut, her poetry frequently rises above that of her peers in that it dispenses with ironic defenses while reaching for the tragic. Indeed, the tragic is the condition in which her work flourishes, as much as disposition toward praise, which, though dormant, one intuits is the baseline of her verse.

In Renaissance painting the deposition depicts the moment of the taking down of the corpse of Jesus from the cross. It begins a time of mystery and suspense: Christ has gone into death, whose outcome now seems beyond the reach of either faith or imagination. It is also of course a taking down of information in legal proceedings, a taking down of facts that bear the weight of truth and lie under the constraints of penalties. Her debut collection, *Deposition,* concerns issues of commitment and absence, staples of faith as these things relate to the ways by which the existential body negotiates an arrangement with the metaphysical. It was a book that signaled the presence of a serious and inquisitive talent, a lyrical mastery, and a high seriousness blessedly devoid of the pitfalls—sonority and self-importance, for instance—that too often accompany it. Some reviewers professed mystification at parts of her first book, *Deposition*, but all recognized the stakes and so paid attention.

Subsequently, she and her husband had to be evacuated during Hurricane Katrina, and she has written about the destruction of the city in poems that register the disastrous tangle of events, culminating in the deadly refuge of the Superbowl, evoking comparison with the Roman Colosseum, a structure likewise eviscerated and left a ruin. These poems formed the core of her second collection, *Colosseum*. The colosseum becomes be an image of the human mind, "also a place of ruin," indicative of the randomness of potentially fatal encounters.

What is both surprising and tonic is the realization that her poems come from the same well as such European poets as Seferis, Tsvetaeva, and Rilke. She has spoken of these poets as antecedents and mentors, signaling an ambition not just to be a poet but, in the German distinction, a *Dichter*, a poet who wishes to plumb moral and philosophical depths and to invite us along. If you are a sucker, as I am, for high seriousness you couldn't do better than to read Ford putting aside for the moment the critical ordnance we often stash nearby as we anticipate our first encounters with new writers. The fact is that these depths and metaphysical nuances have been drying up even among poets (I am even tempted to say especially among poets), for whom it has all too often seemed advantageous to abandon the Verities and move out into a thinner and more hospitable environment less *engagé* than armed with quotation marks. For Ford we are hardly done with the mysteries (or vice versa), and her poems give the impression that we would do well to imagine a world in which metaphysics doesn't leave us stranded at the feet of the skeptic. Blake was another, as was Heaney. Since the '90s when the size of the malaise first threw its shadow across a whole generation—Katie Ford's generation, David Foster Wallace and Dave Eggers understood that the key to rescuing literature's force was not a return to a "new naiveté" (as Žižek conceives of it), not a "reenchantment" of nature, but a reimagining of what wonder would look like, feel like, in a time whose wonders are either radically devalued or negative ones tied to disaster.

Katie Ford's work is significant too in that it points to a way beyond Jorie Graham, whose abandonment of beauty and its aesthetic burdens effectively derailed, in spite of Helen Vendler's interventions, one of my generation's most admired careers. Ford's poems attend upon their subjects without actively imposing either form or theme (though they have both). They do not shrink-wrap their content; rather, they attend, as Heidegger recommended, to the being inside and its absence or suspension. That way they avoid the urge to twist expression into pontification. Here is the opening of "Colosseum":

> I stared at the ruin, the powder of the dead
> now beneath ground, a crowd
> assembled and breathing with
> indiscernible sadnesses, light
> from other light far off
> and without explanation.

Critics have noted that her poems often make connections with animals, and she has spoken of animals as a "remnant force of what's left." Yet her poems move among the effects of the natural world without her appearing a nature poet, which would leave her in a niche, a kind of updated Mary Oliver, but less inclined to promote the general health, in spite of her academic credentials, than a poet devoted to what was left of the truth. A poet, in other words, just as easily offensive to the nostrils of a True Believer as to the plain materialist.

Let me put her work in context. The excesses of irony that have afflicted the entire art world (a form of skepticism directed at both means and ends) have had a profound effect on American poetry, which has tried in ways ranging from resistance to assimilation to recapture the—for lack of a less-abused word—*wonder* for which the arts are traditionally celebrated and for which praise is the touch-stone. This shift was especially notable in poetry because the art, in spite of its dwindling fortunes in recent centuries, still clung to the prestige (or what it conceived as prestige) associated with meta-physical things—of which matters of the spirit and religion were the epitome. There being no spiritual things, poetry's subject base was eviscerated, it was felt, and what ensued was a devil's bargain of materialist theorizing, from so-called language poetry, to a rena-scence in poetry that doesn't rely on subjective premises. The cost has been great, even as the shift allowed the academy to make an ever tighter grip on the art *per se*, in the name of custodial expedi-ency, and its new practitioners, unschooled in the wars' clash of values, exercised increasing control over the production and recep-tion of serious verse. On the one hand, we had the democratic (but false) belief that poetry could be written by everyone; on the other we had the elitist view that poetry was now the niche of a group of tightly trained cognoscenti.

Ford has moved beyond the dangers implicit in this dichotomy just as her mentor Graham sought to collapse (but with less success) the dualisms implicit in a recent poetry wars. And her poems are layered enough to warrant the notion that in transcending old dual-isms she is less about healing contraries than simply looking ahead. For one who would investigate our times by torchlight, past and future, memory and hope, there's surprising incandescence to be had. The present is revealed as the more significant by these lights.

Tess Gallagher's *Midnight Lantern*
New and Selected Poems

Tess Gallagher's early work embodies what has somewhere been called "Iowa expressionism," which might be thought of as *the experience of what it is like to be me feeling the presence (or absence) of you.* The "Iowa" component connects up not only the wheaty gold of the Heartland, but adds its own wash—muted, spiky, or jungle-lush, as the case may be—of internationalism—especially as that term takes root in Spanish and Eastern European Surrealism. Geographic influence aside, what has been interesting about this kind of poetry is the emphasis on interiority as the authenticating agency in the work. Behind this, as you might surmise, is the notion that personhood—and its representation—is a value that transcends even art, that sees poetry as a means, not an end. It is therefore a moral (and political) art, for it comes to rest in a place that is still humming after language has come to a stop. It follows that a robust attitude toward *means* is a good thing to have. Gallagher's poems speak to the beauties inherent in rendered language, but despite the poet's considerable descriptive gifts, the poems are also impatient with decoration.

This impatience acts as a defense against the potentially debilitating onset of irony, that aesthetic malady that renders so much of poetry (and art) insignificant and leaves the door cracked so that even the most feeble strains of nihilism are liable to move in and infect the whole. Gallagher's poems, seen in the light of this early affiliation, may seem *escuela vieja*, but it is the school of her mentors, Theodore Roethke and Stanley Kunitz. Her *Midnight Lantern: New and Selected Poems* shows how the personal, the private, and the intuitive continue to thrive in the midst of cultural and political commodifications of every sort—and why Akhmatova was more important than the Politburo.

The mid-1970s debut volume, *Instructions to the Double,* proved a versatile demonstration of how subjectivity, whose mission is to make sense of the interior, provides the key to that interiority (as opposed to, say, religious or philosophical reflection). Moreover, it does so whether the interior, with its memories and ways, is a made thing or something naturally baked in. It is one of the prized collections of the decade, which is otherwise remembered for the Bee Gees, gas lines, Son of Sam, Watergate and the storm of theory that descended on lyric poets, who were challenged to justify their practices and the privileges arrogated to them. These challenges were issued in ways that would today seem oddly literal and overbearing.

For Gallagher, subjectivity itself holds the lever to every larger conversation, from digging the self's mines to the politics of human survival. As she says in "Second Language,"

> you smoke after a meal, the sign
> of food still on the plate, the two
> chairs drawn away and angled again
> into the room.

The fortunes of language as both social tool and vehicle capable of transporting the private into the thoroughfares are not the issue, although conversation—or the utterance that patterns the diurnal nature of experience—is (mostly) the goal. Not that she is unaware that language has been deemed problematic, but the avoidance of what Beckett calls the "discrediting" of language becomes not only an avoidance—which, after all, is a negative way of putting it, but becomes a *behovely* conviction to carry forward. In the title poem of her second collection, *Under Stars,* that sense of the vehicular integrity of the *letter* of feeling is buoyed by its own fragility and made manifest in the image of a woman going out to the mailbox at night to mail an actual letter:

The sleep of this night deepens
because I have walked coatless from the house
carrying the white envelope.
All night it will say one name
in its little tin house by the roadside.

In the early work, as her first title, *Instructions to the Double,* suggests, the "double" is a person of interest. Moving from book to
book, it becomes variously the other, the echo, the Beloved, the
idealized self, and the interlocutor. In later work, it becomes the
other country—Ireland—a counter-image of her own working-class
origins in Missouri and Washington. For Gallagher, issues of identity
are always to the point, linking as they do, existential provenance
with public, civic, and political consequences. Her interest in masks
leads back to Wilde and Yeats and by a slightly more eccentric path
to Eliot and mid-century Modernism. It also leads to kabuki and the
poker mysteries of gesture, restraint, and understatement.

In the early poem "Breasts," she marks the passing into experience in terms of acquiring a new gender marker that at first seems
more nearly a mask than a fate:

Swart nubbins, I noticed you then,
my mother shaking a gritty rag from the porch
to get my shirt on this minute. Brothers,
that was the parting of our ways, for then
you got me down by something else than flesh.

Gallagher's poems get much of their early energy from the grinding of contraries: her love of masks, of improvisation, versus her love
of stability and the insistence that authenticity is not an illusory quality. You sense sometimes that she wishes it were otherwise, that *she*
were otherwise—and so she praises and is drawn to the authenticity
of others. And yet, her father was the first to show the shortcomings
of such a solid identity, and her poems about him can almost be read
as cautionary tales. In "Black Money," she observes,

Coffee bottle tucked in his armpit
he swaggers past the chicken coup,

a pack of cards at his breast.
In a fan of light beyond him
the Kino Maru pulls out for Seattle,
some black star climbing
the deep globe of his eye.

The poem reinforces the idea that place is destiny. The father knows that the future belongs to Seattle (the globe of his eye—the world is what he smartly sees). There is the ambivalence involved in "settling," instead of striking out for the territory. The sides of this ambivalence are also the largest *doubling* of her early poems. In the powerful and hauntingly colloquial "3 a.m. Kitchen. My Father Speaking," she represents memory with documentary concentration and fidelity to voice:

I quit the woods. One day just
walked out, took off my caulks, said that's
it. I went to the docks.
I was driving winch. You had to watch
to see nothing fell out of the sling. If
you killed somebody you'd
never forget it. All
those years I was just working
I was on edge, every day. Just working.
You kids. I could tell you
a lot. But I won't.

In spite of a keen ear for the *patois*, Gallagher is not afraid of abstractions and wields them with perhaps sometimes too great a facility and zest, resulting here and there in the mannered line. David Wagoner notes that ending on an abstraction is "like ending on a sermon." Wagoner presumably means not only that abstractions end in didactic or solicitous suspension, but because they undertake the business of generalization, they seem to prefer putative to real, lyric triumphs to successes measured by more conventional means:

I was justifying my confusion
the last time we walked this way.

> I think I said some survivals need
> a forest. But it was only the sound
> of knowing. Assumptions
> about roots put down like a deeper foot
> seemed dangerous too.

If she finds in the projected double the proper interlocutor—and that is, in the relational world, an iffy matter—then the world is indeed the size of our language. And this is not only to pay a compliment to language, but to praise the world for being disposed to improvisations—one of which is to let itself be comprehended in conversation and verse.

In later work, Gallagher is more plainly interpersonal, which gives her poems added dignity and poignancy when she shifts, as she does mid-career with the death of her husband, Raymond Carver, to elegy. Now it is a truism that every elegy is a self-portrait, and that reflection, on the occasion and under the auspice of death, is the utmost private double. And it is auspicious, as every poet knows, because death requires that we make our meditations in a final vocabulary, beyond which only the critic can gainsay the poet. Literary criticism, you might say, is the thing death shares with silence.

Her work has matured confidently in its ability to inhabit larger circles and to fathom darker political regions. The lushness and feathering also push her poems in the direction of music, both as a pure object of contemplation and as a skill-set. Her refusal to lapse into the monotone of so much contemporary verse owes something to her gradual adoption of Ireland as her second country. That it is the geographical equivalent of personal interlocution also allows her to apply the political layer more directly, a layer, which, until then had been as much literary as existential:

> Walking back, you tell the story
> of the sniper's bullet
> making two clean holes in the taxi, how
> the driver ducked and drove on
> like nothing happened. No pain
> passed through you; it

did not even stop the car
or make you live more
carefully.

"Disappearances in the Guarded Sector"

Throughout her career, Gallagher has been as much a poet of
thematic richness, with recurrent, even totemic images (animals—
horses, birds, lambs) and subjects (parents, work, travel) as she has
been of stylistic high-profiling. Moving through the ample selections
from each of her collections, you find familiar categories in circula-
tion: much of it the traditional stuff, in fact, of subjective poetry.

There is a tenderness in the later poems, as Ireland, her counter-
land, the land deepened and saddened by The Troubles begins to
enter her work as subject and song. Because Ireland is the Double
writ large, it returns with even more engagement in the volumes subsequent to *Moon Crossing Bridge*, especially *Dear Ghosts,* (2006) and
a final section of *Signature: New Poems*. The geographic and cultural
parallelism begins with *Under Stars* (1978) and allows her to consider
an older, more agrarian world—the fields and woods, the animals,
both wildlife and domestic that have passed not only from her life,
but from the lives of most of us. There is no danger that these things
will open the gate to a false nostalgia. Heaney noted that Lowell was
remarkably "free of the sigh for lost Eden." Gallagher may not be
altogether free of that sigh, but it is doubtful she would march off
into a brave new world, either. Rather, it is the moment—the two
moments, one present, one absent—around which her imagination
makes its images:

They kneel to it, folded
on its four perfect legs, stroke
the good back, the muscles bunched at the chest.
Its head, how the will shines large in it
as what maybe used to overcome it.

"Dread in the Eyes of Horses"

In the earlier (English) volume, *My Black Horse: New and Selected Poems,* the poet is shown on the cover mounted on her horse, Sugarfoot. At once Tom-boyish and Romantic, the girl and her mount, very much in motion seem to be one powerful and synchronized organism. As in Edwin Muir's famous apocalyptic poem ("The Horses"), the horses in Gallagher's poems figure as creatures of transport and willing slaves to the labors of their errant masters; in either case they are redemptive creatures:

> He'd pass his mind
> over them where they pushed their muzzles into
> each other's flanks and necks and their horseness
> gleamed back at him like soundless music, until
> he knew something he couldn't know
> as only himself, something not to be told again
> even by writing down the doing.

> "If Poetry Were Not a Morality"

During the Gulf War, Gallagher becomes quite literally pastoral by intervening and purchasing a lamb on its way to the slaughterhouse and writes,

> You are my army
> Of one, though your brothers and sisters
> Are gone to table. So are we all
> Bought and sold in the coin of the realm.

In "Sah Sin," a poem in which a hummingbird brings with it the death of innocence, Gallagher puts the totemic bird at first to edifying purposes that border on the political and the didactic:

> Lifting my blouse
> and catching it—(as I'd heard
> South American women do)
> under a breast.

> It didn't stir, but I held it there

like a dead star for a while
inside my heart-socket
to make sure, remembering the story
of a mother in Guatemala
whose baby had died
far from home. She pretended
it was living, holding it
to her breast the long way
back on the bus, so no one
would take it from her before
she had to give it over.

Readers are made aware elsewhere that Gallagher had undergone breast cancer treatment, lending a special interest to that shielding and maternal protection of the fragile. The poem ends with a visit by a student who "had become famous in the East /for his poems."

Now he was
a little bored with being
a poet. He asked some questions
about what I might be
writing—courteously, as one
inquires about someone
not considered for a while.
I made a pot of tea
and served it in the maroon cups
the size of ducks' eggs
so it would take
a long while to drink. Fame.
It was so good to sit
with him. He seemed
to have miraculously survived
every hazard to make his way
to my house again.

While she takes the measure of the whippersnapper, she also makes plain that the judgment is subsumed by a common interest that is less literary, than tutorial, and less tutorial than animal. The

equipoise is perfect, calming the jitters with Buddhist forbearance
("it was good"). It even made me think of a neologism to describe it:
freak-quilibrium. The paradoxes attendant on fame (of which Gallagher has had a share) are also shared by the means to acquire that
fame, namely language, as she recognizes in "Deaf Poem"

> Yes, he can step back into life just long enough
> for eternity to catch hold, until one of us
> is able to watch and to write the deaf poem,
> a poem missing even the language
> it is unwritten in.

It is little wonder that she has taken on the musical mission of
Irish verse, with its reliance on the sonorities of meaning. Notwithstanding several barbs aimed at the ability of language to support
disingenuous ends and aims, Gallagher trusts her language to be
fully present to its occasions, be they personal or otherwise. As
such, they are, in the distinction Lowell made, themselves events,
not just the record of events. They also, since the 1970s, continue
to stand in contrast to the language of many of her peers, whose
experiences tend to be ever-so-finely cross-hatched with skepticism
toward means. These poems have a lush interior that always seems to
speak to innate capacities instead of delimitings: the mutual work of
tongue and the ear must take effect before the work of eye and hand.

Be that as it may, there is most power, most tenderness and moral
authority when the existence of these very things is under threat.
Hence many readers will remember the somber yet accepting
authority of the elegiac *Moon Crossing Bridge,* a volume that enacts
the means by which the perfect interlocutor—now lost—must be
internalized. That book was a watershed in elegiac poetry, but I
would have been somehow impoverished had I spent the latter half
of the departed century without the music of her earlier poetry, just
as I am delighted to "have a sit" with the poems of *Dear Ghosts* and
Signatures. I will end this review with an excerpt from the title poem
of that difficult book:

And who's to say I didn't cross
just because I used the bridge in its witnessing,
to let the water stay the water
and the incongruities of the moon to chart
that joining I was certain of.

Jack Gilbert's *Collected Poems*

Jack Gilbert has the odd distinction of being both relatively unknown and legendary at the same time. At the outset, it must be said in his defense that he is not of our literary fashion or ideational ilk, if indeed we could be said to have either. To dip into four or five poems anywhere in his surprisingly big *Collected Poems* is to meet a contrarian persona. But hold on and let me revise the previous sentence in one respect: in Gilbert's poems we don't meet personas at all. The very idea cottons to a notion of realism that would strike Gilbert as itself unreal. The first person in Gilbert's poems is Gilbert himself, period. There's a reason for that. Gilbert wishes to collapse the distinction between speaker and character: he's the speaker, and he's not interested in being taken for a literary character. I mention this because we tend to assume that poets who mythologize to the extent that Gilbert does must be out to make characters of themselves. No doubt this comes from living in a commodity ecosphere where celebrity and fame are assumed to be the same thing. In the world where Gilbert lives, celebrity is nothing—as it should be, and the swelling of subjectivity is not the same thing as the puffing up of one's name or reputation.

Gilbert's long career is also an extended discourse on perspective. In an early poem dedicated to Robert Duncan ("Perspective He Would Mutter Going to Bed") he writes of

> A place
> to stand. To receive. A place to go
> into from. The earth by language.

It is surely the case that this most literally self-marginalized of poets has acquitted himself of a wish to remain apart so that he might more clearly inhabit the realms of feeling Keats wrote of in his grand debut, which lined up art and feeling in a not-to-be-trumped ideal order. Whether you connect the dots the way Keats did will say a lot about how you feel about Jack Gilbert's work, whose dangers are not so much those of sentimentality, carnal obsession and broad language (as other critics have noticed), but the claims to a more robust authenticity, one unavailable to those of us who struggle in the status quo, which in turn leads him to resort to brandishing the didactically tinged and manipulative pronoun "we" (as in "We find out the heart only by dismantling what/ the heart knows"). So we do, except when we don't.

It was Keats who wished for a world of feelings rather than thoughts, and Gilbert, whose language does not opt for the sensuous particularity of English Romanticism, has literalized just such a bias in the course of what amounts to a literary and emotional pilgrimage. The lived journey, as the songwriters sing, has made his career the stuff of legend in some quarters, while being little known in others—the distinction arising according to the litmus test of feeling-as-authenticity. If feelings are of the highest order to you, if feelings are the touchstones authenticating your life, then Gilbert's work may be of importance to you, may well be something consulted and admired, esteemed, even loved. More specifically, if you think that feelings signify in a way superior to wishes, dreams, reflections, and intellectual thought, then Gilbert is your man. There is however the problem, endemic to all poetry, that the feelings of one are strictly speaking unavailable to others, except by analogy (hence poetry—i.e., metaphor). The problem is made all the more vivid when feelings are pressed into the service of values. I would argue that Gilbert's work dramatizes the old debate between poetry and philosophy, between whether content or words chiefly bear the weight of significance. If the former, then translation is possible, and many roads appear leading to the temple. If the latter, then nothing the poem says could have been otherwise, without seriously damaging its DNA. This has been the position of most American poets since the dawn of the MFA, and it is surprising (and it must be admitted, refreshing) to find a student of Theodore Roethke subscribing to a different view of "craft."

His practice suggests that the poem resides not in the words over which poets make such a public fuss. The words are rather like a cloak draping classical figures that are just as happy to go nude, except that the cloaking provides a registration or orientation in history. In fact, in an early poem called "Registration," Gilbert writes,

> Where the worms had opened the owl's chest,
> he could see, inside her frail ribs
> the city of Byzantium. Exquisitely made
> of ironwood and brass. The pear trees around
> the harem and the warships were perfectly detailed.

Is then Gilbert that *rara avis,* a philosophical poet? Well, yes and no. Yes, he believes that poems are, at bottom, metaphysical: they are literary manifestations of emotional experiences, often ones that would be vitiated by particular language or justifying rhetoric. In "Recovering Amid the Farms," for example, the poet describes a young girl's coming and going ("I watch from hiding for her sake"), an experience that comes closer to a Wordsworthian intimation or a Botticelli moment than a description *per se.*

> Except sometimes when, just before
> going out of sight behind the distant canebrake,
> she looks quickly back. It is too far for me to see,
> but there is a moment of white if she turns her face.

The distrust of language must of necessity root itself in feeling, Gilbert seems to say, for feeling rights the ship of grammar, the rules governing meaning's procession, rules that because they are indifferent to our individual experience, necessarily betray our aims. Why then would we want to dress them up further? Understatement is the way forward.

> How astonishing it is that language can almost mean,
> and frightening that it does not quite. Love, we say,

> God, we say, Rome and Michiko, we write, and the words
> get it all wrong.
>
> ("The Forgotten Dialect Of The Heart")

There is another sense in which Gilbert's poems are philosophical, namely, they often proceed by propositions, as in the early
"Poetry Is a Kind of Lying":

> Poetry is a kind of lying,
> necessarily. To profit the poet
> or beauty. But also in
> that truth may be told only so.

The intention to define, to say X is a kind of Y, is tied, of course,
to perspective, to establishing the truth of matters by acknowledging scale and field of view—which includes margins. Gilbert is more
interested in establishing a consistent tonal field than in increasing
diction's dynamic range, of tracking the to and fro of thought by
means of saturation and hue. Hence his poems share a look. They
are, as if referencing the title of his second book, *Monolithos* (actually
the name of the hill behind his house in Greece), monolithic. He
eschews stanzaic form, preferring bolts of language straight down
the page.

Because of their allegiance to the spirit, rather than the substance, the feeling hinted at, rather than nailed down in words,
Gilbert's poems are wary of the forms that sustain and enrich the
productions of most of his colleagues. In fact, the visual impression
is of rectangular lots of words like boxes of type, with lines roughly
suggesting blank verse—which is also a familiar orthographic look
and may well be something of a "ghost meter."

What most clearly distinguishes Gilbert's work and what separates
it from the Standard Model of poetic discourse, is its reliance on
incomplete sentences. In one sense this mannerism reminds me of
Superman self-speak ("Must find phone booth!"), in which the rules
of grammar have a merely honorific status. In a wider sense, the
widespread use of sentence fragments disables the engine of gram-

matical dynamics in favor of a more imagistic standard, reminiscent of Suzanne Langer's observation that the lyric poem more closely resembles a picture than a story. Gilbert's poems may give us stories, but they leave us with the impression of images suffused with strong emotion, of ghostings chronicled by a haunted bard.

Much has been made of Gilbert's associations with women, and it would not be unfair to describe his work as that of a sensualist, properly understood. It is by means of the flesh—in his case, women, that we come to understand the necessity for spirit, or as he writes in "Moreover": "We are allowed / women so we can get into bed with the Lord." In Gilbert's case, three women have become the subject of this degree of veneration, and these appear in the dedication like Seneca's Graces.

An audacity attends these poems too, their references to "the gods" and "the Lord," which are likely as not to land with a thud on the ears of some. They not only reference gods, but something of the godlike infuses many of the poems, as if Gilbert were invoking Muse-like powers with nary a knowing glance at the camera. The astonishment—or disparagement—that goes with such does put us in mind of his relationship to classicism—or one variant of that airy descriptor: the accessibility of the self to myth. The titles alone put us in mind of a mythical propensity ("Orpheus in Greenwich Village," "The Plundering of Circe," "The Sirens Again," "Finding Eurydice," "The Greek Gods Don't Come in Winter"). The seriousness with which Gilbert, who sort of famously spent eight years in Greece near the start of his publishing career, writes of classical figures reminds me of other Modern (and exilic) Hellenes, especially Cavafy. Consider the short poem "Going There":

Of course it was a disaster.
The unbearable, dearest secret
has always been a disaster.
The danger when we try to leave.
Going over and over afterward
what we should have done
instead of what we did.
But for those short times

we seemed to be alive. Misled, misused,
lied to and cheated,
certainly. Still, for that
little while, we visited
our possible life.

Such classical restraint allows actual distancing to sound familiar, especially as the distancing comes from the ample deployment
of abstractions: not the thing (the evocation), but its mention (the
invocation), as if abstraction were language's elegy for the direct
expression of fact. Indeed, it's impressive how much of Gilbert's work
is elegy—not only poems that explicitly reference the death of lovers—say, of his wife Michiko, of cancer at thirty, who is the subject
of many poems here. Elegy is a way of marking the felt journey by
acknowledging the negative power of absence:

In whatever room
Your warm body.
Among all the people
Your absence
The people who are always
Not you.

("Rain")

With classicism the trick is to try for resonance by tying into a
set of references that have cooled from the religious beliefs that
gave rise to them. Accordingly, one acknowledges and is charged
by the passion by which belief itself struggled into existence, while
maintaining the aesthetic distance necessary to keep quelled systems
"literary." The result is that

We cobble love together
from this and those of our machinery
until there is suddenly an apparition
that never existed before.

("Painting on Plato's Wall")

At its best, this kind of poetry can achieve a grandeur and a majestic poise that is, more often than not, unavailable otherwise to the daily agenda of verse. Consider "Bring in the Gods":

> Bring in the gods I say, and he goes out. When he comes
> back and I know they are with him, I say, Put tables in front
> of them so they can be seated, and food upon the tables
> so they may eat. When they have eaten, I ask which of them
> will question me. Let him hold up his hand, I say.
> The one on the left raises his hand and I tell him to ask.
> Where are you now, he says. I stand on top of myself, I hear
> myself answer. I stand on myself like a hilltop and my life
> is spread before me. Does it surprise you, he asks.

One of the propositions most in evidence in Gilbert's work is one with ties to Nietzsche, the Yeats of "Lapis Lazuli," and to the Derek Mahon of "The Snow Party." The purpose of Gilbert's poems, you might say, is to show us a world of reciprocal compensations, not overseen by common herd morality, but by an explicit, unifying sense of poetic justice. Even as a vision, this world has gone by the wayside, and yet until recently, every college student made its acquaintance in the second half of the literature survey:

> There is laughter
> every day in the terrible streets of Calcutta,
> and the women laugh in the cages of Bombay.
> If we deny our happiness, resist our satisfaction,
> we lessen the importance of their deprivation.
> We must risk delight.

> ("A Brief for the Defense")

Likewise, in the same poem, he writes,

> To hear the faint sound of oars in the silence as a rowboat
> comes slowly out and then goes back is truly worth
> all the years of sorrow that are to come.

This is true as far as it goes, but you wouldn't want to make policy on it. On the other hand catering to the expansion of subjectivity has always been a goal of poetry: we fully spend our lives working our way out from the self. The poet reminds us that we also need to work our way in. The process often requires a good deal of unlearning. Gilbert excels in recommending such deconstructions, as in the poem, "Tear It Down":

> We find out the heart only by dismantling what
> the heart knows. By redefining the morning,
> we find a morning that comes just after darkness.
> We can break through marriage into marriage.
> By insisting on love we spoil it, get beyond
> affection and wade mouth-deep into love.
> We must unlearn the constellations to see the stars.

It may be that a life lived in the pursuit of subjectivity runs afoul of our social natures. It is, after all, a kind of reverse engineering of what life lays before us. I would suppose that Gilbert's allegiance to classical principles also entails the saving idea that it's not necessary to proselytize subjectivity. It's enough that representatives of the soul have made their registrations and continue to do so even if they are, as Milton says, "fit though few." Again, it may be that how you come down on this idea of intense subjectivity, of holding on to ecstasy and pain, of feelings long evaporated, will determine whether you think Gilbert's career was worth the price paid to give it such luster and troubadour grandeur. Readers should be aware that revisiting ancient sources carries with it the whiff of ancient values. The aristocratic code to which the poems often allude sometimes remind me of certain stories of Isak Dinesen, for example.

Be that as it may, Gilbert has put in a claim as an American literary figure, and I am persuaded on the basis of his most memorable poems to recognize his stature as approaching that of a major poet, although I often want to consign him to what I call the maverick tradition: not Roethke or Wright, but Vachel Lindsay, Jack Spicer, and Charles Reznikoff, distinguished outliers of our verse tradition. His whole career must look to him like a pilgrimage to deeps and destinations beyond the shores of realism, but to his readers the same journey may also look like an escape. It's all a matter of perspective, of course. And wouldn't you know it that the perspectivalist who demands steadfast pursuit of love over many terrains also demands of imagination's engine that it never succumb to its means, but that it never stay long in idle, either? Thus the poet cannot separate himself from the career of his words and becomes, in spite of himself, what he wished in any case to be: an exemplar of a way of life beyond the reach, if not the imagining, of his readers.

Linda Gregg's *All of It Singing: New and Selected Poems*

When a reviewer bubbled that Linda Gregg's poems were "luscious," I knew what he meant: the romantic woundedness, the stoicism and mythic air, the terra cotta simplicity, the mannered quietism embodied in shards of participial fragments. There was also the impulse toward utterance released from any obligation to circumspection. For example, in "The Chorus Speaks Her Words as She Dances," we hear such apparently artless outbursts as this: "I adore you. I take you seriously, even if I am alone in this," and in "The Beckett Kit," the poet proclaims, "Ah world, I love you with all my heart," to which it would be churlish to add the exclamation point, though one is added in the mind nonetheless. The last poet to accomplish this feat, so resistant to the knowing protocols of contemporary poetry, was Randall Jarrell. It wasn't that Jarrell had a penchant for cheesy lines; rather it was how well the cheesy lines from life bled through the usually protective shell of art and so seemed impervious to art's protection. A male poet I admire once told me that he would never write the word "heart" in a poem. I dare say there are many who would march to the same drum. So Gregg's poems, with their spectrum strung between imploring and withstanding, invite partisanship at the moment the voice sounds.

Most of the poet's work from five previous volumes finds its way into *All of It Singing*, as well as important new poems. While the issue of the voice, like Ariadne's thread, leads readers again and again to something additional the poet wishes to impart—something about where she's coming from and how hard or soft, or again something about the creation of presence, that most kicked around of essential qualities—what I have found most interesting in Gregg's poems is their relation to the life of poetry as such and to myth, and believe me when I say that I'm aware that they can be construed as the same.

Now, a life in poetry is no mean thing. Today the expectation is that the poet's reduced fate leaves her compact with the life of academia, so that the rewards of the poetic life are likewise consistent with the rewards of academic life. Were it not for the academic bailout, it's doubtful I would have thought the life of poetry an issue. But it also breeds, as everybody and his chimp knows, the faults that belong to academe. Be that as it may, the life of the poet in the life of poetry is a distinct thing, university or no. Linda Gregg has shown one plausible—and commendable, if austere—form of what that life might be like in her career of nearly four decades. She has built a body of work that is formally rigorous and thematically recursive, and her work has remained for me as compelling today as when I first read it back in 1976. That year I was editing an anthology of new American poets, and Joseph Brodsky called me up to lay down the law: "David, if you want your anthology to be a *book*, it will have to include poems by Linda Gregg." Already Gregg had attained a certain celebrity without having published a book, owing to a rumor that, returning from Greece where she lived with Jack Gilbert, she had submitted her first seven poems to the likes of *The Atlantic, Antaeus, The New Yorker, The Nation*, and so forth, and all had been accepted. For her fans, this winning luster has not diminished in the course of five collections, and as her base has grown, so has her official recognition, culminating in the PEN/Volker award for 2007.

Which is not to say her poems are not without their detractors. Some have mentioned a certain portentous and emotionally monotonous air surrounding the lyrics. Also to be heard have been the usual objections that accompany first-person free verse: sentimentality, über-subjectivity, and the ongoing attributions that may be laid at the altar of self: sacrifice, loneliness, a late willingness toward anonymity, paradoxically combined with the exceptionalism of destiny. Then there is the matter of the poet's stylistic manner: all those conspicuous sentence fragments and participial phrases, a method used extensively by Gilbert, beginning in his first book *Views of Jeopardy* (1960). I concede a measure of truth to all these charges, but let's get them out of the way. To become distracted by such things in the presence of a talent this original is equivalent to having been thrown off by Berryman's syntax or the scything sweeps of Lowell's assertiveness. It is to miss an experience of the devotion of the other, indeed, to the Other. That there are solemn, even sacerdotal aspects to Gregg's poems is not to be denied, and these aspects, which are inclinations—at once psychological, emotional, and religious—find their source in Greek culture and—very broadly speaking—Greek sensibility.

The mystery that we understand as metamorphosis comes down to the mystery of deciding how we encounter and bear discontinuity. It is the mystery that lies between Ovid and Rilke in their competing accounts of the myth of Orpheus. That myth first and foremost centers not merely on the bard's ability to conjure with his song, but on Eurydice's agreement (or reluctance) to allow herself to be turned back from death. It must be said at once that in the classical, "pious" version of this myth, Eurydice is given by Pluto to the poet as a consequence of the power of his song which, in Milton's phrase, "drew iron tears down Pluto's cheek." Moreover, in this version, she has not been dead long enough to turn her allegiance toward the mere materials out of which she is composed, and yet death, which renders her inertial, also allows her to harken toward a living, intrusive, mission-bound Orpheus. In Rilke's version, however, the cream has turned, and like any of the shades in Hades, she is more like a wisp of memory than a willful revenant. She is disoriented, easily led, clueless. This Eurydice adds a note of poignancy to Orpheus' song because he must have been forced to undertake a private risk-benefit analysis in order to decide whether such a person was worth the extravagant audacity of his lyric at the epicenter of his harrowing.

The figure of Eurydice is central to Gregg's poetry because it includes the problematic of the return from death, which also includes the journey to the apogee of being, the border with its constantly pesky opposite, non-being; the decision to return *contra naturam* toward life; the harnessing of death to love; the *ne plus ultra* of sacrifice, and other such questions worthy of mythic figures. Linda Gregg's Eurydice is a figure poised on the verge of metamorphosis but complicit with her return. She (somehow) manages it again and again, so that self-sacrifice becomes a mode of control. Here it might be instructive to remember Sylvia Plath's "I have done it again," to which Gregg's "Whole and Without Blessing" provides its analogue:

> I was bred for slaughter, like the other
> animals. To suffer exactly at the center
> where there are no clues, except pleasure.

All of her best poems raise similar questions. For example, what does it mean for one to be a sacrifice? What is at stake, and what has she sacrificed in order to become herself? With what gods presiding? In Gregg's poems, not to make a sacrifice but to *be* one ups the ante because you are the thing you desire—or rather, because you want to sacrifice what you are in order to become who you are as an image. Thus self-sacrifice yields an excellent benefit: you gain a new identity. The opposite is also true:

> What if the world is taken from me?
> If there is no recognition? My words unheard?

> ("What If the World Stays Always Far Off")

Reading the poems in chronological succession, one feels that, except for several forays into failed romance—themselves psychologically and spiritually resonant—and a few that meet and largely skirt the violence of politics, the succession of poems makes up a series of emanations from an original big bang. And what a bang it was. Consider the incandescence of "The Girl I Call Alma" from her first book, *Too Bright to See:*

> The girl I call Alma who is so white
> is good, isn't she? Even though she does not speak,
> you can tell by her distress that she is
> just like the beach and the sea, isn't she?

The sleeve-pulling urgency of these questions, these bits of reality-testing, hop up the poem to the point that its discontinuities and non-sequiturs become blurred out, leaving the crash that seems to have been the point all along:

> And the white curtain, and the secret smile
> are just her way with lies, aren't they?
> And the we are not alone, ever.
> And that everything is backwards
> otherwise.
> And that inside the no is the yes. Isn't it?
> Isn't it?

If *Too Bright to See* announced a poet observing alarming quiddities from the middle of her life, her second book, *Alma,* sees from the sidelines: the poet has become her token, has incarnated her own projection. Never was Blake's dictum, "they became what they beheld," truer than in the difference between these books.

Gregg has not followed colloquial fashions, but aimed at a more neutral expressiveness, one capable of classically restrained (and yet passionate) utterance. How else, if passion, when all is said and done, is your thing? Such an instrument is also capable of consorting with silence. Mediating the distance between that passionate utterance and the silence that is the context of any utterance is the figure of Alma, Gregg's avatar doll, double, and household goddess, a wounded but somehow transfigured female spirit whose shifting identity makes her nevertheless Gregg's foil through a number of her early poems. This displaced subjectivity has its rewards. It takes the spotlight off the first person; it redistributes the ego's mission to a flatter, more mysterious bearer, one that comes with a whole different set of premises. We say, a doll? Is she serious? And she is—that is, the poet is serious enough to create a parallel world in which the scars, amputations, outrages, and worship opportunities become staged enactments, allowing expression that threatens to become too emotionally burdensome, otherwise:

> When I go into the garden, there she is.
> The specter holds up her arms to show

that her hands are eaten off.
She is silent because of the agony.
There is blood on her face.
    I think
I am supposed to look. I am not supposed
to turn away. I am supposed to see each detail
and all expression gone. My God, I think,
if paradise is to be here
it will have to include her.

("There She Is")

    This is an address to a doll that takes place in a world where the
gods too have shrunk to dolls, and she is their votaress. Originally
appearing in *Antaeus,* this is one of the key poems that helped establish Gregg as a poet to watch. It had it all: pathos, the sway of authority, the feel of mystery, American passion and violence held in place
by classical and modernist stanchions. Taking seriously the contrast
in figure-ground relationships is what enables Gregg to nail the early
poems in *Too Bright to See* to the back wall of the reader's brain, where
the work is weirdly reminiscent of Heidegger's discussions of being
as a rising into the light in pre-Socratic philosophy. Sometimes, such
constructions turn out to be all-too-literal, as in "The Beckett Kit,"
with its play of matchbox figures and the question of their placing
and spatial relationship:

I finally found a way of using the tree.
If the man is lying down with the sheep
while the dog stands, then the wooden tree
can also stand, in the back, next to the dog.

    The poem will remind readers of the trapped obsessive young
wife of Gilman's "The Yellow Wall-Paper," where the created thing
remonstrates against the oppression of the given. Here the poet contrasts a controlled environment of arranged toys with the dangers
of the city and by extension, with the fate of sincerity in the face of
personal and historical violence, of hostility and cynicism:

The blacks probably do rape the whites in jail
as Bill said in the coffee shop watching the game
between Oakland and Cincinnati. And no doubt
Karl was right that we should have volunteered
as victims under the bombing of Hanoi.

A guy said to Mishkin, "If you've seen all that,
how can you go on saying you're happy?"

"A guy said to Mishkin…" is the kind of risky diction-mixing that, in the right hands, can raise the classical out of its grave and present it to consciousness as new, or it can merely indicate a failure of ear and control of verbal means. Gregg learned the difference.

Her early sublimity ironically derives from smallness rather than vastness, just as her later work derives power from self-sacrifice and acceptance, rather than emotional ostentation. Never was Carolyn Kizer's quip that "classicism is just romanticism without all the excess" more true and in evidence than in the work of Linda Gregg. Partly, the power of these early poems comes from the intuition that her first words are delivered in their final vocabulary form—i.e., there is no gainsaying the terms: meaning stops where the periods do and only silence trails its comet-tail after. She is a *puella senex* for whom California and Mediterranean sun are one in the moment and the mile.

In "The Defeated," she writes, "It was like being alive twice." This declaration, the epigraph to two books (including the present one), is both apt and mysterious, even as praise. Eurydice of all people has to justify why it would be appropriate to be alive twice in a world that scarcely allows for being alive once. In "The Gods Must Not Know Us," she fears that "part of myself will get lost / and I will not be a fitting gift." As for the worthiness of self-sacrifice: we start with the sacred, with respect. And yet, this poet's large ambition runs into difficulty, as she acknowledges in "What If the World Stays Always Far Off":

What if the world is taken from me?
If there is no recognition? My words unheard?

....
What if I continue unnoticed...

Invisibility whatsoever is the subtext here, below the personal (and
professional) fear, although virtue follows, as Whitman knew. But
how can you reconcile, on one level, the wish to be invisible, the self-
sacrifice—even if it is Whitmanian, with the wish, the drive—to be
visible and audible, indeed, to be Keats' nightingale singing "higher
and higher to a screech"? In Eurydice's terms, how indeed to come
back into "the world" becomes the question, always problematic,
always minus the unconditioned embrace. The status of the pure
and the unconditioned continues to exercise Gregg, for whom this
impulse is subject to compromises both temporal and transcendent.
In "Oedipus Exceeding," we find,

> I have returned to mix my blood with our
> earth. Mix myself with what we are not.
> Something happened. Everything
> was sacred.

Does self-sacrifice (added to sacrifice) also help to establish what
we experience as the sacred? It seems as if we are being nudged
toward affirmation, and yet, we have to consider that mixing "with
what we are not" belies purity. It is as if Oedipus wants us to know
that the pure and the sacred don't go together. But the self-exiled
King of Thebes continues to signify because he takes that step that
proffers the mixed as a catalyst toward the sacred. In the myth the
gods, sure enough, recognize his sacred status. Our status, though
supremely mixed, even divinely miscegenistic, is less clear. At the
same time, we cannot deny that we are in the know about things.
In "The Copperhead," Gregg addresses the issue of knowing versus
being, which is central to whether we can ever be sacred:

> Almost blind he takes the soft dying
> into the muscle-hole of his haunting.
> The huge jaws eyeing, the raised head sliding
> back and forth, judging the exact place of his killing.

Those gerunds and participles here cycle the mindlessness of nature's red tooth. But they also show the world they describe with an equanimity that is as much the result of mind's removal as of its application and stabilization.

> He takes the soft thing and coaxes it
> away from his small knowing. He would turn in and follow,
> hunt it deep within the dark hall of his fading knowing,
> but he cannot. He knows that.
> That he cannot go deep within his body for the finding
> of the knowing. So he slows and lets go. And finds
> with his eyes a moving. A small moving that he knows.

Are words themselves (and grammar) epistemological agents? How would one know? And yet there must be something that it is like to be a snake hunting and swallowing prey. And words get us plausibly within reach of what that is like—in the falling—which we can appreciate and in the "knowing," which is much more problematic. For what is it for a snake to know anything? And how does that knowledge relate to ours? The language of the poem has to be conducted quite differently to "fit" the snake and the knowing. One of the dangers of dealing with this kind of material is that it often seems like only all-or-nothing choices work. No alternatives. That limiting is both a strength and a narrowing. It's similar to the distinction between poet and bard, or the German distinction between *Dichter* and poet. George Steiner makes much of this distinction in discussing the difference between Continental and American notions of the poet. For one thing, the *Dichter*, like the snake, "object knows" what it knows aboriginally, without escalating, focus-dissolving abstractions.

In succeeding collections (*The Sacraments of Desire, Chosen by the Lion, Things and Flesh* and *In the Middle Distance*) Gregg turns to the darkness of the partisan and the national will, in war and the shadows of recent history, as much as to the Mediterranean light (from which she never really turns). She also records a doomed affair in her most personally freighted poems. We don't need to reread Freud to be reminded that the prerogatives of history are at odds with the prerogatives of the heart. Remembering her Akhmatova (she writes about her in a later poem), Gregg knows that insistence on prerogatives of the heart, often met with resistance and even disbelief, are one way for poetry to remind us that helplessless in the face of love is one of the sad proofs of our common bond. Yet like all great paradoxes, helplessness may be turned to account as a kind of strength. We find her aware of soldiers, marching to the center of historical events from which the poet is moving to the periphery, peripheries which, we suspect, will become new centers in their turn:

> Maybe morality does change,
> I was thinking, but suffering does not.

Are the claims of love the ultimate claims a person can make? Gregg asks the question in light of recent history: you are aware of the non-simpatico types lining the streets where you wander forlorn, both of you exilic: the one interior, one other, exterior. Their exile is the only thing you have common between you. "The War," "Night Music," "The Foreign language of the Heart" also contain images of people either looking the other way, or simply not acknowledging presence, as if humanity consisted of layers of incommensurable people who only share a common humanity in that they are on their way to becoming "[t]he dead in layers."

In "The Ninth Dawn," which opens *Chosen by the Lion,* Gregg steps back and considers her themes from the perspective, the "place to stand," as Jack Gilbert has it, of a life lived under the sky of classical austerities:

> It is not for nothing we notice a wider theme
> in Virgil's *Georgics* when he speaks about
> the passion of Orpheus and Eurydice. The gods
> want the honey in the hive, are willing to have
> the lovers destroyed.
> I am haunted by Eurydice
> who merely went too far into the wood and after
> lived with the darkness around her forever.
> The gods instruct us to cut

the throats of eight beasts, throw in poppies,
kill the jet-black ewe in the beautiful Italian
light so the bees, who have been the real business
all along, will swarm out again under the pliant
    boughs.

In this signal poem, not only the bees are pure Virgilian: so is the
form. Everything about this poem looks backward to that symbol
of our cultural continuity and forward to our diminishment. Just
so, the bees are "the business all along," the vibrant and constant
process that uses and justifies (if justification were ever needed).
When lovers heat up, they disturb this business, which is not a social
or cultural business, but a "natural" one (i.e., and unthinking one,
one conducted regardless). It is this move toward naturalism that is
at the heart of her later poems. In these poems, self-sacrifice goes
by another name, one denuded of the prefix "self." You can sense
the iciness of acceptance, but the reward no longer belongs to (or
is withheld from) the poet, but belongs to the poem and to the art.

All of It Singing is a beautiful and substantial book that sings of a
fruitful life with a sustained degree of ardor and courage not usually on show. There are at least ten poems here I know by heart, and
others I will remember as long as I live. They are a part of me, and
I would hope they could be a part of anyone who has followed me
this far. Can I break into more unguarded praise?

John Kinsella's *Divine Comedy*

Australian poet John Kinsella has written a massive trilogy of what he calls "distractions" (i.e., riffs) on Dante's *Commedia*, although, freed of Dante's just-so Thomist strictures, it arrives as a series of journal poems filtered through an up-to-date ecological prism. The poems track the fortunes of 5 acres of land (his mother's) in the Wheatbelt Region of western Australia. They also ray out to encompass flora and fauna, family, history, politics, and ethics, as these things, in their turn, hook up with larger (and older) themes of spiritual embodiment, moral escape, the climb to responsibility, judgment, and hope. Ambitious and accomplished it is, and like all epic-sized literary creations, it encounters problems, some inherent, some of his own making. Despite this, *Divine Comedy* should raise Kinsella's profile in America considerably.

Eco-poetry is as good a place to start as any to review the old debate over poetry's social utility. Every poet is haunted by Auden's terse, "poetry makes nothing happen," though that is as likcly to be an expression of pique as an opinion once solidly held. Even so, it seems unlikely that poetry, as a subset of language, could ever completely escape the fate of language in being a social tool. Meanwhile, the epiphanic nature poem, as practiced most conspicuously from the two-and-a-half-century-old Romantic tradition, continues to maintain a busy store, if the adulation of Mary Oliver has any meaning beyond the longing of her bluestocking audience for "self-help and human potential," as William Logan sniffed. And Mary Oliver represents one of the most benign and evolved practitioners of this poem, one in which the benefits of natural communion don't all curve back to smooth the silhouette of the poet. Even so, at the end of the day, such poetry amounts to a kind of meliorism: in addition to whatever degree of subjective enlightenment it discloses, it also asks why we all can't just get along. What eco-poetry proposes is a difference in kind.

While the Romantic nature poem has made purchase on large tracts of the American imagination, it's become definitively clear to us in ways that were not available to John Keats (or, for that matter, Robert Frost) that "nature" exists for itself, not (just) for our improvement. Romanticism was itself in reaction to the rational rigors of Enlightenment over-reaching, a mode of reenchantment for a world where God had been sent packing by logicians. Like Jessie Jackson, we could say we were somebody, in this case by virtue of nature's self-judging—but more to the point, approving—mirror. It should be noted that the spread of so-called "natural religion" was also guilty of contributing its bit of mischief to British and American poetry. Could it be, then, that with the arrival of eco-consciousness, the twilight of narcissism is at hand? Well, or course not, but the privileging of magic moments tied to subjectivity—as in Wordsworth's "spots of time"—has been put, like the figure of the human itself, way back on the shelf among the passing effects of nature, be its tale told by Darwin, Freud, or John Muir. Those moments are no longer hovering godlike before us and leading us forward into some handsome condition of humanity replete with wildlife parks and *jardins* as promenades.

By the 1980s, poets as diverse as Gary Snyder, Wendell Berry, and A. R. Ammons were charting a more naturalistic approach. Now, the pincushion effect of ego-plus-place, of leveraging eureka moments into being—was avoided in favor of "the weathering land /The wheeling sky." The slow but perceptible (and seemingly inevitable) rise of eco-poetry has had more than a recalibration function, since its aim is didactic, though it is a didacticism steeped in aesthetics. What this fact has come to mean is that here we have yet another movement with a problematic relationship to "beauty." In the sense that beauty features and underlines its virtue, descriptions of beautiful things amount to discriminations, and that is—because it is value-added—unnatural. The problem, not to put too fine a point on it, is that the leveling required of naturalism stands to put poetry at a disadvantage, not just because it refuses to reach deeply into the art's old kit bag, but more to the point because it requires a kind of refusal of that kit bag.

Meanwhile, because poetry will always be linguistic and so cultural, it will always be its own species of meliorism in relation to "nature," the very mention of which, as a category, is proof of my contention. There will never be a poetry whose relation to nature is not ultimately cultural. Saying so may say as much about the way we make categories as about how our imaginations engage things of the world, ourselves included. Which brings me back, scholium completed more circuitously than I had planned, to John Kinsella, and his audacious trilogy, a book whose chutzpah gets going with its title, *Divine Comedy*. Each of its three canticles goes by a host of descriptors, but one that recurs is that the poems are—or comprise—a "distraction" on one of Dante's cantos. While that may sound like ADD's fidgety response to the Middle Ages, it in fact suggests that the "responses" here go considerably outside the box of literary theme-and-variations. Kinsella's poems, although given vaguely Dante-friendly titles ("Canto of Listening to Birds in a Tree") otherwise pass obliquely over the Florentine's *topoi*. Instead of topological allegories of Hell, Purgatory, and Paradise, Kinsella puts us out among landforms. His poems are descriptions that, because they aren't geared to do more ultimately than to edify and remind by patient accumulation and sharp detailing, automatically flatten dramatic possibilities, with their emotional heats and troughs, into a more narrowly discursive bandwidth.

And what of Hell? Kinsella writes, "I do not like Dante's *Inferno*. I do not like his judgements nor punishments." Kinsella's work, with its own Inferno, is as much about judgment as Dante's. Kinsella complains that Dante is "not adequately deconstructive in terms of the self," but Dante operated in registers where the buck always stops, where, in the case of the *Inferno*, the process of spinning the truth freezes in the absolute zero of death. So Kinsella has to be on the watch for the way language snakes around truth. He exercises his vigilance against Orwellian language in part by deconstructing his own self, and showing that the language he wields as a prophetic and therapeutic tool can never prove its own premises—it can only embody them. Our own "distraction" is to have followed his journey on the parallel track of our own subjectivity.

So how does the descriptive act hook up with the Dantean template? Well, the connection is not necessarily intuitive, but there is one indisputable similarity and that is that both poets see a call to action, not elegy—i.e., memory—as the final stage of the poem's journey. Don't get me wrong: memory is crucial, as it is literally information over time, but of the shrines that have been built to memory as such, Kinsella has no interest here. These poems, composed in loose tercets, offer another kind of homage, and yet they also prove able forms for journaling because of their ability to process highly articulated conversational descriptions and to contain summaries and dismissals—that is, to legislate the manifest thought of the poem. Still, I am often reminded not so much of the poetry of Dante (nor am I supposed to be, in another sense) as of Alfred Corn, another poet of conversational specifications. By "conversation" I refer not just to colloquial quickness and people-pleasing language, but to the give-and-take mode of higher literary discourse, where judgment runs alongside the *laissez-faire* of casual talk, not runs into it. Here is the ending to "Canto of the Uncanny":

> Tim says he can remember
>
> being in Mum's tummy, or likes
> to be told . . . to be shown the soundings
> taken of him in the world of liquid.
>
> He suppresses nothing. And we
> answer what he asks. There's something
> familiar about this white-faced heron,
>
> stuck over the downed obelisk patch
> of pasture. The tales told me by my
> grandmother whose mother's mother
>
> was Scots held no birds. Later,
> she filled in the blanks with crows
> and cockatoos—not quite generic,

but a loose amalgam of species
seen out and about, as if something
familiar had been stirred up,
stuck up there in the sky.

Like early Dante, Kinsella is fond of commenting on his own purposes. Each of the three collections is prefaced by an essay expound-
ing its aims and purport. These are helpful in their way, though one
senses that he can also sound hyperventilated when, as he sometimes
does, he goes off on a stem-winder. For example, of Paradise, he
explains that

> [t]his work of mine is an attempt at exorcism, exhortation, reclamation,
> rebuilding, celebration, respect and just working out how best to
> survive what I perceive as a massive and unjust assault on the natural
> world by largely self-serving and indifferent—or at best hypocritically
> 'caring'—humans.

In writing, diversity, not condensation, is a devil's bargain: you
extend articulation's reach at the expense of dramatic structure.
And although the Dantean model offers organizational standards,
the temptation to resist restraint, even to expand into bagginess is
strong. Likewise, the temptation to fall into prose: "land prices/are
on the rise and the State looks to secure /its own gas needs." ("Canto
of the Beach"). I am reminded of Pound's wonderfully inverted command that "poetry must be at least as well written as prose." But
happily in this case, the poems are much better written than the
prose. Indeed, as much as Kinsella wants to embody an allegiance to
progressive environmentalism (with its jeremiads and caveats, even
its jargon), he mostly comes across at last as a lover of style who can't
wait to get to the blank page, a connoisseur of the verbal conjoinings
that stand at odds with the gloves-off methods of purpose. This, too,
he knows. Moreover, he finds himself, as an artist, implicitly recommending a similar ironic stance for the reader's pleasure. After all,
the irony of the situation does not subdue the passion of the project,
nor the pleasure subdue the duty.

Blood is the history of horses,
of centaurs. We are cautious

passing a horse, a centaur:
not wanting to spook
it from its path. Well-worn trails

in the long paddock: runnels
blooded, skinned patches
of bush. The flow between

city and country: roads, traffic:
horse-floats, semi-trailers,
shoes on the track.

As suburbs bulge into bush,
cleared quicker than night, blood
still boils in the tannery's vats.

("Canto of Boiling" [Seventh Circle, first subcircle, 12—Inferno])

This is an impressive, even magnificent work of late youth. Kinsella makes a big deal of specifying differences among these canticles, but practically speaking, the differences seem to matter more to the poet than I suspect they will to the reader. The whole reads—as does Dante's *Commedia*—as one long poem, and it is a formal predilection that more closely favors the tradition of Anglophone poetry. It actually reminds me more of *The Revolt of Islam,* in rhetorical reach and sinew, than of the poetry of Dante, who, in his severity, inspired more laconic children: the Eliot of *Four Quartets,* for instance, and the Seamus Heaney of *Station Island.* For ordering is not order; nor is loquacity dynamism. But his is another way of saying that its ambition drives home the hope that the circumstances of postmodernity will prune, without brutally downsizing. And we have already had an earful of pessimistic prophets, all of whom are also of a didactic persuasion. Perhaps it's time to allow for the possibility that ecological hope is unabandoned to the very degree that it seems most under threat. If that is so, then Kinsella stands to be one of its more intelligent, authentic avatars.

Still Cool
Rereading Kizer's *Collected*

When Carolyn Kizer's *Cool, Calm and Collected: Poems 1960–2000* weighed in at a whopping 400 pages, readers were surprised both at the prolixity and the heft. Organized by decade rather than by publication, Kizer's book seemed a recognition of the formal unfolding and elemental power of chronological narrative, and was in effect a wager that the justice of time transcended time's erosions. Against the calm suggestiveness of classical entablature, framing the caryatids of her youth, there now stands, thanks to the block layout of contents, five decades worth of work, in which spin the demotic rush of particulars, of facts. As if in answer to Robert Lowell, who once wondered why invention had to be seated ahead of "what happened," the march of poems in Kizer's *Collected* alternates between lyric and narrative (with the latter seeming to take up more space in later years), dramatizing the most recognizable dynamic in her poems: the actual, remembered past confronts the idealization of event that yearns to transform fact into myth—which is to say, to remove it from history, from narrative—away from further imperfection.

The straightforward chronological arrangement demonstrates not only the evolved contours of a career that moved from the 1950s' neo-Metaphysical formality à la Roethke, Kunitz, Adams, Bogan, et al., through a depressurized period of Chinese impersonations, which we may interpret also as a declaration of independence from east coast aesthetic expectations (back when such distinctions still mattered), to a stretch typified by the brilliant, bipartisan conspiracy of formal achievement and organic, open poetry. We find no dry periods, no queer gaps requiring explanation: the days and years, grinding as they can be, awful as they may seem through history's lens, made memorable, forward-thinking poems possible, not—as was too often the case for her peers—impossible, or scarce. In every decade, there are poems aware of the fault-lines worn by their occasions, passionate alike in love and denunciation, never merely witty when they can be hilarious, never sad when they can be heartbreaking, Olympian, or self-justifying. Intuition knows that ends and beginnings touch, although self-divergence, as Elizabeth Bishop told us, paradoxically mediates such wholeness as it may be our lot to achieve. Wittgenstein likened human life to a rope: although no individual strand goes all the way through, the rope is continuous. What is continuous in Kizer are the conditions for lyric expression, combined with the sense of poetry as a discipline whose longed-for outcome is the union of image and voice underwritten by occasion.

In her work, beauty is not suspect, and this also means that evil (as cruelty, neglect, or despair) is real. Over nearly fifty years her consistency has maintained a realization that voice both chants and enchants. As the lover admonishes in one of her admirable Chinese "imitations" ("Summer Near the River"):

> … Come, tease me a little!
> With such cold passion, so little teasing play,
> How long can we endure our life together?

Keyed to a different register, the same voice—tender, teasing, in-the-know, colloquial—can also sing an ordinary ending into being, as in "Exodus":

> We are coming down the pike,
> All of us, in no particular order.
> Not grouped by age, Wanda and Val, her fourth husband,
> Sallie Swift, the fellows who play bridge
> Every Thursday, at Mason's Grill, in the back,
> Two of them named George.
> We are all coming down the pike.

Reading the early formal poems for many years now, I have always been struck by the fineness of the inlay—not only a reflection of the artisan's pride in construction and line, but of the subtler and, at present very much out- of-fashion notion of "finish." This is the stylistic closure that implies not fidelity to a mimetic ideology, but in Nelson Goodman's sense, a "world-making." In other words, poem-making is not situated among occasions ready-made for recording; rather, it is represented as invention. Robert Lowell called attention to a similar distinction in the 1970s and registered his anxiety not only that invention (world-making) was hard, but that simple mimetic acts—descriptions, say, of facts and states of affairs—might be beyond his—or anyone's—grasp. As a poet, Kizer was blessedly free of such anxiety, and this confidence in the power of words to stay where they've been put gives her literary production a sense that authorship and authority are not simply cognates but synonyms.

In this, she is perhaps less postmodern than she feared. While feminism too began to drift into layers of ambiguity and self-consciousness, what set Kizer's poems apart was their allegiance to an old, and if possible, even older-than-thou way of saying things that seemed essentially new. Kizer gravitated to the work of like-minded old-schoolsters like Louise Bogan, Leonie Adams, Rolfe Humphries, and Ruth Pitter, and set her allegiance there before she ever took up with the likes of Robert Creeley and Denise Levertov. This fact both predates her feminism and, when it emerged, kept it from becoming ensnared in its own curlicues—which has been the fate of both feminism and American poetry itself, when left to the ironic patronage of the academy.

While she began to develop a reputation in the 1950s as a poet of high promise, it was the appearance of (what eventually came to be) a work- in-progress, the (then) satirical *Pro Femina* that announced an agenda both playfully subversive of earnestness and subversively in earnest toward the pieties. However, the formal and thematic connections of *Pro Femina* with the poet's first volume, *The Ungrateful Garden*, make one wonder at its inclusion among the Chinese brushwork of the next volume, *Knock Upon Silence*, a fact that only chronology can explain. The precursor and companion poem to

Pro Femina from the first book is the great "A Muse of Water." In that poem, woman is a shape-shifter connected magically, metonymically, with water, while the "march" of civilization unfolds its stiff-jointed diorama. The point is that insofar as civilization is a march, it can't be much of a civilization: the excluded half is precisely that which doesn't march, but flows freely. It can be "harnessed" to man's needs, but such a need to control can't escape a certain whiff of perversion:

> And yet these buccaneers still kneel
> Trembling at the water's verge:
> "Cool River-Goddess, sweet ravine,
> Spirit of pool and shade, inspire!"
> So he needs poultice for his flesh,
> So he needs water for his fire.

The last poem in her collected, "The Erotic Philosophers," the poem that now concludes *Pro Femina* and, effectively, her active career as a poet, is a rereading of St. Augustine and Kierkegaard, twin pillars of patriarchal rectitude who locate what will become the Western master's (i.e., the male's) self-important dysfunctions in the ambivalence toward sexuality and women. Here Kizer finds the ground-zero of feminism in this same ambivalence. But the stentorian clatter of the earlier revision of Juvenal (the opening section of *Pro Femina*) is superseded by a more bemused I-told-you-so that is notable for its tolerance, as the earlier was enjoyed for its scorn:

> . . . We women,
> Outside, breathing dust, are still the Other.
> The evening sun goes down; time to fix dinner.

Now we see (and the chronological template reinforces) the possibility that *Pro Femina* may be profitably read not as a single poem (although the poet called it that) but as a series of poems related by theme and refined by an evolving dialectic of resistance and homage. "The Erotic Philosophers," we learn, is in part an affectionately ironic tribute to Kizer's philosophy teacher at Sarah Lawrence,

Charles Trinkhaus. And so the dialectic, like the muse of water, shifts in turn from satire to narrative to meditation.

The distance from there to here may be charted by innumerable graphs, but none is more telling than the graph that discloses a poet's willingness to mill privacy into public discourse while managing to retain its affective skin. Many of Kizer's best poems go back to biography and emerge as situated memories, memoiristic descriptions leading inescapably to judgment, with a number leading—as with her poem of seeing (and being seen by) Professor Einstein ("Twelve O'Clock")—to spots of time pure enough to suit Wordsworth. Nor did the increasing forays into memoir and—inevitably—elegy spell a loss of rhetorical muscle-tone. That outer coat for which she has been praised was still being worked until the last published work, though the application is more relaxed, more settled and timed by event and recollection than predestined by form. And there is at every turn that beautifully controlled (and controlling) vernacular.

Kizer once characterized the (male) Western poet's obsession with elegy as an implicit necrophilia. Preferring the chronicles of friendship by which Chinese poetry holds, as it were, a mirror to the West's infatuation with absence, the years since the 1960s and her poetry's purifying journey into *chinoiserie* helped to reinvent for her elegy's utility, as gathering shades took their place in the larger chorus: teacher, lovers, parents, other poets and friends from time immemorial become the subject of elegiac treatment. One of my favorites for the 1980s is the poem "Gerda," which fixes and so in part restores the memory of a beloved Swedish maid and nurse, banished by her parents during the Depression, whom the desolate child can restore only through linguistic conduits years later in another language—English. It is but another step to see elegy as a cover for self-elegy, as in the recent "Trio," where the poet's name rhymes with the very singing it has every hope of becoming:

> Some say sorrow fades.
> I shall carry my sorrow forever
> After I smile farewell
> To those who led me here.
> Only joy endures.

I pace the days along,
Three shadows follow after:
Two who were tall and fair
Are caroling behind,
And a third, who had no song.

As I have argued elsewhere, translations are honorific elegies by virtue of the attention they direct to the absent poem, the poem "under" translation. In Kizer's case, translation also becomes a means of engaging the political imagination, which in other poems is often left to hang fire, though its passive absence is often felt. Indeed, because her social commitments are seldom at variance with her deeper desires (they often are her deeper desires), her political poems are some of the best instances of this kind of poem, notoriously (for Americans) vexed and tainted by the very idealism that gives it character. The early, anti-McCarthian "The Death of a Public Servant" still threatens to make Jeremiah re-materialize after all the elegiac consolations have grown remote: "A poet, to whom no one cruel or imposing listens, / Disdained by senates, whispers to your dust."

Since the start of her career, Kizer has made no secret of her foundational opinions and bona fides. Looking back at her history, you notice the poems to her father, a prominent lawyer from Spokane, who overlooked the comforts of provinciality in favor of an old-fashioned insistence on the reality of art and one's duty to be politically forward-thinking. There you also find her mother, the first female Ph.D. in her state (in biology), and Kizer herself the late and only child of this enlightened couple, who gave her a sense of self-possession and reared her to believe herself capable of orienting her imagination in terms of horizons unavailable to others her age. Who but an artist could incorporate such a congeries and keep course, let alone a straight face? Reading the old poems, I have been moved by the force of their elemental rightness, their intricate solidity, hilarity, *savoir-dire*, existential coherence, and joy in the face of every challenge to the persistence of these qualities (challenges that are often the subjects of the poems themselves). Rereading Kizer, I have been struck by how every deployment of theme invites variation so that an outward-facing, yet self-referential figure begins to emerge with a force resembling logic. This is something you don't see enough of: poetic logic, played out over the course of a career.

But it must be said, too, that the work of a lifetime—a poet's collected poems—can inspire ambivalence both in the reader and in the poet herself. On the one hand, there is the understandable urge to sum up, to take the measure of time, which otherwise takes the measure of us. The same urge may occasion regret in the reader: when we approach an aggregate, aesthetic whole—an *oeuvre*—the figure that this work makes may lose its mystique to the need to be comprehended. Since her debut in the 1950s, Carolyn Kizer has moved at a pace that seems in retrospect the inevitable andante, from presence to eminence, through the decades, but with this *gradus* comes the danger that one's reception will grow less amenable to criticism and gravitate more toward blind reverence—or worse, forgetting.

Nevertheless, there is a utility to a volume like this: it trains us to stay on point, not to be dazzled by reputation, but rather, as she puts it in *Pro Femina*, encourages us to "get back to the meeting." Which means, more broadly, that the limited aesthetic wholes we call poems, for all their fit-and-finish, formal rectitude, sensuous satisfaction, and thematic closure, invite us to consider deeper involvements beyond pure contemplation. Unconvinced by the didactic, yet not content to be merely personal, Kizer's work connects the dots between private and public dreaming by suggesting that private utterance can only derive authority through public ears and the mediation of cultural memory. For her, Herzen's famous "What is to be done?" is not rhetorical.

Carolyn Kizer
Late and Last Poems

I was a student of Carolyn Kizer's in the late '60s and early '70s at The University of North Carolina, Chapel Hill. In those days, boosted by tailwinds of the student and anti-war movements, young people were taking up Bics, Rapidographs, and even Pelikan 150s to write creatively as never before. Kizer had arrived at Chapel Hill with a positive buzz, having resigned from her job as first literary director of the NEA, the first of several significant pushback political actions she would take, endearing her to progressives and eventually landing her on Nixon's enemies list. She had also published "from *Pro Femina*," a didactic wake-up call for women's liberation, as it was then called. It was a thoroughgoing and life-defining stance, not simply a program to arouse righteous indignation in housewives. Yet her poetry, even then, struck many of us as lofty and arch—far from the demotic lexicon that we used. How was it, we puzzled, that her democratic sympathies lay so at odds with the often-aristocratic diction of her work? We learned over the years the uses of pitching language up, as a way of managing acknowledgment of content's importance. Her subject matter left us feeling that we worked on smaller canvases than we might one day be required to do. We were young romantics, writing what it felt like to be alive in such heady times. She was a classical poet who was as likely to people her poems with goddesses as with the ordinary *homo sapiens* who was her real subject. At one moment Olympian, the next understatedly Asian, she was fond of covering herself by saying, "classicism is just romanticism without all the excess." In this witticism danced all the contraries of her subsequent career: desire and restraint, smoldering content and chastening means, the call for political action and philosophical reflection.

Although she could be combative, her idea of the poetic culture to which she offered both loyalty and resistance, seems by present day standards benign. She believed in a tradition that included a laying-on of hands and the creation of artistic families. In her capacities as editor, arts administrator, teacher, contest judge, and literary board member, she helped launch and/or boost the careers of such poets as Lucille Clifton, Mona Van Duyn, Judith Johnson, Robert Peterson, and Richard Shelton. She also performed reclamation deeds for such neglected poets as the Brits Ruth Pitter and Bernard Spencer and similarly sought a spotlight for international poets: Shu Ting, Edouard Maunick, and Nina Cassian. An itemized list of her generosities—all in one way or another recipients of her patronage—could go on for pages.

It should not come as a surprise that she also believed it was possible to envision one day a summing up, to shape a final period that would exhibit something like an achieved coherence, aligning all her poems into a new force-field that would both render them anew and increase the intensity of the light in which they were read. In fact, she sought to give shape to her entire career, and her collected poems, published in 2000, should be read in that spirit. Whether she believed this at the starting out is perhaps moot, but such a belief follows logically from her formalism: to control some aspects of the future—where death, too, is waiting—is a worthy goal for an artist and bespeaks likewise a respect for the past, rightly understood. Such idealism notwithstanding, from the "intentional fallacy," keystone to the New Criticism, to postmodernist assumptions of our own day, the idea of authorial intention has undergone devaluation. Although the devaluations were usually local, they had global implications, including implications for career shaping as a predictor of one's reception. It takes a healthy ego to push back at such intellectual climate change, but Kizer operated under the assumption that it was so and indeed preferable to no attempt. It wasn't that she misunderstood the issues either, or thought that she was fighting a windmill in thinking she could fashion an *oeuvre* from her poems.

She had no patience with what she saw as the machinations of theorists, who sold poetry short. She saw feminism pass through the mill of academic revision until it succumbed, in her judgment, to the worst of fates that can befall a great idea: terminal obfuscation. It is not surprising that she trained her pen on the career trajectories of so many talented, yet minor, failed or compromised poets, whose paths were diverted because they were unable to bring determination to bear through no fault of their own—or for that matter, through venial faults aplenty. The poets whose careers were marred by self-inflicted wounds or premature endings seem somehow to become the objects of contemplation on the struggle of determination and chance in the making of careers. Often the poems suggested that they were concerned with the making of a body of work that might withstand what the existential body would inevitably find daunting.

Like her own teachers, she held to the notion that art provides an image of timelessness, and she subscribed to the idea that such an image is a necessary fiction. It seemed that when Hegel commanded modernity to historicize everything, Kizer did not get the memo. For many of her colleagues, the question was, was this a rock of truth upon which art could build its church, its tradition, its literary culture, in spite of the hungry generations, or was it a necessary fiction to bind literary communities together in mutually flattering (or consoling), even ecumenical relations? In some larger sense, the answer mattered little, as succeeding generations would come along to breach the gap where present artists had fallen short. The main thing was that the larger machine of literary discourse had a kind of honor and integrity. The first beneficiary of this idea that art stood to mend what life could not was the artist herself. As work accumulated, it became both a matter for shaping and upward striving, as it matured beyond the mere sum of individual works. In this way too, poetry stood to correct—or at least exonerate—he life that gave it shape—the life that, unlike the art, knew it would someday come to a close. Why not a conclusion, then, instead of simply an end? Why not a chord, instead of silence only, that airless space where only literary criticism seems to find breathing room and cause for utterance?

I suspect that Kizer foresaw the end of her active writing career in light of thoughts such as this and took pains to conclude it so that the closure resembled the last movement of a classical symphony, with its restating of older themes with the added wisdom of experience: issues finally exhausted in satisfaction, dissonances resolved in consonance. When it comes to the final period, one likes to think that its accompanying style has both the privilege of final speech and a retrospective mandate to brings old themes into a new focus. In other words, insofar as the poet has a chance to give final shape, to do otherwise would be to succumb to a congeries. Of course, death and debility have other agendas, and thus the question becomes who the author of one's work will be—the poet or that poet's end? Preemptive ending is like preemptive criticism, an insurance policy taken out against the chief contingency of authorship—i.e., its very end.

Theodor Adorno, who thought a lot about lateness in terms of style and architecture, was of the opinion that, far from summing up, a number of great artists (Beethoven in his case) twisted free of the conventions that had sustained them and given them both the keys to artistic intelligibility and enhancement and the rewards that go with positive reception. Edward Said took Adorno a step further in showing how poetic power and fame were manifestations of cultural power relations between artist and community in which the art was countenanced and appreciated. For Said, the late period bore the relationship of an exile to a distant, though formative, country.

If Carolyn Kizer had anything like an exilic relationship to the culture that found her muse, it was the unfinished—indeed ongoing—business of feminism in the face of her own sense of winding down. It is in the uncollected poems in *Cool, Calm and Collected*—tellingly millennial in its subtitle *(poems 1960 - 2000)*—that we see two forces at work. In "In the Night" the poet is confronted with shadowy images crowding her bedside, against which she offers a temporary resistance:

> There are spirit presences
> around my bed
> waiting for me to die.
> They are in no great hurry
> nor am I.

In "Shalimar Gardens" we get another warning note, though this one, being aestheticized, comes across as less threatening:

Here spirit is married to matter.
We are the holy hunger of matter for form.

Kizer you enter the dark world forever
to die again, into the living stone.

Then follows a series of poems that pick up recognizable themes: gender, politics and justice, the fate of poets at the mercy of chance, the presence of the past. It is notable that after the alarm of death's presence in the first two poems, there follow four elegies for (male) poets, each of whom is in some way affected by his relationship with a female partner. Once this Beckettian mood of persistence in the face of minimal hope is established, she ends the section with her final poem, "The Erotic Philosophers," a text that, far from assenting to the views of the two philosophers under review—St. Augustine and Kierkegaard—takes these authors to task, and the very tradition of detached meditative thinking that underwrites their philosophies. This latter is the object of the complaint that, more than any other, spans Kizer's career and enunciates the formative issue of her feminism, namely, the contention that "Yes it was always us, the rejected feminine /from whom temptation came. It was our flesh/with its deadly sweetness that led them on."

"The Erotic Philosophers" is Kizer's last *major* poem, and its place among the canonical pieces—"Columns and Caryatids," the early version of *Pro Femina*, "A Muse of Water," "Singing Aloud," and "Fanny," her poem about their wife of Robert Louis Stevenson, gives it something of the status of the last word, and thus it deserves the special attention of her readers. Kizer thought so in another way, as the poem bears a note that it should be considered the last section of the ongoing sequence for which she is best known, *Pro Femina*. When she made a similar statement, annexing the Stevenson poem back in the '80s it caused the raising of some eyebrows, for that poem was a dramatic monologue, now suddenly appended to a three-part Juvenalian satire. Not everyone was convinced that *Pro Femina* grew organically, although "Fanny" was definitely a feminist reading of a woman who had sublimated her career to be the helpmate of her more famous Victorian spouse, the creator of *Dr. Jekyll and Mr. Hyde* and *Treasure Island*. The detour Fanny took was to become an obsessive and finally a masterful gardener, but the obsession overwhelms and nearly consumes her—at a time when her famous spouse goes from triumph to triumph. In the last line of the poem she swears, "never again [to] succumb to the fever of planting," which, in turn, recalls the first line, "At Samoa, hardly unpacked, I commenced planting." With the emphasis on the repetitive and sacrificial nature of the sublimated muse, Fanny is left with nowhere to go, except toward the stance that Cavafy, following Dante, termed "The Grand Refusal." "The Erotic Philosophers," by contrast, tells us what we had all along suspected, that the hands of the masters weren't clean, that in their sense of duty, "Saint A. and Soren had much in common / including fear and trembling before women, the Saint scared himself, while Soren was scared of *us*."

> Yes, it was always us, the rejected feminine
> from whom temptation came. It was our flesh
> with its deadly sweetness that led them on.

The indictment endures long after the resignation sets in:

> Think of the worldly European readers
> who took Soren seriously, did not see
> his was the cynicism of the timid virgin.

Kizer finishes the poem and sums up her career at the intersection where moral responsibility, psychological acuity, and poetic judgment converge:

> In Soren's long replay of his wrecked romance,
> "Guilty/Not Guilty," he says he must tear himself away
> from earthly love, and suffer to love God.
> Augustine thought better: love, human therefore flawed,
> is the way to the love of God. To deny this truth
> is to be "left outside, breathing into the dust,

Filling the eyes with earth". We women,
outside, breathing dust, are still the Other.
The evening sun goes down; time to fix dinner.
"You women have no major philosophers." We know.
But we remain philosophic, and say with the Saint,
"Let me enter my chamber and sing my songs of love."

At this end, Kizer not only concludes with the final installment of *Pro Femina* and legitimates its *in*clusion, which is her *con*clusion, in the process), she does so by conceding that women are still "the Other." But thanks to the courtesies of language she still writes within a tradition by no means exhausted by timid male virgins or corrupt philosophies. Moreover, she asks now only to "enter my chamber and sing my songs of love." Thus the last published word of Kizer's active poetic career is "love" and thus love becomes the auspice under which the *oeuvre* can be seen. We close the book and remember Tillich (justice is "the form in which and through which love performs its work") and Rorty (work "not done under the auspice of love is not worth doing"). Two men, I note, who thought a great deal about the Other and the self's halting pilgrimage in its despite.

Dorianne Laux's *Superman*
The Chapbook

Nostalgia, that Boomer specialty, gets a going-over in Dorianne
Laux's *Superman: The Chapbook*. Being all of six poems (which arrived
in handsome card stock in a clear plastic slipcase), Laux's chapbook
performs the impressive trick of seeming much bigger than it is. It
does this, not by putting the past's faded glory to bed but by bringing
it forward for scrutiny and finding, in doing so, no loss of mystery.
This little collection's title is not just a clever marker: it gets us into the
opening poem *tout de suite*, where we find the Man of Steel overlook-
ing Metropolis like a kindly but bored gargoyle contemplating Paris.
We know he is one of our own because of his evident fondness for
weed ("Superman sits on a tall building / smoking pot"); his super
being notwithstanding, he suffers he ennui of the working man:

> He lifts his head from his hands
> as the sun sets, the sound of muffled gunfire
> in every city of the world ricochets
> through his gray brain. He'll take care of it
> tomorrow, the thankless, endless task
> of catching dirty bombs and bullets...

Like any working stiff, he no longer finds incentives to "leap," and
there is moreover the spreading sense of mortality that cloaks him
better than any cape ("Kryptonite / bending its rays up toward his
scarlet heart"). I remember Carolyn Kizer musing about the loss of
Zeus in the collective memory of usable literary touchstones in favor
of contemporary pop tags like cartoon characters and movie icons.

Her concern was, you might say, the standard classical one ("They'll have to footnote Minnie Mouse."). I suggested (only to be dismissed) that Superman might sub for Zeus in the non-classically trained brain, and here Dorianne Laux, taking up the idea, presciently sees with what result. Deconstructions of this sort generally redound to the poet's credit: she gathers our trust in pulling the masks off nonce gods. As Brodsky remarked, increases in humility are always a good idea. Were we to leave the matter there, we'd be left, however, with the consolation of a good idea but with few extenuating benefits. Laux, to her credit, pushes fearlessly ahead.

In "Cher," she broadens her pantheon's plinth with an ode to the elusive singer ("I wanted to be Cher"), the old Cher, "before they shoved / pillows in her tits, injected / the lumpy gel into her lips." In distinguishing between the authentic Cher and the later, refurbished celebrity, she locates authenticity with green age, but she is shrewd enough to see that such identifications are themselves beholden to things beyond the reach of innocence. It was as if Cher's posing with the doltish, blunt-fingered Sonny ("in front / of the Eiffel Tower, The leaning tower of Pisa, / The Great Wall of China, / The Crumbling Pyramids") never completely painted over the fact that the "authentic" Cher was itself a persona. Her "hit-or-miss beauty" turned out to be a gamble that the imperfect could compete with the perfect. And yet, who could not identify with some version of the adolescent wish to find the ideal in the ordinary, beauty in the snaggle of the given?

> I wanted her
> rouged cheek bones and her
> throaty panache, her voice
> of gravel and clover, the hokum
> of her clothes...

It was this transformation from plain to fabulous that, you might say, authorized Sonny and Cher to sing "the oldest, saddest songs." The poet too knows that these songs have to come after-the-fact (and before not-unavoidable parody sets in), if they are ever to be sung. And so they do: in a sense this chapbook is singing them.

"Bakersfield," for anyone who passed open-eyed through the '60s, could almost have stopped at the title. To say "Bakersfield" is like saying "Bay Area," only the implied content would have factored in the dust and heat, the trailer park, some country music hummed *sotto voce*, and more whiskey than pot. Here the draw is a mopey boy, the kind who will not last a lifetime, but who will nevertheless be linked to memory for the time ("I liked him. That's what I remember."):

> He was a bit slow
> like he'd been hit hard on the back of the head
> but nothing dramatic.

Accosted by the mother for her forward ways, Laux responds, "I stopped seeing him / after that thing with his mother." "How we endured it," she wonders and admits, "Back then / I was scared most of the time." Meanwhile, Taj Mahal intones, "If you ain't scared, you ain't right." The bluesman's quoted *aperçu* is said of the time, perched on the lip of slow-motion come-downs, after the botching of its supposedly meaningful highs. The quotation is meant to be prospective too.

How anyone gets anywhere—to say nothing of why—is the presiding question that hangs over *Superman: The Chapbook*. In "Late Night TV," she watches the flourishes of a commercial actor who demonstrates the cleansing "power" of a detergent, and one wonders about the links of cleaning with forgetting and about the parodic ease with which a filthy shirt is rendered spotless, while memory is often powerless to expunge the tarnish of trivial scenes. For all that, unexpectedly echoing Frost, Laux nicely distinguishes between the mindlessness of the presentation and the destiny that brought the announcer to his inane pass: "By what road did he travel / to the late night station?" Laux is expert in letting details and unremarkable acts leverage deeper moments and more nuanced strata: nothing is left to starve of its own insignificance.

But the fact that so much that is resistant to rational meaning seeps into daily thought while bearing intimations of significance suggests that it is we who are driving around in a lower-than-desirable gear, our articulations stuck at the level of feelings and hunches, not rapid enough to capture nuance on the fly, nor sort through the cacophony of phenomena that surrounds us. The danger is that we come then to a tipping point when too much begins to tip over into whatever. Laux eyes the danger, but she doesn't succumb to it.

In "The Beatles," Laux wonders as everybody born before 1970 does, why the Beatles broke up ("the whole / Yoko Ono thing seemed an excuse / for something deeper." Considering the usual list ("wives, ex-wives, mortgages / thoroughbreds and waist-coated butlers") she concludes,

> Maybe they arrived
> at a place where nothing
> seemed real. A field
> bigger than love or greed or jealousy.
> An open space
> where nothing is enough...

And here I must suppress the urge to clear my throat. The real—the what-is-the-case of our lives—depends, you might say, on editing and the haphazard presentation of things to our senses. The thinginess and ordinariness of life come with no guarantee that they're going to be synonymous with the really real: all too often, our choices flame out into personal preference and favoritism. The heart, after all, has its reasons where rational action (like the Beatles staying together) can't make any further headway.

The follow-up question of how we got anywhere at all, with or without the Beatles, is the subject of "Yard Sale." Here Laux churns up wonder for the fact that the singularity we are told enfolded all of us, all our stuff, including all the stuff we live among and negotiate our way through, was our unbelievably tiny point of origin, before the Big Bang spangled ourselves and our stuff across the vast nothingness. She does this by considering the very preposterous nature of matter's eventual configuration, and the imagines this rabbit pulled from that hat:

> ...a garage filled with spokes and spikes, sections of fence, grand
> hammers and glowing clamps, an extravaganza of penny nails ticking

in row of open jars on endless shelves of darkness, collapsed lawn
chairs, gold rakes, sacks of fertilizer and rock salt...

You get the idea. The poem is Laux's *Theogony*, a poem of creation that recognizes both constant tendency toward devaluation
and waste and the ongoing value of endless division and diversifica-
tion. For us, it's the diversity, of course, that keeps imagination in
play by always showing the player another move. It is "one humon-
gous yard sale burned clear and washed up, lapping at the shore of
the unknown lawn." Just like with the Beatles, there is too much to
know, but everything to desire. So what's the street value of these
nostalgias? There is knowingness to be sure, but between loving and
knowing, Laux gives us a clear idea of where she stands. *Superman:
The Chapbook* give us credible assurances us that the apple of the eye
matters more than what the mind can break off and chew.

Philip Levine's *News of the World*

Philip Levine has always subscribed to the lefty slogan that says if you're not mad, you're not paying attention. Now in his eighties, he is within his rights to make peace with the old angers, political, cultural, and personal. In his superb new collection, *News of the World*, Levine takes up questions of end-gaming, and it will be of interest to his many readers that he has not only such questions to raise, but also some answers—of a sort. Neither the icy Olympian equanimity of a Beethoven, nor the self-conscious *shantis* of an Eliot present plausible scenarios to this poet. And you can forget traditional religious consolations. But his naturalism is compact with Whitman's, and the trump card that this allows him to play releases him to envision the same anonymously grassy freedom that enveloped Uncle Walt, although grass, for the denizen of Motown, looks positively nostalgic in the wake of the Great Recession.

What we might call the "naturalist option" proposes that you give up relinquishing any robust claim of transcendence. This is true whether you are a poet, a soldier, or a machinist. Thus, deciding for a naturalist outlook, you are in for a big sigh of relief (if you can opt for it). Naturalism derives its strength from the justice of matter, with which Levine finds common cause. Consider "New Year's Eve, In Hospital," which encounters still-Victorian attitudes towards mortality, revealing Arnold's cosmic hand-wringing in "Dover Beach" as nothing more than the manipulations of a religious scold and Cardinal Newman (who could refer to "That masterful negation and collapse / Of all that makes me man") as source of the hand-me-down discourse of a young priest making rounds:

> A young priest
> sat by my bed and asked, did I know
> what Cardinal Newman said
> about the sea. This merry little chap
> with his round pink hands entwined
> told me I should change my life.
> "I like my life," I said. "Holidays
> are stressful in our line of work,"
> he said. Within the week he was off
> to Carmel to watch the sea come on
> and on and on, as Newman wrote.
> "I hate the sea," I said, and I did
> at that moment...

Levine is letting his book-learning provide some of the ammo here, which elsewhere he evokes to summon the same refusals that most of us take a literary life to be underwriting. That casual erudition, to be sure, can still snap a whip, even if it can't (or won't) suggest a redemptive system to its hungry readers:

> "You should change your life,"
> he repeated. I asked had he been
> reading Rilke. The man in the next bed
> a retired landscaper from Chowchilla,
> let out a great groan and rolled over
> to face the blank wall.

The knowingness is acute and only marginally therapeutic. That last gesture comes, as you probably noticed, courtesy of Comrade Hemingway, who turns up in "In the White City" (one of eight prose poems) where a lieutenant in the Spanish Guardia Civil who wants to lead American tourists in a Falangist teaching moment. Convictions are scrambled elsewhere, too—especially political ones. In "News of the World," an Andorran shop owner recalls the changes:

> Back then," he said, "we were all reds." "And now?" I said. Now he could
> sell me anything I wanted. "Anything?" He nodded. A tall graying
> man, his face carved down to its essentials. "A Cadillac?" I said. Yes,

of course, he could get on the phone & have it out front—he checked his pocket watch—by four in the afternoon.

The commitments, obligations, entailments, desires, regrets—take a bow—which, as gestures go, is a long way from pacing the battlements. And yet, Levine suggests, there was something about the devotion to human justice, about the acknowledgment of the tragic, even if that tragic continually arrives without its stoic fur. While we are alive, the poems suggest, those of us paying attention struggle against those of us who aren't. Then life, concluding the narrative of us, puts its period to the struggle:

> Think of it,
> my name, no longer a portion
> of me, no longer inflated
> in a rich compost of memory...
>
> ———
>
> a tiny me taking nothing, giving
> nothing, empty and free at last.
>
> ("Burial Rites")

It is a flintiness devoutly to be wished. At the same time, readers of Levine will recall many poems informed by a tenderness made all the more tender for refusing a second helping of emotion, or in any way underscoring the affect, in whose dimension, in fact, most living takes place. What it feels like to be poor, to have been dealt a lousy hand, to be on the wrong side of history—these are questions the gods find unintelligible. One of Levine's strengths is his ability to stir readers at an emotional level, while refusing or holding off more expansive or rhetorically pumped-up versions, often brake-tapping by means of a counter-statement:

> Yusel Prischkulnick,
> I bless your laughter
> thrown in the wind's face,

your gall, your rages,
your abiding love
for money and all
it never bought,
for your cracked voice
that wakens in dreams
where you rest at last,
for all the sea taught
you and you taught me
that the waves go out
and nothing comes back.

("My Fathers, the Baltic")

The working-class paradox, which consists of old-fashioned solidarity versus the wish to experience release—i.e., to escape—has
never found more forceful, intelligent expression in contemporary
poetry than in Levine's work.

In "Our Valley," Levine asks us to hold two thoughts: 1) that
"home" is a nonce term and 2) that naming, that special talent of
poets, waits at the behest of some beyond that is itself just an inkling
("that huge silence we think of as divine"):

Now you say this is home,
    so go ahead, worship the mountains as they
            dissolve in dust,
    wait on the wind, catch a scent of salt, call
            it our life.

That reminder of the ocean, that "whiff of salt" is all you need to
get going with geography, starting from invisibility and zooming all
the way in to your "home." The other thing you need is patience—
which is to say, to make your attendance an extension of the patience
of time ("you can almost / believe something is waiting beyond the
Pecheco Pass"), the recognition of which leaves you "thrilled and
terrified." The sea is there—or you believe it's there—but the point
is that a life is like that attendance, that waiting for the "beyond." Just
waiting is the thing—not getting the wish, not arriving on time, not
the money shot. For a few minutes you might be excused for believ-

ing that this was a poem by Richard Hugo, but Hugo's nostalgias are masculine and Western, hoping to hook into myth. Levine's are urban, suspicious of myth, which so often presupposes the wrong kind of heroism: "You came north / to Detroit in winter. What were you thinking?" ["Arrival and Departure"].

Poets who report from the midst of history rather than from myth are attuned to the narrative and the question of its control. "A Story" is a meta-poem that offers the suggestion that, whatever the story—even the one that didn't happen—there is more than meets the eye. Beginning with the domestic mundane ("Let's begin with / a house.") Levine, like a master draftsman, begins to make the crosshatch shade the line to the point that we can come to feel this is a family—not just a poem. Whatever there is about this family, moreover, there must be included its spectacular, yet banal demise:

> This was the center of whatever family life
> was here, this and sink gone yellow
> around the drain where the water, dirty or pure,
> ran off with no explanation, somewhat like the point
> of this, the story we promised and may yet deliver.
>   Make no mistake, a family was here.

The diction incidentally marks a distinction: the poet no longer fits squarely within the class he is describing. Or does he mean to suggest, like Whitman, that this class now possesses the diction that politics would prevent? In other words, does his poetry itself stand as evidence and elegy of the educated, blue-collar poet's crossing over, or does it extend the franchise? What we learn is that the hypothetical family in this poem gives way to a real one (presumably the poet's own)—by virtue of being named—and the new reality is defended against the aggression of the hypocrite *lecteur.*

> The worn spot on the sill
> is where Mother rested her head when no one saw,
> those two-stained ridges were handholds
> she relied on; they never let her down.
> Where is she now? You think you have a right
> to know everything?

Like a film director, as well as a custodian of family history, Levine widens and heightens the perspective to aver, "If those questions are too personal, then tell us, / where are the woods? They had to have been…" The poem ends, "there has to be more than dust, wind-borne particles / of burning earth, the earth we lost, and nothing else." Does the opening proposition, "Everyone loves a story" yield an answer in "there has to be more than this"? Long story short, there is, because the force of *there has to be* pushes the narrative until it topples into *is* (*pace* Hume). We know this because the old distinction between *ought* and *is* is meaningless in hindsight, where both are—we might say—poetry. This poem begins with "Everyone," considers a concluding image ["no more than dust"] but finishes with the adverb: *else*. It may be that the narrative line is obligated to take readers to "else," which, after all, promises deliverance from the likes of "is."

The biggest historical event of our lives is up for grabs. For the Greatest Generation, however, it's not arguable. It's WWII. Levine's brother (brotherhood is the template of several poems here) appears in "Innocence," where, years after the war and now grown blind, he lives in a Neutra glass house. When someone passes along the received toll of the Air Corps, to which he belonged, the brother shows why the events of that history never leave:

> When I tell him
> of the 50,000 airmen the gardener told
> the novelist about, his blind eyes
> tear up, for above all my older brother
> is a man of feeling, and his memory is precise—
> like a diamond—and he says, "Not that many."

The brother's probity in "On Me!" explores how coming-of-age is configured by money:

> In the next room, my brothers are asleep,
> the two still in school. They just can't wait
> to grow up and be men, to make money.

The question raised here is whether bearing is the same as bearing up. But events can queer the arithmetic: where once coming of age equaled being a man, it now finds a *tertium quid*: coming of age equals no money, which in turn equals anger. Coming of age, in other words, means coming to recognize one's own ongoing baseline of rage:

> Now it's so clear,
> so obvious, he wonders why it took
> so long for him to get it and to come of age.

Levine's poems often search for a way to accommodate failure by considering what is authentically empty, the seal of authenticity becoming a placeholder for value, offering peace of a sort. In "Homecoming," the poet considers the nothing that comes after the something:

> An actual place in an the actual city
> where we all grew up. you and I pass it
> on the way to school or on the way home
> after work. It's where the old house
> once stood, it's wide eyes open day and night,
> replaced by nothing.

This "nothing," then, becomes a theme, surrounded by the accoutrements of language, for the sake of which, you might say, it becomes an honorary thing: "Call it an empty log / though it's not empty." It's here in this poverty that Levine works best. He may not be religious, but he likes the presence of virtual things made present by virtue of language:

> If we're quiet
> we might hear something alive
> on the move through the dusty alleys
> or the little abandoned parks, some-
> thing left behind, the spirit of the place
> welcoming us, if the place had a spirit.

Reading a poet so admirably and reliably hardheaded, you might conclude that naturalism is just a green version of nihilism. But nostalgia and desire (even anti-nostalgias and desire's refusal) come to the rescue because memories and hopes—even faulty memories and daft hopes—supply a metaphysical layer on top of materialism, on top of things. A denial, a dismissal, a lie—all require the energy it takes to propound them. They could have suffered indifference, which is the badge worn by meaninglessness.

Levine's devotion to what Heaney calls the "redress" of poetry is the subject of "Library Days," where in wartime (Korean), stealing time from his job as a beer delivery truck driver, he treats himself to "these treasures, for Melville was here, Balzac / Walt Whitman, my old hero, in multiple copies..." Guarded by a harpy ("gone gray though young") he makes his way through Dostoyevsky ("every page of which confirmed life was irrational"), Tolstoy, Turgenev, and Chekhov, noting that

> Outside I could almost hear the world, trucks
> maneuvering the loading docks or clogging
> the avenues and grassy boulevards of Detroit.

The resistance that this hungry reader and future writer puts up adds another, more personal chapter to the dilemma posed by this book: deadening work or no-money-making imagination? It's the question raised by a previous collection, *What Work Is,* for if what work is *is* work, then the work of literature is either a transvaluation or a lie.

> In the offices and shops
> out on the streets, men and women could curse
> the vicious air, they could buy and sell
> each other, they could beg for a cup of soup,
> a sandwich and tea, some few could face life
> with or without beer, they could embrace or die,
> it mattered not at all to me, I had work to do.

The work of literature, this insistence on world-making either in the void or else contested by pressing, often violent contingencies, is in its purest form an instance of creation (not recreation) *ex-nihilo,*

even as its miraculous happening is a trick of the eye or ear. In "The
Music of Time," he notes,

> I can lie awake in the dark
> rehearsing all the trivial events
> of the day ahead, a day that begins
> when the sun clears the dark spires
> of someone's god, and I waken
> in a flood of dust rising from
> nowhere and from nowhere comes
> the actual voice of someone else.

He is "on [his] way / to nothing" ("Two Voices") when he hears
his name, as if from a voice in a cloud, which turns out to be a crowd
("kids in Rollerblades/ kids on skateboards, kids on foot"). In "Alba,"
the poet travels with other tourists in still-Franco Spain, where he
encounters the story of a mass execution by a young commandant,
González Brilla, whose killings are preceded by speech-making:

> You who are guilty, who are about to die,
> to leave the stage of history, behold...
> behold...something or other."

"Something or other" is all his friend can remember, while Brilla's
widow "swears he never spoke / that way his whole life." Skipping
to the point, the poet finds the friend in a hospital ("he remembers
nothing, / not even the war"). The poet asks,

> Can we hear them now, the words of Brilla,
> the elusive lesson worth all those lives?
> Above the cries of seagulls, the message comes
> transplanted into the language of water and wind,
> decipherable, exact, unforgettable, the same
> words we spoke before we spoke in words.

In a similar spirit in "Magic," the poet muses on the fate of a
friend "back from Korea / with graying hair and a flying cross,"
and both noting and wondering why he notes such changes, lays his

poem to rest in as positive a note as he is able to summon, witness
and chronicler that he is,

> It took me years to learn
> a way of walking under an umbrella
> of indifferent stars, and to call them "heavenly
> bodies," to regard myself as no part
> of a great scheme that included everything.
> I had to put one foot in front of another,
> hold both arms out for balance, stare ahead,
> breathe like a beginner, and hope to arrive.

Although history forces us away from our pretension to timelessness—a notion dear to many poets of Levine's generation, it
also enables the tragic register to come into play. The fallacy lies
in believing that the tragic kicks in as the metaphysical (the timeless, religion, Platonism) ebbs. To refuse heaven is courageous, even
macho; to refuse the tragic is sublime. What Levine shows, to his
credit—is both the desire to be free of history and yet to have experienced it deeply—where winners and losers vie for the narrative.
The paradox lies in the insistence, clear in this book as never before,
that to be free of history, to return to the dust and meaninglessness
after a life of engagement is itself a kind of metaphysics, for it returns
us, shorn of sound and fury, to natural structures once designated
as harmonious. Getting in touch with our inner-Dostoyevsky, rail-
ing against the dying light and all that, look from the perspective
of Alpha Centauri, quaint. But that was never our perspective, and
while we railed, we were as big as our contradictions: only the living
know this. And the silent *who cares!* of the beyond is a boorish hurricane compared to the whisper, the whimper, and the sigh.

Sarah Lindsay's *Twigs and Knucklebones*

As we have been reminded in louder warnings than in any year since Y2K, this is the Year of Darwin. That being so, we might well ponder the passing of vast time, the clashing of tectonic plates, and extinction of animals in the dark backward and abysm, as well as speculate about the course of evolution way into the future: Sarah Lindsay does. Lindsay, the author of two well-reviewed collections (*Primate Behavior*, 1997, and *Mount Clutter*, 2002), has leveraged a syncretic imagination into a niche industry. Her new volume, *Twigs and Knucklebones,* should go a long way toward securing her reputation as a poet with a specific itinerary and the engine to get her where she needs to go. She is literary, learned, acerbic, and funny, as well as possessive of more than a little tenderness, the quality that is historically least in evidence but most in need for her subject: the extreme decentering of human wishes and the chilly specter of Mother Nature Redux. Her poems suggest that it is to this that not only should we turn, but turn we will, both because of a kind of weariness with ourselves (Lowell: "I'm tired. Everyone's tired of my turmoil.") and because the future is a big place. If you want to know how big, just ask the past—and not in terms of human time, but of Deep Time.

Naturalism provides, as it were, a green alternative to the conventions and traditions of western poetry with their metaphysically indentured ways and means. It frees itself from these ways and means by avoiding the usual stuff: first person engagements with the outside world, the accumulations of conventions and gestures,

the themes and *topoi*—the literary noodling with which poetry, historically, has more than a passing interest. A poetry of naturalism,
on the other hand, ought to strike us as not unfamiliar, thanks to
a lineage that stretches from Lucretius, by way of Bacon and Darwin, to settle on our shores—and switching time for place—in the
persons of Louis Agassiz, John Muir, and Loren Eiseley. Lindsay's
poems remind me of essays of Loren Eiseley as told by James Tate:
the last wisps of metaphysical melancholy disperse to make way for
the brighter lens and clearer vision of science. Gary Snyder is also
there, but in a different register, as he specifically deletes Milton and
all that he stands for as if performing an act of *feng shui*.

Lindsay doesn't go after the tradition from which she emerges,
but like an evolved poet, simply points her horns forward, sparing
no tears for the vexations of past cultural angst (if any). Much of
the difference in her poems amounts to a matter of perspective:
she prefers the long view to the subjective, the telescope to the love
letter, the microscope to the folks in the office. She moves easily
between microcosm and macrocosm—a specialty also of Eiseley,
and, as strategy, this yields its own brave-new-world spectrum of
emotions, replacing elegy with awe—which is to say replacing the
past with the future.

As Emerson noted there are two tribes contending for our culture, the Party of Hope and the Party of Memory; Sarah Lindsay
is a member of the former. Emerson, and later Rorty, used these
categories to describe social dispositions. Lindsay's hope is not a
secular paradise where human progress finds its true Jerusalem;
she subscribes to the sense that "hope," whatever else it is, is an
evolutionary trait. As for memory, it's problematic, as a moment's
reflection on the subject of archaeology will confirm.

There is a shrewd ambivalence that lurks under the question of
what absence "feels" like. It surfaces in "Elegy for the Quagga." Since
extinction is evolution's equivalent of forgetting, it is of interest to
the poet, who is not merely content to put us in our place, but wishes
us to contemplate the plain swept free of quaggas and other creatures that have fallen on their departure buttons. She suspects that
forgetting is also part of the housekeeping of love: forgetting cleans

the place up. So how we get down with "death's second self" (a.k.a. oblivion) is an index of our capacity for wonder. Wonder and love both become, as it were, free-standing; they're no longer required to be relational or interpersonal to be real. A blow to subjective poetry? You be the judge. But Lindsay's poems ask us to consider if taking the long—and I mean really long—view is one way we manage to exercise our species' maturity: saying adieu to the quagga, to whole branches of the tree of life, and finding in that the consolation of the really real? Brave new world, indeed.

For all that, it's also steady as she goes, for while the scientist's eye is nearly always busy focusing on little-noticed phenomena that she will pick out and describe, she never abandons the craft she learned as a poet. It is also true enough to say that being a poet, she cannot have gone over completely into the naturalist's camp, as her craft entailments alone tie her to a mast where the whole cultural barge of poetry's discourse, from yawp to Elizabethan splendor, sails on into any and every sunset that the dolphin and the cloud enjoy.

One of the marks of a gifted poet is the ability to sweep up disparate filaments of fact in masterly fashion and to dish them out, suitably summarized, evaluated, and skewed (which act—skewing—is the compliment language pays to mundane fact). With Lindsay, this gift is often on show. "Destruction" describes the difference between the old-style archaeology of the amateur, the "ruin-bibber," in Larkin's phrase, and the lab-coat-clad scientist of romance-less modernity. Her swaggering antiquarian and *roué* is himself the ruin he seeks: his life consists in grabbing with acidic, unscientific hands, hands that "were restless ... / not to amass or study, but / to spill, to jingle, to give away grandly." This baron also brings with him the colonialist's combination of obtuseness and derring-do, finished with a dash of Paterian aestheticism:

> They say the Baron von Hausknecht traveled
> nowhere without a valet, a chef, and a mistress;
> and cursed in nine languages, some of them dead,
> which he taught his mynah bird.

———

Madly rich
and wildly in debt by turns, he left a trail
of women smitten or well amused,
partridge bones and empty bottles,
rumors of duels, a few of his teeth,
and a newly chic fascination with ancient lands.
He wore black lambskin gloves, they say, at all times,
and had crates of fine wine carried to every dig.

Part of the fun of *Twigs and Knucklebones* comes with the realization that the spirit of Indiana Jones hangs over it. While on the one
hand it is as if Sarah Lindsay stowed away on the Beagle; on the
other, it's as if her discoveries are served up Hollywood-slick, not
with the groaning and creaking of the mast, nor with the motion
sickness and boredom of the protagonist. Lindsay brings a swash-
buckling tone to bear as science reveals the future, while canceling
any vanity we might have presumed to bring forward. Whether it's
the old-school archaeologist, half-drunk on Assyrians and Hittites,
or the negativity of left-brained explorers, she's too poised to be
bummed out by either. Neither does she let her tools drag her back
down into holes from which no poet can emerge. Either it's the sheer
abundance of life, prolific and overcoming adversities, or it's the
threat of extinction (especially in the first poems). Is there somehow
a fear of extinction lurking in her poems? If there is, there is nothing
to be gained by not looking catastrophe in the eye.

The more you grow into naturalism, the more tragedy comes
to seem unintelligible. And if that is the case, does the naturalist
transcend tragedy? The pathos of classical literature was precisely
that the tragedy of heroes was unintelligible to the gods; we gained
dignity as a result. By contrast, the triumph of Christianity was that
it grew into and through tragedy, thereby marking it as a "human"
religion. In Lindsay's poems people appear obliquely, not front and
center. Even when they are the subjects, they are frequently seen
in shadow. But naturalism is vaster than tragedy, which seems by
contrast, smaller, self-important. And if tragedy is small, then what?
What with the conquering vastness, some sublime would seem to be
the next stage, but Lindsay knows better: the vastness that begins

at the ends of our noses outstretches any sublime. In the end, our stance toward vastness is just fashioned by tweaks and quirks. It's mental tourism, and that's just another version of species vanity. So she keeps her distance, both because "awe" still carries the taint of hoary old encounters and because the vasty deeps that stretch before her imagination are often of a microscopic variety, as in "Why We Held On":

> But the reasoning minds of the twenty-third-
>   century institute,
> having found the cause of our
>   counterproductive affliction,
> can move ahead toward a cure. Although
> some researchers instead will find
> they cannot resist pursuit of the abstruse mystery
> of the parasites' motivation.

To Lindsay's eye, history is corrosion; impact craters pile up until the planet's surface is as pitted—and significant—as a bad case of acne. In "Valhalla Burn Unit on the Moon Callisto," patients take advantage of the "soothing views," recuperating in an environment "never close to each other or anything." The self-important present gets warehoused as unceremoniously as does the ark in the final scene of *Raiders of the Lost Ark*, an ending that would have raised the hairs on Diderot. And as it is to the elements of creation, so it is to the components of recreation, especially art. Ozymandias meets Ryder Haggard In "The Museum of Damaged Art: Audio Guide," where,

> A broken air conditioner flooded
> Brice Marden color fields, and they bled.
> A portrait of Eubie Blake was slit
> across the face as its shipping crate was opened.

If ruins are your thing, it doesn't get any better than that. A museum of unpreservable objects is no paradox—all museums are in the business of non-preservation, even featuring non-preservation:

If we had funding we could show
Rembrandt's Danaë in a time-lapse sequence:
first overcast with age, then bubbling and running
with sulfuric acid, then propped while a row
of curators gently spit water on it,
finally with its monotone repainting
As it is, just another vandalized Rembrandt,
    Gallery Five.

But just as the Age of Reason knew that *memento mori* are always good, so the Museum replaces the feel-good mood of tragedy, with a glance at new horizons—almost as if this were an anti-privilege— where we will also not be invited:

Step through the door marked EXIT now;
the cracked sidewalk leads to Parking.
Observe on your left the beaten grass
where not one stone is left on stone
of the building that stood here once, before ours,
and on your right the city skyline
and distant mountains, faint in the corrosive haze.

The centerpiece of *Twigs and Knucklebones* is a series of poems called "The Kingdom of Nab," which Lindsay describes as "a fictional realm in the neighborhood of Hittites and Assyrians." You might say the congeries of her ideas in the opening poems are systematized and applied to an entire civilization; there are subsections ("Late Kingdom," "Middle Kingdom," "Early Middle," and "Early Kingdom") reversing the Rise-and-Fall cliché to give pride of place to the fall. In this dusty-shard-filled sequence, full of displaced gods and domestic objects, Lindsay works the same territory George Seferis did in his great Modernist poem, "The King of Asiné." For Seferis, the question was one of retrieval: what lives on in the word? May we "retrieve" the king merely mentioned in Homer's list of combatants? In Lindsay's version, linguistic archaeology directs its attention to the barest threads of present humanity's connection to lost humanity. For some, the dwindling returns speak for themselves, and their lack of interest gets no censure here. But for the impassioned scholar, everything turns on nuance, placement, and conjecture:

> Hundreds led in battle, hundreds slain?
> A thousand times beloved, nine hundred sheep?
> And the standard translation of this word, here,
> is either "desire" or "need." But did he write
> of a homeless yearning, or mercantile requirements?
> Was he a "singer"? The scholars who care disagree.

In the manner of "The King of Asiné," how would we know the difference? But even if we don't and basic meaning itself occasionally flips over into nonsense, have we no business then producing scholars and scientists? As meaning gets weaker with age, as contexts erode, what happens when we "sample" the past, construing meanings and forming conjectures from dwindling circumstance? "Estimag and Sililit," dappled with ellipses and lacunae provides one answer:

> Therefore the people...
> ...gather up and...
> ...even the widow and the infant...
> ...as if the smallest grains...
>
> *The rest is missing.*

In "The Ruins of Nab," Lindsay continues the theme:

> We prod and whisk and deduce what we can
> from marks and clay, from the trace of a wall.
> But the way the king tossed and caught his
>   adoring daughters,
> the foolish songs he improvised for his wife,
>   and his furry voice—
> these have been safely forgotten.

The excavator-poet sets about deducing "what we can," and we have to be satisfied with that, filling the gaps with imagined bits of plausibility, a set of repairs that this book also accomplishes. In a way, losing "fact" through time and replacing it with imagination is not a bad bargain for the significance-seeker, when you think about it. Lindsay suggests her approval when she lovingly gives us a sunset, dorsal view of the archaeologist at work repairing the filaments in civilization's fraying braid:

> See! Behold! Look! Lo!
> they cry in season, rapt, in love,
> chipping away with their pocketknives,
> pencils, rulers, fingernails,
> but some have tunneled so narrowly and deep
> that those behind see nothing but slivers of light
> around an excavator's haunches.

("The So-called Singer of Nab")

The question of passion versus being-in-the-know surfaces here, the passion of the archaeologist is suggestive of Billy Collins' familiar image, the self-hugging trick that from one angle looks sexy, from another like a straitjacket. Yet for all that, as she says in "Sililit the Ungraspable":

> *I have found my desire.*
> *I have breathed on it.*
> *I have barred it to plundering light.*

Thomas Lux's *God Particles*

To witness Houdini, or, for that matter, David Blaine, squirming out of his chains is to understand that immortality, that gray but fecund arch-trope, is more about finding fissures in the monolith than about banishing Terminus. It's about coming to see necessity as a dubiously curtained wizard, laying down the same law that the poetic optic nerve sees right through as just another metaphor, not the bluff-free ultimate in realism it claims. Lux has been that Houdini among contemporary poets, enacting that wish not to be pinned down and yet not fade into ambiguity, either. For this reason, the formal aspects have to be in good order, because the weight of situated and craft-maneuvered form keeps imaginative liberty from collapsing under the weight of its own exfoliating inventions. Keeping a balance is the key, and this Lux does.

The kind of poem Lux writes is now one that he consistently nails. In *God Particles,* his 11th collection, we find him nailing it again. Several earlier reviewers of this book, while generally weighing in with praise, have also felt obliged to complain that Lux's poems are facile and academically complacent. I would take issue with this characterization: I think it misses the point, since it seems really just a way of pigeon-holing poets of his demographic and of consigning him to a comparable or slightly lesser meadow on Parnassus than the ones inhabited by the poets with whom he has been often compared, such as Knott, Tate, Edson, and Simic. Although Tate seems lately to be an unstoppable font of the humorous narrative prose poem, Knott is, as ever, Knott, practically *sui generis.* Meanwhile, Edson continues to generate subversive conundrums, and Simic to refine and adapt the Eastern European surrealist lyric to American ears. While Lux's work does bear comparison with these poets, his signature belongs to him alone. And readers who have followed his career of four decades will note that the radius of his talent keeps widening, the Emersonian circles ("the first of forms") also disclosing something that readers of poetry hope for—that "under every deep a lower deep opens." Although Emerson's shade may seem an unlikely ghost to preside over Thomas Lux, I note that an Emersonian *aperçu* stands as epigraph to the volume.

"The Pier Aspiring" reminds me of a midwest relative of mine who once innocently inquired on first seeing an Atlantic pier: "Does it go all the way across?" Lux is on the case ("See? You can't see the end!"). This pier the speaker has built himself (but not for himself: "pier" is also "peer"—peer-building.): "the theory / is this: it's my body's habit..." So the answer to whether it goes all the way across is moot, being redirected to the fact of habit (including the secondary sense of habitation) in the act of making "one board laid down after another." Here he also hints that habitual practices bring one to the point that it is natural to "nail" pieces.

> It's good to wear an X
> on my back, to bend my back to the sky, it's right
> to use the hammer and the saw,
> it's good to sleep
> out there—attached to one distant end
> and tomorrow adding to that distance.

This is not sacrifice but generosity, the giving, almost a self-emptying. Such self-gifting seems to be an important component to *God Particles*, as it builds, not only the seemingly impossible bridge to others, but the protection from what would otherwise be a world of such contingent mechanisms that we would stand to be continually disengaged from participation in our own fates. "It will be a bridge," Lux asserts against common sense, and yet it is an assertion of such application that it glosses both this (and any) poem and the poet. But less important than whether the pier becomes a bridge are the things that, by repetition and habit, go into making a character. It is an old question: the poet or the poem? There is still an argument to be made that the former takes precedence over the latter. And there is reason for this: the seen without the seer is unintelligible. Alas, much ink has been spilled and many keypad keys worn down in support of the idea that the poem is more important than the poet (an idea that would have raised Keats' eyebrows).

"The Pier Aspiring" itself makes a bridge to the title poem, a cognate poem but in another key, about the supreme act of self-emptying-as-gift (first line: "God explodes..."). In this poem, God brings on another Big Bang—that being Himself—showering bits of the divine substance confetti-like over His creation. This poem stands in some contrast to "The Pier Aspiring" not only in scope, but in bias. Lux locates this benign catastrophe in an unspecified time-out-of-time where people drop what they are doing to experience the shower of God particles. The moment is reminiscent of the 1950 movie *The Next Voice You Hear,* that religious melodrama intended to placate the conscience of a post-Hiroshima America in which God addresses fellow Americans on the radio. The message: do your homework and be good. But Lux updates the moment with his God revising the distribution of Self à la mode (and there are allusions—sly, knowing, melancholy—to suicide bombers elsewhere in this collection). So the inconvenient query, "Who just asked: Why did God explode?" is equivalent to asking the kind of pointy-headed academic questions that inhibit action and bring one to the slippery slope of irony. Now the problem with irony is not that it's not called for: in some sense it's almost always called for. The problem is that it's reactive, secondary, and, straight up, a lie: not the kind of reaction befitting the Deity's legacy. The particles: we are to be given them even if they're too good for us. God becomes His legacy—our redemption is our being pardoned for previous lack of imagination (and then, presumably saved by ourselves). It is a coming-into-fullness, not a perfection.

> ...and He wanted each of us,
> and all the things we touch
> and are touched by,
> to have a tiny piece of Him,
> though we are unqualified
> for even the crumb of a crumb.

There's that moral voice-over. One can't escape the feeling that the tongue-in-cheek, the un-saying, cushions every positive assertion. That's the irony I mentioned, the quality that leaves us "unqualified," though not, for all that, empty-handed.

For a poet of Lux's shrewdness, a book of blessings would be incomplete without a curse. In this case, it is the poem, "Invective" ("I pray your son wish to be a poet"), which may be read as a blessing with the switch flipped to *off* and the stream of (God) particles thus neutralized and pushed to their logical conclusion minus the key ingredient of self-emptying, of giving. This poem stands as a little presentation piece, a coded bit of equilibrium, a mirror-image of the title poem.

As has been the case in earlier poems, there is an incoming tide of poignancy here—the allusions to childhood, the memory of tenderness, the people standing about like characters in Magritte, trying to act resolutely ordinary. This is the case in "The American Duel," for instance, where absurdities are interchangeable with niceties:

> This
> is an American duel, how we fight,
> how we respond to nose-pulling,
> unlike the foppish French
> or the English, who wrap their umbrellas
> so astonishingly tight.

Pathos seeps in along with Lux's intuition for whimsical opportunity, even caprice, which is always at least a nod in the direction of imaginative freedom and hence is capable of providing satisfaction by showing us other fates and vocabularies than the ones to which we've become, as Blake warned, too early habituated. Lux's syntax also tells us something about other fates and possibilities by giving us alternative grammars that leverage English into nuanced enactments both of emotional states and of the gradations of thought. As they record, they also embody. Consider the multivalent closure at work in facing poems, "Man Pedaling Next to His Bicycle" and "Her Hat, That Party on Her Head." The former ends,

> Where did they
> go—that which, those whom, he was meant to glide
> past,
> or love, on his journey?

You see the shuffle of pronouns giving way to verbs. The inter-ruption of syntax often maps the by-no-means logical processes of thought. It would not be inaccurate to say that Lux's syntactical (syn-tactics) manipulations (and stylings), especially as his poems move toward closure, record barometric pressures of emotion and surpris-ing moments of realization—then recreate them in the reader. In the latter, he writes,

> whose absence
> made her wear this hat
> to help, but fail, to let her absence go?

Lux did American poetry a solid when he found the scope and fit of the Lux poem. His poems have never strayed far from the well of theme-and-variation; he has not been observed staking his talent on attempting great American "masterpieces" or big production numbers. He is not a poet out to write *Four Quartets*. But this is not to let his ambition float, either. There is a lot of real estate here, and the magnitude of Lux's importance starts to become clear as the poems stack up. His is an amiable poetry finally, although the stations of his cross are the old absurdist ones made familiar by a generation of poets influenced by surrealist juxtapositions (mostly E. European, not Hispanic) and various strands of "anti-poetry." His is a horizontal poetry, too, in spite of its surrealist pedigree that finds inspiration in the unconscious depths. This horizon is popu-lated not only by characters of fiction (as in "American Duel") and bourgeois propriety (amicably vexed), but of Eliot's rolled umbrella-bearers and Continental suburbanites who refer to themselves as "one," thereby heralding the approach of irony and behind it, of the intuition of vanity.

There are at least three reasons why we ought to assent to an absurdist view: the irrationality of people, the contingency of nature,

and the silence (or death) of God. Lux taps into each of these reasons, hinting at what it feels like to be directly in the beam of each.
His poems, by and large, are not directly autobiographical (for which
he is to be complimented), but this is not to suggest that he stints
on subjectivity. On the contrary, he knows all too well its sorrows,
as suggested in "Autobiographophobia," where the speaker avers,

> . . . because I'm telling the truth,
> it is right that I talk only of myself
> and never of you, or you, and you, or you.

Lux's poems sound like narrative because they often have what
Frank O'Hara called the "I do this, I do that" way of versing. The
cadences are also those of speech (or of thought, as noted) and
therefore are capable of a sweetness, the *dolce* touch, beyond the
reach of the rest of nature with which we are surrounded. In "Sugar
Spoon,"

> a tiny hole opens
> and thenceforth it will leave a dusting of its cargo,
> a trail, a grainy Milky Way
> across the maple table
> from the bowl of my father's, my mother's, coffee cup.

The sweetness often accompanies the absurdity, and their inter-
changeability is mirrored here and there like the work of the artist
Rachel Whitehead, who makes plaster casts and hence, negatives of
real things: bookshelves, whole rooms. . . . In "Put the Bandage on
the Sword and Not the Wound," we hear that "It must hurt, too, the
sword, heated to red. . ." Likewise, in "The Harmonic Scalpel,"

> The patient hears
> the tune (the anesthesia local) and is soothed.
> Sometimes a nurse (oh white
> on white and her nylons too!)

Peter Stitt found that Lux's strongest poems "are those written in
his most difficult tone—an ironic mingling of humor and sincerity

which betrays a ferocious anger at necessity." In the Luxian universe, the reverse is also true: manifest ferocity betrays a tenderness and humor at the core. One of my favorite poems in this volume is "The Ambrosiana Library." This Borgesian place caters to the dying breed of which Lux and anyone reading this can identify:

> On its onyx shelves: every book you've ever read,
> and the tone you felt, which pierced you,
> when you did....
> The library not only caters to readers, it honors them:
>
> Each reader is assigned
> his or her personal librarian,
> and each librarian is paid twice the average income
> of orthopedic surgeons....

The point of this *embarras de richesse* is as simple and unobjectionable as it is impossible and yet desirable: "...citizens sit and read themselves into another / world." And that world, in catering to this one, pays it the compliment, as in the title poem, of the greater deferring to the lesser, which is the paradigm of things done under the auspices of love, of caritas, pity, all those things books go on about.

Anne Marie Macari's *She Heads into the Wilderness*

Anne Marie Macari's *She Heads into the Wilderness* does show the reader at least two ways out of town. The book's two sequences (and an epilogue) take us in the direction of eco-poetry ("Earth Elegy") and of Edenic and post-Edenic myth ("Their Eyes Were Opened"). Her form of choice, unrhymed and heavily enjambed couplets, reminds the reader of the missing *tertium quid*, history, because the formal backstory of that form, in turn, points to a time when the couplet was poetry's version of Q.E.D. and the poet and reader complicit in unpacking its connections and implications. History, which is at the other end of the title's wilderness, can make of any trek a pilgrimage. Meanwhile, Macari's frequent use to the unrhymed couplet underscores its other capacities: its ventilating pauses, its sinuous coursing, while holding in reserve its potential for pulling up and making a statement stand pat, even occasionally sounding the decisive click of the lock.

The poems of the section called "Earth Elegy" work by denying the human its usual self-empowerment and/or enlightenment at the expense of nature and of denying, further, the exceptionalism with which poetry grew famous, attaching to the spread of subjectivity. In truing the perspective, her poems find what is moving in the world beyond the subject and its reality distortion field:

> I watched from my kitchen
> as it gathered in leaves and needles

bleached, dissolving, though I hardly noticed
how the slow orgy

of weather took it season after season
into the pelvic

trench of dirt...

("Earth Elegy")

That trench is guilty not only of a Stevensian concupiscence, but
of a barometric "orgy," for its wheeling and grinding puts us in the
way of the tidal forces, where deep time and high time embrace:

a company

of beings, billions,

dying as we were dying and other beings driving
through the debris

and living off it—the dining and dead together,
unseen sinning and tilted

like us on our axis, pitched toward some
ever-place

of crashing trees...

("Earth Elegy")

Pelvic energies, as we see, bind nicely with the dying, as mori-
bunds make way for the hungry generations. In poetry, nothing is
more trite, and at the same time, nothing more profound. It's the
process, the breathtaking systemic blindness and milling violence
that is all the show, not the fact that we perceive it, or mark it up
to experience. Naturalism always features desire reliably separated
from love and yet never failing to turn up its inexorable tractor

beam. The pulverizing Macari describes moves thematically in the opposite direction too, that of Eliot's love that is not the product of desire—which is hardly a "love" at all, except in the strict sense of compliant self-emptying:

> Tell me
>
>   there was a reason, more than hunger,
>   that drove me here. Then leave of me
>   what's left, scattered on the roadside,
>
>   for there are so many travelers
>   and they are forever hungry.

    ("American Tree Sparrow, Platte, Nebraska")

While the milling of death in every register not only shows the necessity of self-emptying, it also lets the poet make a plug for Whitmanian anonymity, as does the off-hand "once I read that..." attribution. Clearing the decks, as it were, makes way for a return of the gods, in the sense made familiar by Heine and Heidegger. Not only that, but naturalism can be its own religion, as Darwin knew. Macari is closer to the naturalistic point of view in her particulars, but closer to these antecedent poets in her interest in the strategies and tactics of continuance:

>   I leave everything I have to you—dirt
>   and dust. Make what you can of me. I was
>
>   born here, return me to grass lullabies,
>   the black tea of creation. O broken-rib earth,
>
>   red orb in the tree, I touch you, my fruit,
>   my flesh. I eat you, my forbidden.

    ["X (It's Just the Starting Place")]

In the longer second part of the collection, she moves into myth mode, knowing that doing so allows her to derive a narrative as readily from nature as it does from history. This fact suggests an answer to why so many American poets seem to find the naturalistic option tempting. Whitman showed how porous the borders were by redescribing history as nature with such aplomb that it grew obvious to succeeding generations of poets what he had done. Similarly, pushing the subjects of poems into the realm of myth released them from the old obligation to pay heed to traditional religion, while at the same time saving for themselves something like the timeless. In other words, myth folded time in on itself and so departed from the laws of sequential development, to which history was tied. Myth meanwhile benefitted from the prestige of timelessness that formerly belonged to the eternal. In incorporating time, the mythical poem supersedes the cascades of historical event, even as it incorporates those events. It likewise folds in nature's sequences of birth-death-reproduction. Yet what the reviewer detects only magnifies subtleties, leaving the poet to recede behind a feline smile. Macari has the grace to avoid the behind-the scene positioning of big templates, and yet her work provides the stuff that converts variables into verities:

> And she who writes
>
> about the lost sea cow,
>
> tell her the air she moves in
> is singed with extinction.
> We are waiting. Remember how
> we turned the other cheek?
>
> ("Steller's Sea Cow")

That sign of humanity, that cheek-turning (from the "Earth Elegy" section) merely raises the wilderness' eyebrow, as does a Biblical reworking worthy of Kierkegaard:

> Whoever, like Abraham,
>
> rubs your neck and leads you to the altar,

whoever asks you to choose and bow down,
will be against you."

[“XV (The Cord Between Us)”]

Can one ever say enough about estrangement? “It’s good to be
unknown, a stranger, / good to know nothing and no one and say
now, now…, says the speaker in “XXV (Empty It, All of It).” It is the
work of a lifetime, of balancing faith with doubt: faith that future
generations will make good on promises uttered fortuitously; doubt
that promises framed the right-healing spaces:

Not your country
I tell myself as if
I could know any place as if I were
in a place but am not

really that is the happiness
The grasses sing

(“Ireland”)

An Eve-like figure presides and moves through the poems of the
book’s second part, “Their Eyes Were Opened” (“We always ate from
that tree. The women / with child craved its fruit, sweetest, most
red.”). As the title suggests, her talent is for perspicuity, and the first
question her appearance raises is how to match the seen with the
said. This figure is first presented in the third person, but as the
sequence progresses, she becomes the speaker. Mother Eve is also an
aspect, an emanation, of the poet ‘s will to impose a particular story
on her experience, which is to say her history. At once other-worldly,
timeless, and eerily familiar, the voice loses its authority by succumbing to the itch of moral indignation only once, in a Katrina poem:

See Noah wave from his plane, smiling like
God’s own secret above the broken levees,

below him the whole world a sick brown sea,
survivors begging from roofs, bodies

floating, cars in the trees...

["XXI (A Scratchy Radio Voice Whispers)"]

Reapproaching history need not only leave one in a state of political high dudgeon. One of the most approachable poems in the volume is Macari's affecting elegy for the mezzo Larraine Hunt Lieberson, who died of breast cancer in 2006:

> On stage in hospital gown and socks, IV
> Hanging from her arm, she is what she'll become,
>
> A woman not wanting to die, and all
> That applause, audiences crying—stay with us,
>
> Don't leave—flowers flung at her.

["XXX (Octave to Octave She Passes)"]

Lieberson is of interest to poets because, shortly before her death, her last concert appearances involved songs based on poems of Neruda (set to music by her composer husband). Not only does Macari's spirited pilgrim eulogize this singer who fell, even as she seemed to be ever-ascendant, and not only does she summon the shade of Neruda, her phrasing also manages to suggest that his erstwhile comrade, Chilean poet César Vallejo, come along. In *Poemas Humanos*, Vallejo writes of a corpse that, after repeated attempts from an ever-swelling circle of friends to affect a resurrection, finally relents and allows itself, in the crescendo of wailing humanity itself, to be reanimated. The repeated phrase, "Don't leave!" emanating from the crying audience, sets the lament backwards to touch Neruda and Vallejo—or pulls them forward to join Lieberson's audience. Here one must succumb to the temptation to quote Carolyn Kizer who, in "Singing Aloud," rushes out "to impose a form on what I don't understand / or that which I have to transform because it's too grim as it is." That story, now myth, brings with it the solace of what a book like Macari's offers: formal coherence, proportion, linguistic precision, dynamic control, and rhythmic delight:

She heads into the wilderness, weeping
and stunned by shame, her eyes open. Into

another country, bent and becoming,
fibrous and heavy in her body, feeling

that she is the tree, or that she is the fruit
that ripens and falls, that falls and will keep

falling her whole life.

["XXXVI (She Heads into the Wilderness)"]

The problem that Macari sets herself is how to mediate the mythical persona with the familiar voice. Self-authorization can be a continually foreshortened labor, but it is labor nonetheless. It is also
a task worth engaging, and with her new collection she seems, as
Louise Gluck once slyly remarked about her bardic self, poised to
write "the great poems of her middle period." I hope she does: her
intelligence never confuses Eve with Tallulah Bankhead, never the
tragic with world-weariness.

Al Maginnes' *Inventing Constellations*

You don't have to read far into Al Maginnes' *Inventing Constellations* to find a man haunted by contingency and trying his manliest not to be made giddy by time, even as he is a man acclimated to stoical adjustments. Much of Maginnes' fourth collection finds occasion to comment on our sojourn under stars, discovering music's timeless transport as body and soul age, taking both specifically human and generally mammalian pleasure in securing his family against threat and clearing the brush to the main road. He knows it all could have been otherwise: the there-but-for-the-grace-of-God theme runs throughout:

>   I admit
> and deny nothing because I know
> a mile beyond the heart of town
> waits the house of a man caught
> and convicted for all the wrongs
> I committed and got away with.
> He spent years locked away and now
> sits on his stoop carving figures
> out of soap or soft wood. When
> he sees me pass, he says nothing,
> and I don't look in his direction,
> the two of us disciple
> to our divergent paths,
> our twinned and broken fates.
>
> ("In My Good Life")

Going nuclear notwithstanding, the family too is invented, and
the very idea that it is not sequenced by nature would be, in another
time or place, one of the risks. Here it is one of the rewards for selecting old verities to apply to new opportunities—in other words, of
improvising. The poet's humility in the face of his evident luck (and
of the common humanity he holds with the *un*lucky) is an appealing
quality here, as is his wish to characterize the exact caliber of his
gratitude at finding himself the fifty-something father to an adopted
Guatemalan girl. This urge is made all the more poignant because
that gratitude, whatever its merit, shades into melancholy, just as
encomium desaturates into elegy. The "shading" invokes all the associations, from relief to suspicion and the generally ominous. It is the

> ...shadow that deepens my joy at chasing
> my daughter through the morning
> of a day that will not last and likely
> will not be remembered even if
> we breathe it all the way in and use
> the best words we know to write it down.

("Before Elegy")

If you thought for a moment you perceived Roethke and Justice
peeking out from the leafy shade here, you would not be wrong.
Nature takes on a metaphysical weight, even as it is exonerated from
the willful destruction "we" excel at, either *in potentia* or in fact.
Maginnes frequently resorts to a complicit "we," and it's the drive of
"our" desire to experience the art within the poems that keeps us
from resisting such a consensus-wool-gathering as the first-person
plural so often implies. For who does not feel the urge also to think
hell no, I won't go along! I won't be caught up in the poet's language net!
This is especially so, one notes, when such language makes that
90-degree turn into the moral and ethical neighborhoods where
the poet himself lives. But just as the edge of the lawn alternately
threatens and beckons both child and protector, so too its coverage widens, to be coped with by means of art. In "Light Remains,"
this takes the form of movies—visual narratives riding piggyback

on streams of photons: what could be more dreamlike than the as-yet-unplumbed mysteries of our newest art? The old theater, even as it molts its magical identities and settles into more secular and provisional forms, somehow retains the memory of its beginnings. It is more haunted than any canvas or book:

> The Grand rises from the dark
>> of its lost lease to house
>>> community theater, a gallery
>>> for local painters. The bottling plant
> of my childhood is a museum
>> of county history now, the drugstore
>>> where I read comics
>>> and wrestling magazines a gift shop.
> Memory, like light, changes
>> but remains, its accuracy
>>> a matter for archivists,
>>> backyard astronomers, those willing
> to guess the age of a stone or star,
>> to catalogue the dust caught
>>> in the cone-shaped beam
>> that blazed the screen white
> as the beginning of time, before sound,
>> before cartoons and coming attractions.

More typically, it is music that provides both the succor of, and the belief in, invisible things. Shorn of religious hope and consolation, he feels duty-bound to pay honor to the steadfastness these things once bestowed: "A song on his kitchen radio promised / we have a home in heaven waiting." ("Prayer for the Imponderables"). Music—rock, bluegrass, folk, jazz—provide him a platform, not only for emotional expressiveness and sorting-out, but for mirroring and improving upon reality (knowing too the fact that music makes its *own* reality). In "The Shape of Song," he realizes that the setting down of music still requires the performance, just as a composition leaves open a space for a whole gamut of acts and enactments, from interpretation all the way to improvisation. It is the latter where we pause, before stepping into the unknown:

Absence is not silence,

                    but the slow beat

of a band trying a new song,

                    each player alone

with pitfalls of melody,

                    the snags and snarls

before the threads begin

                    to weave in the same direction.

Our lives are mostly mistakes

we are trying not to make again,

living as we do

           without rehearsal....

Because music, as Yeats saw, presents us with an image of the time-less, it is a swinging bridge to an ideal realm. Maginnes plays on the ambivalence inherent in the dual nature of bridges, as structures that allow leave-taking and connecting alike. He plays upon this ambivalence in "The Bridge," the collection's centerpiece and his riff on Hart Crane, whom he sees, rightly, as both enabler and blocker of imagination's reach. The poem moves easily between quizzical meanings and the effort of language itself not to be problematic:

The first time I heard a singer cry,
"Take me to the bridge," it was not James Brown
but Robert Plant imitating James Brown,
though my knowledge of music—and most things—
ran so shallow I didn't know anyone was
being imitated. Before I knew words could claim
two meanings, my mother told me
her friends were coming over to play bridge.

In spite of the tendency of meaning to proliferate, preferring the plural to the singular, we know that simple language puts us in the position to hold true beliefs not shaded and cross-hatched by irony or semantic creep. When language can do that, it complements us as rational beings. But poets know that we are far from rational much of the time, and language does not shake off slipperiness like a dog who has just run through a sprinkler. It is routinely slippery,

as parson Eliot reminded us, and hints at cracks in the façade of
our rationality. At the same time, most of us dismiss the slipperiness
in our daily rounds. We are, as Brodksy said about Cavafy, rather
bourgeois about language: we don't want to catch it sashaying when
we have stuff to do. Hence, the image of a bridge itself tips the hat
to an inbred ambivalence in language at the same time as it exists
to find connection:

> Thousands of CDs, many thousands of songs
> and I'm still not sure what purpose
> the bridge serves in a song.
> "I never write a song without a bridge,"
> I heard one songwriter tell another
> while I listened as silently as I had listened
> to my mother over cards with her friends.
>
> ---
>
> We believe our lives make a shimmering whole,
> but revisit moments, each an island
> in a series of islands, isolated and come upon
> mostly by accident.
>
>   And now and then
> we believe we've reached the place where
> the span of the past shines clean and whole
> as an architect's plan, a bridge
> where the band can vamp.

Notice how he nails music's need to "vamp"—away from our quotidian destinies. He makes the same point another way in "The Missing Language":

>   we know this is language
> that has no need for us.
>
>   -----------------------------------

> I wonder
> what murderous silence fell
> on some of them when they were among
> the ones who knew them best
> and what it cost to choke the flow
> of words designed to fill the hollow
> men have not learned to name.

> -------------------------------------

> And it is not
> desire for poetry or God
> that starts her speaking a language
> no one can answer, only desire
> for the women who could hear
> what she said and reply.

Yet again in "Blue Collar," he turns to a different set of problems inherent in the use of language, namely the political dimension of utterance and silence. I note too that the class context here puts Maginnes in the tradition of Philip Levine, whose tracing of such divisions marks a thematic meeting place where poetry and politics share a wardrobe, and where class certainties begin to seem as chancy as they had also seemed locked-in:

> They were the frayed shirts with company logos
> and names stitched over the pockets,
>
> worn
> by my friends' fathers as they came home
> from the bottling plant or the mill with no good words to say,
> who opened sweating cans of beer and slowly
> unlaced their shoes, mumbling half-sentences to their sons
> and nothing at all to me.

The bridge between the work of the poet and that of the musician figures as one of the themes here. Maginnes is like a number of poets of my generation who came to poetry more or less by way of

music, be it as inspiration or accompaniment. And we all remember
the universal academic lament that went up when we learned from
our esteemed professors that poetry and music were divorced in the
Renaissance, thanks to the rise of the printing press. We all dreamed
of a reconciliation, though in a fuzzy way, and this fact led to the
purchase of many a used Gibson or Martin. It also led to poems
about music (though not vice versa, thank goodness):

> First, believe with me that music becomes
> our default language after navigating
> the grave.

> And the music involved in the bargain
> for eternity must be epic, its performance
> flawless. Onstage, singers claim, the mess
> of daily life falls away. Cold dressing rooms
> and bad management, divorces and tours
> poorly planned all evaporate. So the soul
> trying to sing its way into paradise
> must believe the past, the life ill-spent
> on earth, will be forgiven if only
> the right note can be reached and held.

("Opera in the Afterlife")

Maginnes finds that connection in family and art, in family *as*
art. He makes no pretense at programming his poems to reflect
intellectual derring-do. Nor should he: he desires that his daughter
and we make up our own constellations, not from fabled antiquity,
but from newly conceived stories that reflect what have become our
myths. It is enough that we have stars at all, he seems to say, but like
a good provider, he also slips in a little bonus from time to time: the
unexpected quip, the unlikely *volta face*, the grace-notes of gratuitous invention.

In his astronomies, Maginnes suggests that humility is a survival
mechanism aimed as much at Nietzsche's god-like self-creation as at

Darwin's (or God's) down-sized determinism. As he puts it in "Two Horizons": We have all traveled enough to know / every horizon is imaginary." This then is the new belief. In "The Wine Resurrection," he makes the point explicit:

> Each time my friend plays his song about turning
> water into wine, I hear a new verse,
>
> and then one I hear tonight is elegy for his bandmate
> who died last summer of cancer. Because
>
> he was raised to believe the transformation
> of the material is possible, even probable,
>
> I think he is sometimes saddened, as only
> a believer could be, by the world.

Likewise, Maginnes writes through the register of his *maestro,* the late revered poet and novelist James Whitehead. He can also channel other stalwarts whose echoes provide a susurrus of his tradition. In "The Edge of the Field," you could almost write your own *Road to Xanadu,* following the tracks of Frost, Roethke, and James Wright, and their particular notions of a "field," with sidebars dedicated to the fate of stars as images in contemporary poems, to say nothing of the last four century's devotion to the imagery of shadows. You could then put your ear to the rail and hear Rilke ("tongue," "courage,") Creeley ("insistence"), Roethke ("the edge of the field), Bly (the "silence / waiting there"), Stevens ("deeper than music"). It's not only the protocols of rhythm that motivate Maginnes' pen, but also the echoes of keywords from the singing masters of our white, American souls.

> Each one of us
> will take our turn crossing that field,
> far from the lights of cities, nameless
> under nameless stars.
>
> You can walk into the shadow
> early, singing a song whose words

you forget as they leave your tongue
and believe it is courage, not fear,
marching you forward.

the soft insistence of the wind
urging you to the edge
of the field and the silence
waiting there, deeper than music.

("The Edge of the Field")

Maginnes is a tender poet, one who looks out for the underdog
and a poet capable of laying out the promises and perils of domestic
love. How often in contemporary poetry have we been subjected to a
sustained sense of love? Maginnes grafts sinew to the tenderness, like
teaching a child to be tough, but the toughness takes a back seat to
the tender instruction. His poems operate on the border between
feeling and sentiment that are these days subject to policing according to the ideological moment. In the title poem, he writes,

                                                    Tonight,
I wish the ones I love were with me in this small field
near our house to see earth's shadow cross the face
of the fire-reflecting moon. But lately I've let
too many small angers burn, said too many things that can't be
excused or taken back. I've wanted too much time in fields alone.

                              After she dropped into sleep,
I lay on her floor a while inventing constellations, giving names
to those soon-to-vanish formations: The Bad Father,
The Child Rising, The House of the Family Dreaming.

                                   In the morning
I'll tell my loved ones about the color of the moon
and all they missed, but morning has its own business,

and they know the moon will be there tonight to preside over
this constellation, this body of light, we made and remain.

Is the sentiment an issue? For readers who no longer choke on a
steady diet of irony, probably so. I imagine this is why Maginnes situates so many of his poems in the context of night, the sky, and memory. These things, depending on which way your aesthetic hangs,
will either give modesty a modest bump or be ignored. His poems
are composed of scrupulously observed details that carry weight, if
weight is what you think words hoist. They pace slowly—even the
poems about musicians—rarely accelerating past an andante. While
the gait may be old-fashioned, the underlying apprehension is both
of the moment and universal. His poem about the decapitation of
Daniel Pearl, for instance, draws out the sense of dread that connects, in its own version of a bridge, to the shadows on the edge of
the lawn and culminates in a shock wave of horror, where beauty
and other tonic truths used to be—and still await incarnation in
violence's despite.

Peter Makuck's *Long Lens*

That old head-scratcher Emerson famously (as Harold Bloom and Richard Rorty have not failed to remind us) said that we either belong to the Party of Memory or the Party of Hope. Peter Makuck, whose *Long Lens: New and Selected Poems* has been one of the happy arrivals in my mailbox this year, belongs to the former. Yet this new book will also show a man on a three-decade's-long mission to argue that as far as these parties are concerned, it's a distinction without a difference. For without memory the very idea of hope is fatally impoverished.

What the Sage of Concord had in mind was that too much obeisance to the past amounted to a kind of cultural necrophilia. In our (post-)modern day, it no longer takes a sage to see that excessive respect for the past calcifies, enabling a rigid conservatism. We witness evidence of this fact daily in political arenas, and yet my undergraduate political science course, combined with my life's reading of Whitman, reminded me that others, who also have a legitimate claim on a portion of America's soul, have evermore trained a moist eye on the future. Now, let it be said straight up that Makuck's poetry is not political. More specifically, his is not a poetry that takes historical reverberations as its subject (although it does take them in its stride). And yet, it is impossible not to feel that his work it is a continuous and conscious registry of the times in which the poems were composed.

That it is a poetry of "feels" as much as insights and epiphanies is only to say that Makuck takes subjectivity seriously to a degree that pays homage to his predecessors (James Wright, et al.), leaving the niggling problematics of subjectivity, with its various cans of worms, to the hungry generations of workshop poets doped on the steroids of theory. Makuck's allegiance to an older, nearly superannuated aesthetic is no more a problem for him than it was for the Yeats of The Last Romantics, who took pride that his poetry was a beauty-bearing form. The past, in this view, comes to the aid of the present. In both cases, it comes to the aid of a poet embarking on senior years, for whom the past is a senior right, and because it is significant, it gives hope a more distinct outline. Blake, who argued for distinct outlines, understood that hope first appears, then takes shape based upon shadows cast. The resolving power of Makuck's poems seems to have just this dynamic in mind.

Makuck's connection to the picturesque South where he took up residence is not that of a sentimentalist. At the same time, he knows that pathos drives the icon. It's the medievalist's knowledge, and it makes me wonder if it isn't perhaps time to unearth and dust off the troubadours' interest in *pity*, a concept our age has summarily dismissed but which, after all, is sponsored by aesthetics. Although his wit is at the ready, it is not Makuck's tendency to reach for the ironic toolbox. Educated before the School of Irony raised its plastic towers, Makuck knows that the problem with irony is not that it disses the subject and prefers being in-the-know to being in love. The problem is that irony is always, as it were, in second place: it's reactive (and reactionary?). Poetry for him is a believer's art, but from that readers would not be entitled to conclude that he is a *naïf*, although naiveté can be as much a capacity as a fault. To say the least, it makes wonder possible, and wonder is expansive (irony is reductive). Makuck, in other words, is of that school for which poems provide a larger figuration to memory and experience, and the dignity of the journey—nowhere found in ironic encounters, except in pinched, parodic versions—accrues in that very space. It is in such a sense, one would suppose, that poetry becomes therapeutic—it is the therapy of enlargement, of freeing Ariel from being wedged in the claustrophobia of matter.

The "long lens" of the title poem is not simply the objectivity of the long view—appropriate for a *New and Selected* (and yet it is that too) but the reach of emotional attentiveness. The alliance of emotion and objectivity is a tenuous one, and Makuck's poems explore this tension as a dance of contraries. "Long Lens" is itself sectioned into three, telescoping like an old spyglass, each section a focal length corresponding to a scene appropriate to art:

> …she gave me her camera
>
> for my weekly trek through three counties
> and asked for photos of anything
> she might improve into a painting…

If you think that Makuck's book arrives shod in Hush Puppies, you would do well to chalk the impression up to protective coloration. The poet's downward mobility into gentle academic and benign editor conceals the fact that nostalgias of such an order are meant to be reenactments of wonderment, retrospective scenes that seem to have escaped time, yet unfold in the double cadences of the poem and of the existential poet, doing time in the prison of his days (as Auden has it). No wonder the title poem extends its tube, as though the real 20/20 is piercingly telescopic, reaching out to what, minus the poem's optic, fades down a lane bordered by the cryptic on one side and the anonymous on the other. As Dickey reminded us, the poet is the enemy, not of forgetfulness, but of insignificance. Makuck's way is to approach, so to speak, each poem with Dickey's distinction in mind.

It is an unfortunate fact of writing that the really important often seems to border on the fatuous. Indeed, too much significance can, all by itself, put us in mind of airy nothings. That's why Makuck's poems carefully turn down the rhetorical engine on the excellent theory that understatement such as one finds in Socratic irony works best. The Socratic bottom-up orientation is as near to art as the top-down is to demagoguery. As a matter of fact, one feels that the method itself challenges the speaker to bring it on, with the result that the small volume feels large and stays in the ear and mind, growing that reader-configured abode Rilke spoke of. The majestically cranky Ivor Winters objected that conversation was an unfit model for poetry, that its vessel was too everyday to heft the Verities. Winters opposed the ambivalence of this kind of Wordsworthian poetry, a danger he thought especially powerful to American poets working with democratic armatures. But just such a reliance on meandering is all right with Makuck, whose recurring images include the fisherman setting out and the Tom Sawyer-style wanderer trying his luck, immigrant-American-style against the body and time of America itself—and where, as that body shrinks, time lengthens.

Likewise, in an earlier poem, "Into the Frame," the father-son dynamic—conventionally a way of seeing generations as engaging in negotiations, not merely mutual invasions of personal space, the knowing boy, who is the poem's subject, "scoots" a shark look-alike over a shelf in the channel, defying caution but underscoring self-reliance and experiential knowledge. Rereading Hemingway is not required to remind us that the fisherman is a quester after knowledge—knowledge that rewards the thoughtful seeker and attenuates danger. Following this alarming moment, the poem concludes:

> The scene becomes a painting again.
> Go ahead. Step into the frame,
>
> descend one step at a time
> to all that white sand, jade and windy light,
>
> the boy still in you, latent but not lost,
> running to tell you his tale.

The tale that the boy tells is precisely this poem. Its clarity—its willingness, we might say—finally to tell becomes a gloss on autobiography. The negotiations between Keats' hungry generations are acted out in the self because those generations already exist in the self, all time folding into the present. The poet knows the dialectics of generations require no greater scope than selfhood. And yet in another sense, scoping is the master trope Makuck has bestowed on his *oeuvre*. It could have been the figure of this peregrine immigrants' son, going down a towpath, a towpath that he domesticates with his very footsteps. It could have been that of the angler, the poet who works by "angling," who holds temptation this way and that, until nature rises to his bait. But Makuck chooses an image—the

long lens—that empathizes perspective over these images of enactment. Or rather, he chooses an image that encloses our understanding of all enactments.

Perhaps the key poem in Makuck's earlier work is "Against Distance," a poem of rescue:

> I reached the boy
> with just enough breath to blurt,
> "Stay with the tube,"
> then over and over told him not to worry,
> though I did
> because the current was wicked and fast
> and the pier hurried back and away.

"Wicked" here carries just the right amount of kid-tuned menace
and resistant swagger, already bonding the boy to his accidental
savior. As the riptide carries both toward danger in this nonce-cama-
raderie, the poet becomes aware of other currents:

> *E.T.* was his favorite film,
> baseball his favorite game.
> His father lived in another town.
> Mom's under the pier with her friend.

Plucked from the mundane to the marine ("Less than an hour
ago / I had stood on the porch of our rental"), the poet comes to
the rescue of the kid, but even at the site of danger he finds that his
heroism, like the unhappy moment of which it is a response, is subject to the vicissitudes of chance. Wishing to exercise some measure
of control over the arbitrary sway, he imagines the face of an idol on
the façade of an isolated house:

> For a moment,
> just a moment, I was ready to believe,
> to sacrifice whatever it wanted...

And then with just as much fealty to the unforeseen the riptide is
itself mastered and gradually brought under control:

At some point, unnoticed, the wind
turned about...

What follows is that moment of phantasmagoria, of dreamy, retrospective wonder, that one had experienced something of mortal consequence and survived:

I lay on the sofa,
trying to focus that other world
within this one
wavering its magic light on the ceiling,
heavenly proof
of the buoyancy still in my limbs...

Makuck would know that there are many glosses to this event, for which "That when I woke, I cried to dream again" from *The Tempest* would not be inappropriate. Indeed, when the poet writes in the final lines that he was thinking of the boy, "who could have been my son / and kept me from drowning," we understand, almost before those lines appear that it was not the sea only, wherein drowning posed a danger. It was not even the sea mostly, riptide or no. Nor was it a riptide that created the chance for a heroism poised just beyond ordinary decency.

The easy-going manner of many of these poems should not blinker us to the fact that they are also polished and load-bearing when they seem least to be. *Long Lens,* in fact, is as accomplished for what it doesn't do, as for what it does: it reaches for depths without succumbing to the usual sonorities of *gravitas;* it radiates feeling— the from-the-beyond feeling of absence (so closely tied to desire) and the (necessary) pity of closure, without becoming sentimental; it's formally adroit without being arty, and its manner invites the reader without manipulation.

McFadden, Patrick, Parks and Chang
First Books

I think it was Alice who remarked on the information overload of "six impossible things before breakfast." Whether these were things pleasing or odious, I don't remember, but Kevin McFadden asserts that impossibility's bounty comes courtesy of words, and by way of demonstration, he offers *Hardscrabble,* one of the most extended and complex forays into wordplay poetics ever to worm, sew, and knot its way across 101 pages of text.

For a while there was a fear that the theory-fueled scrutiny trained on the non-metaphysical side of poems—i.e., their materiality, their homely is-ness—would dry up what remaining good will there was toward the art, especially after the diminishing returns on confessional and first-person subjective lyricism that finally exhausted *tout le monde.* Be that as it may, Joyceans, Poundians, and those who followed to the flutes of Kenner and Davenport knew that the "materiality" of words or "words alone," in Eliot's phrase, could still plow some fields once claimed by sensations, thoughts, prophecies, politics, all those things anterior and prior (or so it was thought) to the fact of words. For example, what's up with the pun? The anagram? Indeed, what's going on with rhyme and all the homologies and terms of recurrence with which words escape their loneliness and emerge, patterned with an invitation to cock the ear to the lexicon rather than the newspaper or the diary? Questions arose as old realities fell out of focus: does the pun's ambivalence pry anyone's fingers from their hold on the moral compass? Is there perhaps a further, comparable dimension down the rabbit hole of words that shift, that "will not stay in place"?

With disarming modesty against evident ambition, McFadden seems to subscribe to the Blakean notion that the fool persisting in his folly is bound to become wise. Of course no one with linguistic pockets as deep as his could begin a feat of his scope from a fool's starting blocks. But wait! That's only because this "fool" was never fool in the first place, foolishness being a matter of perspective ("Your ability to find the silly in the serious will take you far."). McFadden has, *pace* Jonathan Williams, turned the genteel poetic convention of nesting novelty poems among more serious siblings (or at least among poems that have taken the time to arm themselves against irony). He has written a whole, impressively fluent collection that avoids the pitfalls of standard sincerity and revelation, in favor of maximum wordplay, as though in the thickets of letters, paths will emerge—to the temple, I mean. An example:

> I'm a rain. Let America be a cage;
> I remain a gate, a Mecca. I blare
> Niagara, I accelerate, maim, be
> a beam, I emanate a grail, Circe
> mirage. America, a neat cable I
> tie in. America, a gala embrace.
> Let America be America: a gain.

("Meditate Sea to Sea")

Language is not dumb to its own felicities. You see here the glaring half-truth that it is language that writes us, with the poet as conductor, rather than creator, whose royalties are finder's fees. I always wondered whether we were seriously supposed to commiserate with Keats' fear that his name would not be among the English poets when he died. If language behaves as McFadden believes, then his own name's boost into any sort of literary orbit—although I hope otherwise—is moot, yet no matter. He seems to suggest as much,

> Want a wild time? In Glasgow time was tame.
> See the town? You had to hear the tune. New loans,

including my name: I began saying Cave-in
if I wanted the right introduction in a pub.

("Famed Cities, XII. Loan, Glasgow")

What's amazing about *Hardscrabble* is not just the unstoppable playfulness, but the fact that his tsunami of wordplay lends itself to architectural form beyond the word and its immediate neighborhood. This ample collection has legs in the form of longer poems (and prose poems). The longest two, "Famed Cities" and "It's Tarmac," indeed work in autobiographical narrative: the first takes up the poet's life itinerary, while the second riffs on a winter drive from Charlottesville to the poet's childhood home outside Cleveland. *Hardscrabble* will not satisfy your longing for emotional transport, but it will do something as divine: make you wish you could vacation in the bowels of a dictionary. Did not the old gods survive by taking refuge in letters?

Patrick Phillips' *Boy*, as the title hints, works within a generational register and is (while it is many other things as well) an immense gloss on two classic poems of generational overlay, transition, and reflective order: Robert Hayden's "Those Winter Sundays" and Donald Justice's "Men at Forty," which haunt *Boy* as antecedent poems. In fact, "Those Georgia Sundays" is an imitation, homage, and resetting of Hayden's well-known example of *le mot juste* in action, answering the key, "What did I know?" with a terse, "I knew damned well." What the poet knew was, "I heard death hiss / through those austere and lonely offices." Like discovering death, playing with fire is a boy's perennial adventure, instant high, and eventual come-down. In "Revelation," the poet and a friend, "setting army men on fire," watch as

... the purple flames
leapt up his arm
and around his throat.

Here the poem turns on its title, one that finds Auden and Kunitz at once within its ken:

I saw things clearly
for the first time in my life:

the perfect sky
still perfect as he burned.

Patrick's poems, spare, terse, formally ventilated, have an adroit sense of timing. One of the volume's most memorable poems, "What Happens," works by retriggering its initial *volta* to accommodate a three-part format. Phillips sets up the poem with what will become a trolling assertion: "What happens here happens on its own." The first section recounts an auto accident ("My father's Pontiac began to slide"), during which Hendrix "would not stop wailing." In that moment between the precipitous event and the recognition of damage, he recalls,

spotlit figures clutching their knees
and sobbing in the grass

as Jimi shrieked and shrieked out of the past,
until finally I found the knob

I'd cranked in my euphoria, just before
the gods let loose their wrath.

The second section picks up the thread with "And sometimes what happens / must happen more than once." Here the news of a friend's death, delivered while the speaker is camping, is bracketed away, until

...I was showered, shaved

and halfway down the mountain
when a twig snapped, and he died.

The final section begins, "And sometimes what happens doesn't even happen" and proceeds to its evidence in the wife's obstetrical nightmare:

...she pushed so hard
the screen flatlined.

So hard the heart stopped
and the whole room began

to flash and beep, like on tv.
Nurses streamed through doors

and in an instant we were childless.

This horrifying scene brings a moral revelation in its wake: "And
it was then I knew for sure / that nothing cares for us." But he later
comes to recognize that this unflattering, Hemingway *nada* can also
bestow arbitrary and impartial blessings:

...I've learned
to pretend I do not know

what can happen and unhappen
in no more time than it would take

an angel or a devil to descend into my wife
and pass through her into my son,

who was miraculously born into this world,
where everywhere and always

hearts are stopping for no reason.
And for no reason, starting up again.

The wonder that supports Justice's "Men at Forty" is situated not
just on coming of age, but on the full and not-gradual realization
of what it is to be a father, of having sired offspring, the hungry
generations' next act. In "Untitled," Phillips describes that pure
moment before one is saddled with a name ("your mother / was
in no hurry"). In that briefest stage, before the responsibilities that
attach to even the most innocent are affixed, it's possible to imagine

a love so pure, so unencumbered, it doesn't know which route it's
coming down,

> She cooed and kissed
> and cupped your throbbing skull,
> and lingered.
> until they brought the yellow form,
> in that moment
> when we could have called you anything.
>
> When you were you,
> beloved,
> and had no other name.

Elsewhere ("Our Situation") this same love is described as "reck-
less" and "naive"; it becomes a questionable proposition "to love a
thing / so fragile and weak." Yet the sense is that the speaker pre-
approves of his naiveté in the same way that we sanction any new
love, though we know that both will become barnacled with conditions eventually and lose the freshness that was the boutonniere that
graced our having started out. In "Kitchen," he imagines sprawling
with his sister on the floor, overlaying his consciousness of time at
the site of her Edenic innocence,

> the same age and in
> exactly the same mood
>
> as my son, now, in this kitchen
> where soon we will
> have lived so long ago.

The boy of the title is a figure of beauty, perhaps the last convincing emanation of that goodness that began with the nameless
infant. In any case, the assignment of goodness with beauty lines up
an old aesthetic, by no means superseded or exhausted, that beauty
is a reflection of the Good. The allegiance to this aesthetic in the
face of more robust challenges is the subject of "Ars Poetica," which
recounts the tale of the quartet playing as the Titanic sank,

a melody from Brahms—
not as a consolation

or a sympathy, or solace,
but because the violinist

didn't know what else
to cling to

In "A History of Twilight," the poet observes,

I lie back on a Star Wars pillow
and give the performance of my life:

playing the role of my father, reading
a bedtime story to my sons.

Phillips has given a lot of thought to the refractory ways we encounter, grow into and out of, our identities. If we shift among these, for example, do our actions become performances? And if you answer yes, how does this answer alter sincerity, devotion, and other big nouns where we stake our lives? The thought is another version of Yeats' stone troubling the living stream:

I laugh my father's laugh:
It has no other home.

The future is a myth.
And then it is a stone.

("Living")

If this is so, then it is—strangely—the past that has stability. In Phillips' negative theology, the past is "heaven,"

It will be the past,
and we'll live there together.

Not as it was to live
but as it is remembered.

....

It will be the past.
And it will last forever.

Cecily Parks' *Field, Folly, Snow* is into the basic "gotcha" of surprise: "As I watched my dog roll inside the ribcage of a long-dead
cow I thought of you. Your name escapes me, but please allow me
to describe the cow... ("Letter to the Pistolsmith"). This inventive-
ness keeps poems going when their manifest occasions have receded
into the (mostly western) landscapes they inhabit. "I Lost My Horse"
begins,

> I was looking for an animal, calf or lamb,
> in the wire, metal and hair along the fence line.
> Wire, metal and hair and there, in the gully, a man
> I was pretending was dead.

And ends,

> The man left before I could leave him, and I pretended
> the world was afraid of me because I was alone.

Parks has no problem adverting to imagination's caprice. In the
best lyrics, both the western pastoral contexts and her sheepdog tercets corral strangeness into familiar forms. She is able to convey the
push-pull between wild and compulsive registers, as Willa Cather
loneliness and tactical self-control vie for memory and consciousness.
"Miss Peecher's Rivers" is among the volume's most assured poems,
rehearsing a spinster's stores, the quotidian inventory of domestic
things that impose symbolic order and substitute meaning through
feats of ritualistic control as the dust of boredom rises over life:

> Pincushion, gingham, pins. A picket case
> of rulers, nibs, and pens, Miss Peecher writes
> slate-length essays in chalk that always end

at bottom right. She calls herself housewife,
meaning: catchall for cutlery, a vat
of tape, a sheaf of tables, numbers, measures

and trouser legs.

The absence of a man ("there is no husband") is but another fact transformed into her household wisdom:

... (A thimble weighs as much
as the stone it holds: a man's inseam will rarely
surpass the compass of his chest, a lady's

likewise.)

For Miss Peecher, her very name fructifies meager portions of meaning into a pattern where "light machinery—treadle / spindle / mangle...suffices." Her Linnaean domesticity also allows Miss Peecher a way into the world, rather than what it at first seems—a retreat: "Never has she been underwater. / It is a gown, she thinks, one cuts and enters." The beauty of such austerities, since they depend on accumulation over time—and hence a narrative, even a plot—customarily belongs to novelists, in this case those who chronicle the plains: Cather, Wright Morris, Marilynne Robinson. It's good to see a poet of Parks' talent submitting similar materials to the lyric's resources. As she says in "Trapline," "The landscape holds you in no clouded thrall / but holds you nonetheless."

Landscapes are also on Jennifer Chang's mind in *The History of Anonymity,* as is Patrick Phillip's *topos,* childhood. Chang's poems are charged with competing voices, floating and shifting identities, and elliptical narratives. Chang has spoken in an interview of the draw that confusion has for her, as being more relevant to the perspectival nature of facts and identities. Whether one responds to the lure of confusion with appreciative wonder or reduces and dismisses the project as a species of the Fallacy of Imitative Form is less a matter subject to verities than to taste. But Chang's mentor is Charles Wright, and the latter's flattened journaling and drop-out lines are in evidence here too—and familiar to readers.

Chang's collection begins and ends with quasi-narratives, the eponymous "A History of Anonymity" and "A Move to Unction." Both poems allow for rolling ellipses, mentions standing in for history, and monologues doing double-duty as unsecured identities and numinous voiceovers:

> In The History
> of Anonymity, the glacier longs to be water,
> and each granule of salt
> begs a lesser atom.   We will know each other
>
>   less, the voice writes I am already
>   in this afterworld.   You will find me where the
>
> I am two parts...

The act of journaling, of noting language within the day's scope, takes at face value something noted by Barbara Hernnstein Smith in *Poetic Closure*, namely, that lyric poetry manifests a deployment of words that mimics narrative's dynamic structure, but it does so, as it were, in the absence of narrative. Chang's poems recognize lyricism's more natural allegiance to what Helen Vendler calls the "cloud chamber" effect of poetry written with this degree of realism, which is to say, perspectivalism. Such poetry invites a different degree (if not of kind) of participation and collaboration than is specified by straight-up workshop lyric poetry. It's the kind of "participation" that language poets thought they were going to get before they "hummed the auditorium dead," in Lowell's phrase. Chang's invitation may indeed open participation in new ways, and I for one, would like to see it happen.

At the same time, there are the usual pitfalls for words as relational entities in this same cloud chamber. Aside from abandoning the quest for a specious clarity, there is also the matter of the effects that attend the abandonment of that quest, such as the keying down of diction and grammatical muscle. Notice, for instance, how the static this-is-that of the following passage is enabled by the substitution of the verb to be for more dynamic options:

... It is all wait
and wilt. In the ground,
        there is a secret to grief

which is only a door
with a face drawn on the threshold.
This is who stole Mother's spine
and splinter, leaving her

a morsel of dirt and a filthy hand
to raise at her children.

(A Move to Unction: "In the night, I seek a meaning before I sleep.")

Be that as it may, I am willing to trust the teller whose version of candor includes such encounters with anonymity, cloudiness, and discontinuity: I find it a more plausible assertion of realism than keyed-up lyricism. These meditations that touch on childhood wounds, loss, and looming spirits are finely wrought, even if the question of their uncertainty to ears raised on Frost and Bishop sometimes competes with their bright intelligence. Chang is a poet whose access to mysteries is something that will be worth waiting for in future poems.

Each of these poets has ears tuned to matters of language to a sophisticated degree that was not the case when I was doing workshops back in the day. It would be nice to think that this collective sophistication is a sign that poetry is a progressive art after all. But whereas language comes forward now, I still remember the civil wars between enchantment and disenchantment, naively assuming that authenticity of purpose put poems out of the reach of any but aesthetic criticism. But who is to say where naive and sentimental poetry now makes its bowers, where enchantment's swells and diminuendos are niggling, if at all, the stern Muse and her next darlings?

Joseph Millar's *Blue Rust*

What do we care of the past, with its issues and death, its leathery solemnities, its errors, and faded passions? It's by no means self-evident how backward gazing will get us any further along on the way to the Promised Land, nor how the imposition of past things on the present will be accomplished without a lingering whiff of that old mortality that sent the past spiraling backward in the first place. I remember hearing an account of a literary set-to that took place between a prominent American poet and a British critic. The critic went over the familiar ground that western poetry was based on the stupendous past and on meditations of a mortal and meta-physical sort. But the poet chimed in that much Chinese poetry, by contrast, was based on friendship, to which the critic retorted that so was Western poetry...from Dante to Milton to Tennyson to Yeats. "Yeah," the poet replied, "and all the friends are dead!" Now I take it that the proposition that all one's friends are dead is indeed something to inject caution in the most carefree imagina-tion. The sneaking suspicion behind the exchange is that the poets leveraged these finished friendships in order to strengthen their ties with the doings of yore, orienting themselves backwards, so to speak, even if the result looked to the less deceived like a kind of creeping necrophilia.

Joseph Millar's new collection, his third, more than touches on loss, though it would be damnable to leave it at the word, which has gathered its implications and entailments into the figure of a yawn. His poems engage in Boomer retrospection to be sure, and it is a question that must be judged by each member of that genera-tion (I am one): how much indulgence should be given to nostalgia, however aggrandizing; how much to origins, however unusual or for that matter utterly common? The title, *Blue Rust*, hints at temporal erosions and at a possible instability of the two terms, "blue" and "rust." It also signals that the poet is going to take us to sites of origins, and that in doing so he may drag their baggage into the present. Quite aside from the deeper questions of origin search and query and the effect of origins on the present—of the dead on the living, and the past on the present—what emerges is a persona, begetter of these poems cast as image, a man keen to true the level on language without betraying much anxiety over language's ability to underwrite authenticity. Here is also the kind of person you would like to knock back a few with, whose indictments against life's injustices don't spread out and try to guilt-trip the other bar patrons. It may be that in evolving this persona, Millar is speaking to capacities of subjectivity to create not just images for the past, but the type of person who can resolve the contradictions such images present—by creating the further image of a persuasive literate man whose opinions and poetic strategies have not been chiefly formed by literature. In another poet, this would translate into a bemused persona, but Millar has just enough of the tragic and the contingent flowing in his veins not to fall for that dodge. This is a poet in some sense satisfied with the results of his dice, though chance doesn't quite get the image I want. It's more like emotional *savoir faire*, the statesman's natural grace toward his small host country.

When James Tate quipped that American poetry was predicated on the notion that "something kinda hurt me once," he was a referring to, well, a lot of poets and to several thick strands of our poetic history, not the least of which was the School of James Wright, one of whose spiritual students is Joseph Millar. But if that is the case, it's the difference, the way in which Millar's poetry escapes Tate's illuminating japery that makes Millar's poems so humanly appealing. Behind Wright's poems was the danger of sentimentality, and it wasn't a long throw from that to formal error to the moral dead-end of self-pity. Millar shares Wright's blue-collar creds; indeed at times he seems to near Carver's land mass, except that Carver's vulnerabilities are all too clear, his temptations not only a matter of record, but a source of literature. In America the secret, often subconscious, shame attaching to origins is also the source of power for many of our best writers (think any number of southern writers). There also appears the writer who learns to transact the distance minus sentimentality or chagrin. For this writer, such are divergences from the objective, namely to represent what Blake called "the products of time," of which that poet assured us that eternity—read the most *complete* viewpoint—was in love. Millar's poems might even be poems of sensibility, except that the very concept seems snagged in the moss of the past and hence of little explanatory power, except perhaps to remind anyone reading that tonality—aesthetics, tact, balance, wit—can almost be enough to smooth the chafe of the noose.

It's not surprising to find then that Millar's poems are filled with highways and marriages: the former the image of mobility and transport; the latter the temptation to rest, sometimes to settle. Such twin temptations were already on show and waiting for the poet at birth:

> My mother wrapped me in her robe
> fragrant with camphor and sweat,
> hushing my desolate howls.
> She loved me and she hated me
> through those early months
> when I wanted everything she had,
> and all my father wanted
> aside from her warm, pale body,
> was to finish his hitch and get
> the hell out of the army forever.

("Nativity")

But it's not all William Bendix-style post WWII self-rearing that we witness in these poems. Millar has a sharp eye, and the vividness of particulars prevents him from settling for aesthetic platitudes. So on the one hand he avails himself of pop culture to set the stage—a stage indeed framed in the confines of lyric poems. On the other, it's the feel, the look, and the smell that authenticates the journey, not the celebrity matrix. Indeed, celebrity turns us away towards fancy and desire, but settling—in both senses—is as much a temptation as Frost's woods:

> You could settle down by her woodstove
> turning your back on the road outside,
> hidden away in her kitchen
> smelling the spaghetti sauce
> like a child or an old man. You could
> live easy and die happy, a candle burning
> in every window, the blue compass needle
> and hands of the clock pointing north
> through the field's wavy grass.
> You could make your grave in her.

("Romance")

It was the hippie dream, after all, combined with earthy, working-class, what's-in-your-lunchbox solidarity, that drove the Boomer nostalgia engine, the one that initially eschewed corporate creep and universal commodification. In its way, we Boomers lived through as rich and mucky a period of romanticism as any Wordsworth or Keats, and when the pendulum swung back—the one sharpened on theory by poets in neckties—it knocked off a lot of well meaning but ultimately feeble wannabes. It's amazing, when you think about it, that so little memorable poetry attaches to this vaunted generation about its circumstances and the feel of the time. Most of the populist energies went to popular music, and our musical bards turned out, often against their intent, to be our chroniclers.

Millar typically writes a medium-length lyric that's strong on voice and exact with image, lifting what nourishes memory from a submerged narrative. Pop culture icons frequently get a shout-out in Millar's work, like ne'er-do-wells in a hipster's gradebook. He ticks the names off: Jackie Gleeson, Sarah Vaughan, Little Anthony, The Del-Vikings, Paul Newman, Chuck Berry, The Grateful Dead, Michael Bloomfield, Mickey Rourke, Carlos Santana, Bo Diddly, Willie Dixon, The Who, Quicksilver Messenger Service, Michael Cimino, Elvis, Fellini, The Beatles, Karl Marx, Dali, Joe Hill, Bunuel,

Gene Autry, Randolph Scott, Jean Cocteau, Sam Peckinpah. Compared with this rogue's gallery the roster of poets might seem slim: Villon, John Clare, Vallejo, Allen Ginsberg, James Wright, Larry Levis. And yet there is a personal logic to such pantheons, and we are way past the day when homogenous cultural literacy required remote, classical resonators. I seem to remember my own teachers telling us to beware where you get your mythologies. They were afraid that references to The Doors or Dustin Hoffman would obligate us to footnotes by and by. They seemed to have missed Hegel's advice to historicize everything. Millar's use of this familiar yet personal constellation reminded me more than once of the similar, but preppier, Mark Halliday, just as his orientation toward his own version of the *mysterium tremendum* is reminiscent of the cosmic middle-American, horse-breaking, Zen-and-image-master Dan Gerber, but lighter on the Zen and more narrative-friendly.

And what stories they are. Millar writes a poem tight in its unfolding, as befits a former fisherman, working the boats like the character in the marvelous and unexpected "Ocean":

> One summer night the fisherman told us
> he'd run aground in the river mouth, hull
> mired deep in black mud. He said he saw
> the hour of his birth, the swamp slowly
> filling with light, kelp stretched out
> like a vestment covering the flanks of the marsh,
> the sea's wretched age, monstrous and fecund,
> hair full of dead leaves, rayed petals clustered,
> shoals of dark gravel exposed.

> He told us sometimes he'd rather be dead
> than face the gray rooming house
> and a day-job, his heart like iron
> remembering the sea and staring
> at grayed pallets stacked in a warehouse
> smelling of creosote.

The poem goes off in quite a different direction from every other
in this collection. It is consciously mythy, and the experience is closer
to reading George Seferis than Philip Levine or David Ray. By that
I mean it quests at the level where our commonalities thin, and the
ocean, as life-giving mother, seems at once true and a stretch, a mere
literary *frisson*. We seek authentication on the slimmest of evidence,
and when it comes to scattering and generally mystifying, the ocean
doesn't disappoint. It's also comfortable in its role as Mother and
Other. For the old fisherman,

> No place will be open now
> except for the sad bar, barren of women,
> except for the motel near the dunes
> with its flocked wallpaper
> and rusty heater that moans
> in the night like a tired swan.
> The next day no one will look
> in your eyes, transparent stranger
> belonging to no one,
> not the children sledding on cardboard
> down through the frozen parking lot,
> not the waitress humming a song
> you wish you could remember...
>
> if she asked you about your family
> you could show her their silhouettes
> in a drop of saltwater
> from Wingaersheek Beach
> you keep in a jar by the window...

The ocean in its anonymizing comfort recurs in a poem many
will find painful to read, "Stove." In this poem, the father has found
himself reduced painfully, almost absurdly, when he suddenly must
move a lighted stove across the floor and to try to keep it from walking, with its claw feet, down the stairs and setting fire to the house.
He heaves to, saving the house, but suffering serious burns in the
process. This is just the kind of freaky circumstance that appears in
the better poems of Raymond Carver, and readers will be reminded

too of some Carver's better poems. But Millar's work is more consistent, less willing to countenance the slide into sentimentality. The poem ends,

> Now he sleeps on, smelling of medicine,
> forever deeper and wider, his legs
> which once ran The Hundred in ten flat
> float apart in the water. God
> only knows how far from this world
> the fins of his dream have carried him,
> the ocean breathing outside in the night,
> its metal voice blistered with fallen stars,
> its pale fans opening and opening.

While Millar stays clear of sentimentalizing fate, he doesn't shrink from revealing the odd and even grotesque planks of which the ordinary's house is cobbled. The disclosure of the particulars of our humble origins and in handmade craft is poetry's equivalent of the moribund's privileged speech, of Rorty's "final vocabulary," and Adam's names. I began this review by introducing a distinction between the possibly necrotic grasp of elegiac practice and a more salutary model of interpersonality. While it's clear the poet must face discontinuity and death if he would write of his past, Millar's welcome book avoids the somber reach of the first and the overreaching sentiment that often befalls the second when rendered in poetry. The privilege for which he works in view of his own sources suggests a third way: that of an authenticating muse. And that is good enough to live by (or die), as "Nightbound" makes clear:

> Nothing to see or hear or hold onto,
> blue rust floating away from your
> touch, dark mosses crumbling under
> your tongue, nothing to carry back,
> curled on one side with your knees drawn up:
> father, mother, grandmother, uncle,
> naming your dead one by one.

Mihaela Moscaliuc's *Father Dirt*

Marina Tsvetaeva once remarked, "all poets are Jews." It is the condition of the poet—socially marginalized, spiritually central—that both provides the down-and-dirty equivalent of a God's-eye-view of human behavior and history and gives the poet her bona fides with respect to authentic speech. How much more relevant the irrelevance of Gypsies, those gleaner-wanderers of uncertain provenance? Now renamed Roma, combining both a national identity (Romania) with a rebranded cultural imprimatur (Rome), this population retains its mythological status as outsiders. In the context of what most of us probably surmise Romanian society to be—i.e., as fringe Europeans—the Roma are Jews' Jews. As for how they fared in the annals, ask anyone with first-hand knowledge of the thinking, from the Teutonic right to the Iron Curtain left, concerning where this race was headed. Mihaela Moscaliuc's *Father Dirt* is the debut collection of an American-Romanian poet, who grew up under Ceauşescu and arrived in the States in 1996, after the parting of the Iron Curtain. Like a number of other émigré poets, Moscaliuc finds much matter in the systematic duplicities of state Communism, and whether that matter finds its response in outrage, satire, or elegy, it succeeds by holding a mirror to a mirror. Between the fate of the Roma at one end and the dictates of Communism at the other, Moscaliuc finds a doleful spectrum, in which ordinary people managed to maintain (or not) their humanity in the midst of constant surveillance, forced optimism, and brutal discrimination.

While the judgment of literature on history does not favor the latter, it does enjoy a good deal of discretion in the imposing of its sentence. There is a tradition among modern Eastern European poets of rendering the harshest of judgments by pronouncing the malefactors and their mindset absurd and doing so by following the trail of consequences with a straight face. The surrealism on the ground is the new realism, as everyone from Mandelstam to Popa to Herbert to Szymborska knew. While she tempers the sometimes marmalade quality of surrealistic presentation into a more documentary style suitable to the era of video and CNN, she retains surrealism's sense of the absurdity. What she also adds is an acknowledgment of the price paid by truth to stupidity. The calculation of that price is, among other things, the measure of a poet's worth:

> When I bring you to grandmother's grave,
> behind the Dacian fortress, she'll be armed
> with questions: how hardy your love, how soft your fingers,
> and your dead, how do you spoil them?

("How to Ask for My Hand at My Grandmother's Grave")

Remember the Dacians? Trajan does. He slaughtered them to annex the future Romania as Roman territory. Slaughter and appropriation have a long tradition, as do their more modern enablers: spying and innuendo. Moscaliuc hints that these things may even have been around longer than the tradition she wants to promote: the history of family continuity, of intimacy and close feeling.

> At ten we had at least one
> alcoholic parent (your father the only one mentioned),
> at twelve we used few words to seal friendship,
> fearing each other—anyone could be an informer
> —even this baby waiting to turn in the birth canal.

("To Ovidiu, Whose Voice I Still Don't Remember")

The production of babies, unlike the production of truthful poems, was sanctioned by the Ceaușescu regime in a big way, as the opening to "Destroy the Family, You Destroy the Country" shows,

> When she complains to the school nurse about her bile,
> —it's been filling her mouth with green anger—

she's given the prerequisite "fertility" check and found
two and a half months pregnant. *Ninth to twelfth grade*
the speaker booms, *emergency assembly,*
and our uniformed bodies pleat into a perfect rectangle.

Dear comrade teachers and united young communists, as you all
know, last week a disgrace befell our school: the suicide of student
Isabela B. Volovici. Today, however, we are proud to report and act
of deep patriotism: Maria Pop has decided to contribute a new life
[to our multilaterally developed
society.

Unlike history, which requires the resistance of words, images,
being what they are, don't require commentary, but Moscaliuc's
image-driven poems run along a bias refined by a skilled hand at
wielding up-to-date poetic devices. And although she peoples her
poems with family, classmates, childhood friends, and teachers, she
knows that one of the most history-resisting techniques is to create
an identity—an individual—to oppose the mass anonymity the State
required to maintain conformity and control. Hence in "Portrait":

I thicken coffee with chocolate,
language with accented mistranslations,
love with foreign words
oblong and trammeled and plum-brandied.

Conversely, the withdrawal of identity is also seen by the authori-
ties as individual caprice and criticism. Moscaliuc celebrates the
life of a fellow poet and friend through her suicide ("Suicide Is for
Optimists, Cioran Said"):

When we blacklist the teachers who threaten
To fail us if we attend the funeral—
Suicide is the ultimate insult
To our harmonious communist life . . .
You wink in approval.

The language, like laughter, carries a burden the more frightening for the lightness of its expression, for the poet is suggesting that

the suicide expresses her critique of life quite literally with her own death, and that death in turn inspires the life—the resistance—of her survivor friends. The mention of Cioran, the Romanian philosopher who lived in Paris and carried out a one-man campaign to pull away any remaining metaphysical cushions to lessen humanity's fall, alerts us to the fact that suicide also inscribes its literary criticism on the prose of time. It is "optimistic" because it hopes—or has hoped—for something better, a hope that underwrites even its exit. In "Cold War Redux," she writes,

> I don't understand why history twists her own arm
> but I saw her do it: eyes squinted, lips thinned,
> she clipped our vocal chords, blew echoes into our gas stove.
> We grew delirious with want behind the screeching Wall...

With modern poetry's derivation from such straits, it sometimes seems as if there is a more direct commerce between words and things: words "mean" more, having acquired a more dutiful heft from the things they designate. This is, again, a strategy evolved to resist the State's appropriation of the means of expression. *Father Dirt* is a case in point. Because the strategies needed to keep truth afloat are complicated, it's refreshing to see an apparently artless expression of relief, as in this from "Minds Touched by Happiness Tend to Forget Their Bodies' Sores":

> How about the Christmas our breads
> burned to ash in the oven: kneeling in front of the TV,
> I waited breathless for the Ceaușescus' execution.
> When the firing squad punctured their hearts
> a hundred times and they crumpled like ragged dolls,
> I wept with happiness.

Even here, the artlessness is only apparent. The ashes and ovens recall the poetry of another Romanian, Paul Celan, whose most famous poem ("Todesfuge") elegizes beauties transformed to ash and smoke by the ovens, a moment in history in reaction to which the establishment of the "Iron Curtain" was itself a protracted, if ostensible, response. The journey in Moscaliuc's poem is a peculiarly Eastern European Christmas journey, from ashes of burnt bread to the gift of a triumphant retribution.

At the bottom of the poet's indelible memories are two things: the Gypsies, whose fates haunt her, and her new destiny as an American, with its attendant hauntings and hopes. In "Annunciation," she plays a bitter satire on the Biblical sign that a new, surpassing being is going to be bought into the world. As she says in a note, "In the 70s and 80s, many Roma /Gypsy women were sterilized, often without their knowledge... The children of 'unsettled' Roma were taken away and placed in state orphanages." I will quote this at some length:

When the State seized her boys

—"saved" them—she wished she'd never
had them, and when they pried out
her last "dead fish"—she didn't know
they'd scraped and clamped her
clean, blind with pain on that spilling
mattress but not deaf—"dirty sow,"

"retarded gypsy." Only later she remembered
the heat of the head crowning, the sharp cry
breaching the nurses' laughter. How she'd
touched him before they touched him,
so he may not be dead, just taken.

As for her life as an American, Moscaliuc is in the position of other artistic exiles who understand the elegiac remark of Wittgenstein, who said, "The limits of my language mean the limits of my world." In her case she says, "I want dreams that don't wade into yesterday's waters. / I want dreams in the American idiom..." While I am tempted to respond by saying be careful what you wish for, what I really mean to conclude is that here is a collection that is *not* in an idiom washed in the waters of MFA workshops (although she is the product of such a program). And that's the good news.

There are too many good poems here to discuss individually, but
this fact notwithstanding, I am left with the impression of a woman
who has experienced a life that seems something out of the century before the century before this, full of needleworms, nettle tea,
cauldrons, glass eyes, and cuckoos. There is wonder in that alone,
though Moscaliuc goes way beyond that wonder to touch the moral
at the end of the aesthetic reach. As if in answer to Eliot's question,
"with such knowledge, what forgiveness?" a child asks in "Everything
Touched by Darkness Knows Itself,"

> in the name of Father Dirt
> I be granted absolution until my tongue
> learns the texture of rubble, the taste of clay.

Gregory Orr's *The River inside the River*

As an idea, the "Beloved" (note the capital) has a fine pedigree: Plato's dialogues and The Bible are as good places as any to start. The idea involves the privileging of someone—or of something personified—outside the self, that potential maximum-security prison. From there, zoom ahead to the Middle Ages, Dante, the Provençal poets, then down to Keats and Shelley and in our own historical neighborhood: Rumi, Arthur Waley and his avatars, and Kabir, by way of Robert Bly. We should also add the sophisticated *ars poetica* of Allen Grossman, whose notion of the Beloved arrives by way of many of the postmodernist thinkers, who find in it an ideation worthy of psychoanalysis and phenomenological probing. What these have in common is a near-mystical idealism whose object is to reconcile our mortal place in nature with our ability to conceive of and desire, *per impossibile*, something timeless, by means of art, specifically poetry. As Gregory Orr puts it in his substantial *River Inside the River: Three Lyric Sequences,* his latest installment of a recent series of books exploring this and related themes:

> What was inside Adam
> Swirled about, but outside
> All was still and held
> Its shape.
> How negotiate
> Between these worlds:
> The one that whirled,

The one that waited
To be designated?

("To Write")

    Poetry, along with music, means to accomplish this reconciliation by way of formal devices whereby time is rewritten in such a signature that we are, for once, not at the mercy of the slow hurtling of our days and years, but rather in possession of a more accommodating human measure. Poetry and music come to represent such a reordering and to fasten it to the Eternal, that which stands by definition outside the depredations of time. This aesthetic has also raised the hope that what we lost in Eden, we can build in Jerusalem, to use the Biblical terminology made safe for secular consumption by one of the hidden ancestor poets behind Orr's work, William Blake. The aesthetic of the Beloved also ties the matter of poetry to the matter of spirituality, from little hints of spiritual longing, to full-blown religions. But as religious belief starts to lose explanatory traction, and science and materialist dogmas feed our need for empowerment, poetry becomes a natural successor, as Coleridge foresaw, in the human desire to manifest things of the spirit. The Beloved is both the source and recipient of these works:

"O, thou opening O ..."
Roethke
Begins his ode.

O, poem
Of the beloved.

O, beautiful body
Whose every
Orifice is holy.

O, porch
Made of breath,
House made of air.

The door
We go through—
So small.

The rooms
We enter—immense.

("O, thou opening O...")

In 2002, Orr published *The Blessing*, a memoir. Readers of this
book know that the catastrophe, a tragic hunting accident in which
Orr shot and killed his brother, became, like Philoctetes' wound,
both the epicenter of pain and the possible means toward finding
significance for and in his poetry. For otherwise, with the sudden
withdrawal of meaning, where was significance to be had? Where
was forgiveness? Since forgiveness participates in resurrection, to be
forgiven suggests that two died in the death of one, and two could
be resurrected in the forgiveness of one. Not surprisingly, Orr's first
critical book—a study of the poems of Stanley Kunitz—tracks a not-
dissimilar trajectory in the career of that famously wounded poet,
whose father committed suicide before Kunitz was born and is the
subject of his most famous poem, "Father and Son." It would sound
facile to suggest that out of terrible guilt and the threat of despair
emerges a silver lining, to say nothing of "a blessing," a word that
itself connects up with the multiple disheartening backstories that
give depth to the poems of another kindred spirit, James Wright. But
Orr does precisely that, and he does so by hewing to the sustaining
verities of poetry (and prose), to "impose a form on what [we] don't
understand," as Carolyn Kizer has it. As a result, such is the haunting beauty of *The Blessing* that the book all by itself restores the good
name to that aardvarkish hybrid, "poetic prose." It is certainly one
of the richest, most moving, vivid and deeply truthful memoirs to
emerge from his generation. Memoirs are useful in disclosing where
the silver is hidden, and this is useful in particular for a poet of Orr's
poetic past, with its mysteriously affective surrealistic beginnings. It
was how his poems seemed uncannily to participate in the very Mystery they also approached that established his early popularity and

relevance in a field and at a time already more than infatuated with surrealism, in each of its thickest branches: French, South American, and Eastern European. His work subsequently moved in the direction of myth, a more congenial indirection, in light of his eventual aim, which was to lay his *agon* at the foot of a healing tradition, for it may be said of surrealism that its further therapeutic value lies in finding the exit from privacy.

> If someone had said, when I was young,
> That poems made life bearable,
> I wouldn't have believed them.
>
> My world had closed in
> On all sides.
> I could hardly breathe.
>
> If someone had told me then
> I would feel free...
>
> A place where every poem
> Is a house, and every house, a poem.
>
> When I first came here
> Fifty years ago—the moment
> I arrived, I knew this city was my home.
>
>   ("If someone had said...")

The other defining event in Orr's biography was his participation as a Freedom Rider in a program sponsored by C.O.R.E. (the Congress on Racial Equality) and S.N.C.C. (the Student Non-violent Coordinating Committee) in the mid-'60s to bus northern activists, principally youths, to the Deep South to register black voters. To the indigenous whites, they were trouble-makers, and their presence alone, a *casus belli*:

> Eighteen and a volunteer
> In the Movement,

I was kidnapped at gunpoint
In rural Alabama
And imprisoned
In a solitary cell
In a murderous town.
                    Oddly,
After the beatings and threats,
They let me keep a book of Keats.

I was sick and scared. It seemed
Likely I would die there.

I read his nightingale ode—
How he rose above his woes.

The poem was my ladder:
Rungs and lifts of escape.

I read it at dusk, climbing
With each line.
And I was there with that bird
I could just glimpse
By shinnying up
The bars of my cell:

Mockingbird in the magnolia
Across the moonlit road.

            ("Eighteen and a volunteer...")

With *The River Inside the River*, Orr shows us that, move as he might out from the central events of his poetic life, his preference is to circle back to the ever-fecund wound and to find the pattern and path from personal to mythical, singular to plural; these movements also corresponded to the move from nonsense to sense. The first long section of the book relates to another ever-significant story, that of the Garden of Eden, a tale of the journey into significance as paramount to our culture as any death is to the individual. And when something is as important as death, there is little left to do but, as Donald Justice wrote, close the door softly.

> Love overwhelms us.
>
> Or death takes
>
> One more
> Of those
> We cherish most.
>
> Where else?
>
> Where else can we go?

("Love overwhelms us…")

I note that out of thirty six titles in this section, twenty seven are infinitives ("To Spcak," "To Write," "To See," etc.). The effect of this is to understand these actions as propositions, the weighing of options, the resistance to heavenly Necessity. It is in line with the conversion of the human type from archetypes to creatures entering time. At length, it is the human city, not the eternally bounded space of the garden, wherein we are situated. Orr follows Blake in finding our earthly habituation sufficient, both in itself, and in its ability to stand as a (perhaps elegiac) signifier of that other, Edenic habitation. I used to tell my students that many poets and all novelists are believers in Original Sin, and by that I meant not only that that all things being equal we could call the glass half empty. But I also meant that the "sin" was our alienation from Eden: both our (necessary) disobedience when it came to knowledge, but also the recognition that the place wasn't for us. We needed to build, not just receive. Without the work, dignity was a concept null and void, and tragedy something not within our reach. Orr knows that tragedy befalls us because we live in time, and in writing poems, he is able to make images that reference the timeless, when ugly consequences do not follow from a moment's surrender. Yet in that imagination of

timelessness, he knows we can only find temporary respite; hence, a
paradox: we fall into history where the monsters are, but our poems
rescue us by showing us images of the timeless. It is in our works that
we are forgiven, and so the process works.

This also means an allegiance with the low:

Note to self: remember
What Emerson said
Of Thoreau—
That he loved the low
In nature:
      Muskrats
And crickets, suckers
And frogs.
      Not stars.

             ("Note to self: remember...")

His poem for the dying Richard Rorty, famously atheist, suffuses
the philosopher's last days with a sense of poetry's place:

The old philosopher, dying,
Writes a last brief essay
In which he confesses
He wishes he'd learned
More poems by heart.

"The old chestnuts,"
He calls them,
By which he means
The rhyming ones
He loved when young.

"I would have been more
Fully human," he writes.

Reciting, in his last days,
Those he remembers,

As if the Book
 Were in his mind,
 And he was reading them aloud

 Which is the resurrection
 Of the body of the beloved,
 Which is the world.

("The old philosopher, dying...")

The poem is, you might say, Orr's version of Stevens' poems for Santayana, "To an Old Philosopher in Rome," both poems providing test cases, so to speak, of poetry's ability to confer significance, even as spirit is suspect, even discountenanced by the respective subjects.

Orr's "City of Poetry" is his Jerusalem, or to use Blake's esoteric name, Golgonooza, the City of the Imagination, the appropriate habitation and sustaining vision of the renewed Man. And this "Man," it should perhaps be noted, is itself a metonymy for the spiritual condition (for no other creature has a "spiritual condition"). Here I would refer readers to the last chapter of *The Blessing*, where the young Orr, just now entering poetry's tractor beam, finds himself standing in a field at night, marveling at the large, iron works of sculptor David Smith, on whose property he stood. In this scene is both a striking meditation of art's free-standing place in the natural world and of the feeling of rightness, of restitution, even resurrection—not of bodies, but of the sense of having been justified and hence forgiven by the thing that we do, this art.

The final section, "River Inside the River," naturalizes the spiritual journey, moving beyond the large and no doubt eye-opening claims of poetry's power. Here, the vision of the City of Poetry gives way to the reminder that, although we have conceived of eternity and made images that both reflect and connect us to this healing realm without change, it is time that claims us—and that in turn we must claim:

 Time is a wound that can't
 Close—it flows, it flows.

All that's begotten rots—
It's not anything
Personal the world
Has against us—
That's the way it goes.

Tune we first heard
In our mother's womb
And never even asked
If it was sad or happy,
Because we knew it was true.

("Time is a wound...")

This admission brings Eden once more to mind, and so the journey of this book, transformative as it is, is also circular, a form that
will be familiar to readers of Romantic and post-Romantic poetry.
The enfolding of energies, and the transformations that accompany
each phase (culminating in the mantra introduced in *Concerning the
Book That Is the Body of the Beloved* (2005)—"the body of the beloved,
which is the world, which is the poem of the world, which is the
body") take us in the mythical and thematic direction of Eliot's "Little Gidding." Here, the accordianed, all-enveloping finale affirms
(in his vision) that "the fire and the rose are one." Indeed Orr's last
three collections, as well as the sectional, thematic trinity, stand as
his *Three Trios*, testaments that set out to find a sustaining harmony
and not finding it, construct it, thus allowing the poet to accept both
the natural world and the history that shaped it. The proximity of
the Christian literary tradition that lays out the template is as much
unavoidable as it is avoided.

Poems that are this charged with the cadences of mystical contemplation may not be everyone's cup of tea. There are other ways
poems have used to manage paradox, and the equation of Beloved
to body of the world may strike you, if you haven't had your morning coffee, as vague as Kubla Khan's floating hair. But Orr, by now
a veteran pilgrim of the great wound-like void that separates imma-
nence and transcendence, knows that theme-and-variation isn't just

a method: it is itself an ancient and approved pilgrimage, and gathers to itself a richness over time. Indeed, repetition is the earth's way of knocking on eternity's door: to repeat is to resist, and in that resistance lies the image of a timeless wish: Adam and Eve "Making the holy human city, / Making the wholly human city"—a way of putting it that is as true as it is unfashionable.

Monstered-up Sweetness
On Robert Pinsky

The poem "A Refinery" from Pinsky's *The Want Bone* (1991) and reprinted in his recent *Selected Poems* (2011) shows the first of two qualities that the poet possesses and that usually, as Lowell reminds us, stand apart. I refer to the ability to invent, and the obligation to remember. Invention, because it imitates the gods, stands higher than memory, but the latter, it must be noted, because it generates the Muses in the first place, has the prestige of precedence. Just as familiar dualisms leap to the aid of scholars keen on pigeon-holing literary producers of one kind or another, so similar taxonomies— continuous-discontinuous, formal-free verse—and so forth bring us to the brink of useful insights. The invention-memory distinction points not to incompatible dispositions, but to some useful things to be known about the ether, that medium where poetry itself is air, before it becomes a strapping thing of sharp, often heavy detail. In this poem, the gods are awakened and descend, by special train, like Lenin to the Finland Station, across the star-sprinkled sky down to Northern California, where they arrive at their real shrine, an oil refinery, which gleams at night like Disney World or Pandemonium, whichever you prefer. Now the very idea, abstracted and pitched, is likely to strike sober folk as darkly whimsical at best, frivolous at worst. But this is to neglect the dogged and dark muscularity of the language.

> Their long train clicked and sighed
> Through the gulfs of night between the planets
> And came down through the evening fog

Of redwood canyons. From the train
At sunset, fiery warehouse windows
Along a wharf. Then dusk, a gash of neon:
Bar. Black pinewoods, a junction crossing, glimpses
Of sluggish surf among the rocks, a moan
Of dreamy forgotten divinity calling and fading
Against the windows of a town. Inside
The train, a flash
Of dragonfly wings, an antlered brow.

I was recently driving to Baltimore, some 5 hours away from my home, and I happened to put on the audio book recording of Pinsky's celebrated translation of *The Inferno*. I had read a few cantos when the book came out, and I had no doubt that it was a more-than-commendable effort. I was certainly not expecting the sound of this Anglo-American Dante to exhibit the density that Heaney brought forward from his Irish Anglo-Saxon when translating *Beowulf*. After all, that poem alternated between fanfare and cudgels. Yet the liberal Jewish intellectual from New Jersey and the medieval Catholic conservative from Florence shared a natural disposition to take language away from abstraction and return it to its demotic angularity. Moreover, it stood to reason that a poet of Pinsky's canny surveillance and sizing-up of opportunity would mine the words that supplied hell's Final Vocabulary, this no-place where sensory overload kept the hero on the verge of fainting like a Victorian heroine, much to the exasperation of his stern and belaureled poet-guide. The sinew and knotted energy of that translation are apparent in his poems too. Dante, that consummate hedgehog, liked to work in the muck, finding and wiping off the meanings found there. It's a closed system, after all, and the whole, infernal as it is, echoes point-by-point, as if reverse engineered, the living creation above. Pinsky is drawn to the muck too, but there are no closed systems available to him. Still, there is the modern irony of the living dead. There is, as well, the acknowledgment of surprise, of the pathways out into strained nonsense and inarticulate wonder both (see "Ode to Meaning"), just as the inward tracks land our Masters before their viscous hive, the refinery. And what better word could there be for the work of the poem, or for that matter, the descent of barbarous gods, more at home in the chthonic stone than the ethereal reaches?

> The muttering gods
> Greedily penetrate those bright pavilions—
> Libation of Benzene, Naphthalene, Asphalt,
> Gasoline, Tar: syllables
> Fractioned and cracked from unarticulated
> Crude, the smeared keep of life that fed
> On itself in pitchy darkness when the gods
> Were new—inedible, volatile
> And sublimated afresh to sting
> Our tongues who use it, refined from oil of stone.

The wonder extends, too, to the child's discovery that aphids are suffered servitude as the chattel slaves of ants, and that therefore function and ownership, including hierarchy and directive, operate according a system of ancient behests that seem to bypass Darwin to land at the feet of these monstrous Originals:

> The gods batten on the vats, and drink up
> Lovecries and memorized Chaucer, lines from movies
> And songs hoarded in mortmain: exiles' charms,
> The basal or desperate distillates of breath
> Steeped, brewed and spent
> As though we were their aphids, or their bees,
> That monstered up sweetness for them while they dozed.

That "monstered up sweetness" could have come from the alternately fraught and stingy pen of Jack Gilbert. It is, you might say, cultural memory. I suppose the dozing gods a nod to Yeats' sleepy emperor, himself nodding, for whom art is a distraction to keep unconsciousness at arm's length. Pinsky also performs the work of personal memory, raising and placing it in the historical stream. Several of his best-known longer poems, including "Sadness and Happiness" and "History of My Heart," arise out of specifically personal regions to be re-emplotted in larger settings. This trait has contributed to the sense that he is as close to a "public poet" as we have had, *pace* Robert Lowell, i.e., Allen Ginsberg, and Billy Collins. He is also the bright student of his destiny, approved alike of parents, friends, and critics. But such patronage can be a liability, as Lowell sensed. Better to clock your father, as Lord Weary did, or veer off into Cheeverian caricatures, as Collins does, to make a public place for the inner poet. Pinsky gives the impression of being just such a smart student, but he dodges the eventual resentment that comes back to haunt preciosity, and he refrains from biting the hand. He does this by showing how this intelligence, following its own nose, leads inevitably from memory to imagination and back again, like Ezekiel's ladder to and from heaven, like the railroad of the gnarly pagan gods, until we arrive at those aphids and the micro world is now the world *in toto*. In his final essay, Rorty remarked that "reason can only follow paths that the imagination has first broken." He goes on to note that words—imagination's transport mechanism—precede all moral and intellectual progress.

Pinsky is fond of anecdotes, particularly as they hint at tears and anomalies in the cultural fabric. At the basis of every image casting its glowworm light on the poetic line, there lies a story, a bestirring that gets the molecules going until, at length out of gas, they are handed over to—to some—regrettable circumstance; to others, the utmost in consolation, namely to metaphysical existence. Here is one from "The Street":

> Once a stranger drove off in a car
> With somebody's wife,
> And he ran after them in his undershirt
> And threw his shoe at the car. It bounced
> Into the street
> Harmlessly, and we carried it back to him;
> But the man had too much dignity
> To put it back on,
> So he held it and stood crying in the street:
> "He's breaking up my home," he said,
> "The son of a bitch
> Bastard is breaking up my home." The street
> Rose undulant in pavement-breaking coils

And the man rode it,
Still holding his shoe and stiffly upright
Like a trick rider in the circus parade
That came down the street
Each August...

It's that old school "dignity" that makes the youth flinch when it shows up shorn of quotation marks, but here it's exactly *le mot juste* because it raises the prospcct, not only that the humiliated cuckold's possession of the qualities present in this noun suddenly lies under threat, but that it's a word whose moral coverage is shared by the onlooker, the poet, and, it is hoped, the reader. To which half of a room of readers will respond, "Thanks for sharing!" but which the other half, his half, gather instinctively around the wronged man in solidarity, giving his sense of personal laceration the widened significance of a tribal wounding. Such a solidarity provides a justification for cultural memory. In "If the Dead Came Back," Pinsky observes,

The dead who know the future require a blood offering
Or your one hand accuses the other both lacking any
Sacrifice for the engendering appetites of the dead.

"Engendering appetites"—that's fine. The prepositional phrase "of the dead," on the other hand, has caused no end of mischief for lesser poets, as Pinsky is aware. There was a time, not so long past, when you could easily find poems (and book titles) with howlers like "Valentines of the Dead." You get the picture. Sometimes such a solecism is a necessary component, and one is put in the paradoxical position of using a dead phrase to propel a live one into place. Thus the poet, in laying out the fact of paradox, spreads the cards in their spectrum before us, like a croupier in a smoky room of serious players. Pinsky understands the paradoxical configuration of his lyric matter, indeed of his status as a public poet who is deeply drawn to memory's images, the hallmark of privacy. The welcome success of his status notwithstanding, his intelligence learned quickly to finesse the contrary, often obscured claims: one requesting articulation before the polis, the other demanding the language that gestures

to the mystery of subjective feeling and utterance. The finessing
becomes itself a subject and comes to stand for the difficulties inherent in all mediating poetries. I am not suggesting that the poet
wishes to represent some aspect of poetry's difficulties of address in
the midst of words' sometimes-Elizabethan ease, even eloquence.
Like the man who has been returned his shoe at the site of his
outrage and humiliation, Pinsky wields something like a dignity of
circumstance that transcends the bullshit besetting lesser bards.
Sometimes playing against type, he declines to show that he can,
once more, orchestrate the polysemous parts of larger narratives
by selecting the Beckett option of downsizing the means, both to
discover what will suffice (that's a given) and to put the less-is-more
paradox back on display as an emblem of the poem's inverted reach
in the face of baroque temptations. His well-known "Samurai Song"
shows the type:

> When I had no eyes I listened.
> When I had no ears I thought.
> When I had no thought I waited.
> When I had no father I made
> Care my father. When I had
> No mother I embraced order.

Pinsky manages intelligence so that it doesn't snuff out magic on
the one hand or succumb to self-consciousness, which Baudelaire
taught us was death to the artist, on the other. By intelligence I'm
not referring to IQ, but to the literary manager's highest degree
of consciousness and sweep. When you cross the Wittgenstein line
that separates what can be said with what can only be turned back
from (most poets would substitute gesture toward), Pinsky is more
willing than most to accept the glossolalia that brings the ineffable
to mind, although it doesn't try to take *per impossibile* the ineffable's
measure. He makes a distinction between what lies beyond articulation's reach, which might on a better day be said, and what properly
speaking, and in fact, is unutterable. In the first instance, he writes
"thing" poems, poems of definition, as if to suggest both the precision that can be brought to the definer's art and the infinite Borge-

sian pathways, of time and perspective, that neutralize the very concept of demarcation. In the second instance he nods to neologisms and scat-singing (his love of jazz evident). That which is not (words) then becomes the picture (in nonce words) of a condition we may now experience. Poems with this feature are not numerous with him, but where they occur, they stick: in "Gulf Music," for example, the title poem of a recent collection. The renaming of assimilating ethnicity is another instance of this linguistic slippage ("...you could say "Morris" was his name. A Moshe."):

> The New Orleans musician called
> Professor Longhair was named Henry Roeland Byrd.
> Not heroic not nostalgic not learned. Made-up names:
> Hum a few bars and we'll home-la-la. Who ohma-dallah.

They also accompany disaster, and it doesn't take an Adorno to tell us that words are not adequate to describe. *Gulf Music* brings us to the national disaster that was Katrina, contingency itself bearing down on the cradle of jazz (itself the cradle of musical contingency). Thus the definition poems are intended in some way to show the reach of articulation as such, the formation of clear and distinct sounds in speech, as the dictionary has it. It's the old Elizabethan confidence that whatever can be conjured out of the depths or met in experience can be offered forth in language. Consider the opening of "Jar of Pens":

> Sometimes the sight of them
> Huddled in their cylindrical formation
> Repels me: humble, erect,
> Mute and expectant in their
> Rinsed-out honey crock: my quiver
> Of detached stingers. (Or, a bouquet
> of lies and intentions unspent.)
> Pilots, drones, workers. The queen is
> Cross. Upright lodge
> Of the toilworthy, gathered
> At attention as though they believe
> All the ink in the world could

Cover the first syllable
Of one heart's confusion.

From the Neruda-esque and Adamic thing-poems that open the *Selected Poems*, as if qualifying floor exercises, to the magnificent long poems on which his early serious reputation rests, Pinsky's career has been in some way a meditation on and demonstration of the vexing relationship between intelligence and language, on the ability of the former to monitor its idiosyncrasies and adjust accordingly and on the latter to supply the right word horde. It has also been a career that steers between the two towers of fact and imagination. Indeed, these markers correspond roughly to the contest between articulation and the intimation that something important lies beyond the Wittgenstein limit.

Doubtless if Pinsky never received another kudo or epaulet, it wouldn't make any difference. He doesn't need more name recognition or face recognition (in some benign way he doesn't look like a poet. He looks rather like a physician—"and that," as Yehuda Amichai once remarked, "is a good thing!"). Pinsky needs readers worthy of the full-voiced challenges that deal in reckonings, that examine the ways we must finesse experience to accomplish our pilgrimages, readers who understand how divergent pathways have origins in disruption and discontinuity. He needs readers who do not turn up their noses at having to do their own metaphysical, psychological, and literary work. These are readers who likewise have a hunch they may find themselves momentarily exalted, both in the poet's public struggle to fashion the image until it gets as close as it can to iconic status—and in the image itself. And yet, I despair that Pinsky, for all his honors, can get his due. For that, we would have to meet his ambition in making poems with our own ambition to complete such a circuit with a stranger, accessible and well meaning though he is. Such a meeting almost always falls subject to diminishment by the deflationary expectations on the part of the readership, that is, poetry's readership. I am reminded of the ending to Chana Bloch's "Tired Sex," where she says the subject is "like turning the pages of a book the teacher assigned— / You ought to read it, she said. / It's great literature." And yet the teacher is right.

Preface to Margaret Rabb—
Greatest Hits: 1987-2009

Margaret Rabb (1953-2010) had studied with Carolyn Kizer at the University of North Carolina, where Kizer's workshops were renowned for their classical heft and notorious for the inspired prejudices of their lecturer. Peggy absorbed the biases of her mentor, as did I, but she did so until they had settled at the DNA level (I still remember Kizer asking me what exactly I *liked* about early Ashbery). Stanley Kunitz, Theodore Roethke, Louise Bogan were still the gold standard, along with her contemporaries: James Wright, David Wagoner, and Adrienne Rich. Following the *via Carolynae*, Peggy found much to approve in the work of A.D. Hope, Richard Wilbur, Richard Howard, and Ruth Pitter. She cared less for the alt-Pound side of Kizer's pantheon. The Christopher Middletons, Robert Creeleys, and Gary Snyders figured less, although the *paideuma* had its appeal.

After college, Peggy settled down in Chapel Hill and proceeded to start a media company with her husband and raise a family. Immensely kind, devoid of her teacher's barbs (while admiring their directness), she didn't return to poetry until the late 1980s, betting on the promise of seedfall. The poems that did follow in the next two decades were much honored and admired, winning a brace of prizes. Readers were drawn to the tensile imagination that arose from the formal rigor. Hopkins now was a hero, as were Auden and Heaney—poets for whom traditions and poetic language bore an intelligence shaped by time. She was also drawn to the example and discipline of Julian of Norwich, that proto-feminist whose signal utterance ("And all shall be well, and all manner of thing shall be well...") provided a strong silver thread for late Eliot. The desire to create coherent structures, a reflection of the idea that things hang together rather than otherwise, is tied to just such a promise as Julian made, which in turn reflects an outlook that knows the tragic is not thereby disarmed. Far from insisting on the chimerical prerogatives of the present tense, her work demonstrated that time was itself a power that, for the mediocre poet, eroded meaning, but for the superior poet, sculpted the cacophony of the present into the frozen music of a published poem.

For Peggy, music—the music of poetry—was intelligence because it joined means and ends, reconfiguring the medium of our mortality into something both intelligible and consolatory in its double-wielding of beauty and control. It was also an intersection where aesthetics and spirituality crossed paths, where believers outwitted irony and wit itself secured the poet's freedom from the drag of conformity and empty convention. This same time brought her to the end of her pilgrimage—much too soon for her devoted friends, who perceived a cruelty in fate that she was far too humble, far too accomplished an artist, to countenance. What she left, though, was as dappled as Hopkins, the shimmer folding doubt into faith's garment, the edge into the middle. Astonishingly, she reversed Yeats, which is to say she led art back from its two-dimensional prison to 3-D life, preferring the rag and bone shop to the decorative tinkle, the sleepy emperor and the caged songbird's weary treble. She also shook a master from the Middle Ages she loved, namely Dante, whose judgments lose some of their time-enabled and mythic authority when the modern female poet's motives respond, "it's complicated!" to the beloved master's strict rules. This descendant of Confederates, this servant of transvestites, cloud-chronicler, bibliophile, Anglican and Romantic, knew that the distance between the searcher and the bookshelf was intercontinental and yet intimate, that the time it took to find the special poem, the one addressed to the reader (and written by that same reader), was a lifetime and yet an instant. She wrote her own elegy with characteristic finish and self-distance, finding a life's direction in a mythic moment: "I left the right road. But the good I found / may be told... / I stepped into the stream, sleepwalker woken / midway..."

Rorty from a Poet's View

Until "Pragmatism and Romanticism," "Philosophy as a Transitional Genre," and his late essay in *Poetry* ("The Fire of Life"), Rorty's relationship to poetry was not what was uppermost in the minds of readers who thought of him as busy (perhaps too busy) diversifying the genres of literature. Of course Rorty knew that there was plenty of bad old Platonism to go around in poetry circles, and in *Contingency, Irony and Solidarity,* he had made it clear that the imaginative writing he found most useful was the narrative kind that provided edifying discourses. Fiction fit the mold best because its province was the march of character over time. Poetry, by contrast, seemed fixated on the timeless, and since there was little edification to be had in such contemplations, poetry, once the queen of arts, was ordered toward the back of the line. But the distinction was not so simple. In the first place, Rorty was schooled by poets (as I remind readers in my poem "Rorty") and was habituated to the reading of poetry to an extent that, I would guess, easily bested his peers among public intellectuals. In the second place, he would often use poetic examples in class to make a point: for example, Wallace Stevens's "Anecdote of the Jar" to lead into a discussion of perspectivalism, or Walt Whitman's "Crossing Brooklyn Ferry" to illustrate process in William James. But he also understood that turning to Heidegger was another way of preferring the imagination over rationally constrained discursive routes—that is, another means of transcending the regime of metaphysics. Thus, for example, we might find ourselves renewed to think of epochs in terms of the stanzas of a poem rather than stretches of centuries contending in sequent toil. He seemed to take delight that I had written a dialogue modeled after

Cesare Pavese's *Dialogues with Leuco* concerning a peripatetic Black Forest encounter between Rilke and Heidegger, the former's angels becoming the common readers of the latter's newfound errancy. Now another thing that may be said in favor of a poem is that it doesn't pretend that its relationship with time is anything other than subjective, but neither in doing so does it loosen its grip on prediction and control. Putting aesthetics (back) in the driver's seat, it seems, was an idea not far from either Dewey or Nietzsche.

The coming of theory in the 1970s was thought by many poets of my generation to have a deleterious effect on art, one that worked its evil by rationalizing virtues and denigrating craft. Those who hearkened to theory's call were thought either to be Bolsheviks or poetasters, and the elevation of the critic over the poet was viewed with grave alarm. The status of poets and critics had, it would appear, changed places. I remember the feeling that poets were losing caste the first time I saw one wearing a coat-and-tie to his own reading (Michael Ryan) at about the same time that I saw critic Fredric Jameson arriving for a (well-attended) talk clad in macho leather. Over beer, Andrei Codrescu, who had connections with the San Francisco Beat scene and nodding acquaintance with its successors of the L=A=N=G=U=A=G=E group, told me there was reason to fear the latter, as they had assimilated theory into their poetry, and the result was a barricade mentality whose worst effect was the *coups d'etat* of creative writing programs by theory-crazed pod people posing as professors. "You have to watch out, man," he said, "these people are *serious.*" So having something of a background in later Wittgenstein, I began my study with Rorty in consequence of the idea that I would get behind the curtain of theory. What Rorty contributed was more than enhancements to my wish to arm my advance toward literary exposé. He both assured me that it didn't matter if poets were not up-to-date, theorized, and materialist, or for that matter, *démodé*, naive, and metaphysical. As if to make the matter plainer, he confessed that his favorite poet was the decidedly non-PC Philip Larkin. Even more to the point, for the autonomous poet, *his* approval ought not to matter, nor his disapproval strike a blow for justice: literary, philosophical, or linguistic (if such can be imagined). The point was that what you loved most was most likely to work, be it ever so incorrect.

I got the idea of "Wised Up" from a story Rorty told, which I relate in the poem: that is, the time he found himself on a panel with the Dalai Lama and had to suppress the urge to ask His Holiness to levitate. The occasion came about when I was looking out from the terrace of our borrowed Seattle *pied-à-terre*, which overlooks the Puget Sound toward the Olympic range. I noticed that the color of those distant mountains matched the color of the sky, once your eye traveled down past the snowy peaks and before it stopped at the boulder rubble at the base. That missing middle reminded me of the erasure Rorty made as he related this anecdote by sweeping his hand, as if to show how easily and with what zest illusion can be swept away. The irony, of course, lay in the fact that, notwithstanding the spiritual leader's compliance with the request of his fellow panelist, it would take an actual levitation to accomplish the exposure. At the same time I was aware of Rorty's sheer puckish charm at being ready to expose the pretensions of a holy man by getting him to fall for a cliché about holy men, the perpetration of which would be the equivalent of tying his shoelaces together. That is why the poem ends with the image of a boy. Readers who have followed Rorty's career are aware that his own boyhood gave him much to think about, despite his self-description as a precocious nerd. And the mature man honored the boy's audacity (and antecedent cluelessness) while forgiving the boy his obtuse persona.

When philosophers speak of Rorty, the word "love" doesn't spring to mind as a keyword in the same breath as others in the neopragmatist's kit bag. Yet Rorty speaks of love in the same voice as of imagination; that is, both are manifestations of the will to progress. "*[A]ll* human relations untouched by love take place in the dark," he wrote. He once said to me, "It doesn't matter whether you're studying the right poet; it only matters that you love him." He would later call this (following Tillich) the "symbol of ultimate concern." I was fortunate to learn that the injunction to love is compact with pragmatism, which, in the round, is a philosophical view that specifies our concern be not about our relationship with the immaterial ideal, but rather with each other and the past. Does poetry stand to suffer from such a view? I used to maintain that while poets may be content with asserting that their art was, in Keats's formulation, therapeutic to mankind, in the privacy of their garrets, they were probably working from quite another set of premises. Or as I wrote in another poem—quoting Dr. Johnson—they are right in private to prefer a duke to a genius. I thought of this as an instance of the public solidarity /private irony distinction. I offered this opinion to Rorty at his house once, adding that the private premises were, more likely than not, platonic, and he smiled and shrugged in that laissez-faire way of his that let me know accommodation need not entail agreement. It also let me know he took my point.

Gibbons Ruark's *Staying Blue*

One of my friends once said that he always picked up a new book of poems by Seamus Heaney with slight trepidation because he knew there would somewhere soon be a word he'd have to look up. I have that feeling about a number of poets I admire when it comes to botanical things—flowers, trees, grasses. Of course this speaks to my lack of Adamic potential more than it does to any obscurantism, willful or otherwise, on the part of poets whose work I esteem, esoteric finesse notwithstanding. I mention this because I feel the same insufficiency in reading Gibbons Ruark's fine *Staying Blue,* and the poet wastes no time in getting down to detailing. While I had to look up the exact shade of blue for two flowers (flowers that I knew in a "literary" way—but what is that?—but would not have been able to identify on a walk), the opening poem, nonetheless, struck me as the best poem I had ever read on a color. In it, Ruark informed me that the aim of discriminating nuances was about working among articulations to discover "the blue John Lee Hooker's gravelly / Voice in the sundown field was looking for." The task of discernment, in other words, is not finally Adam's penchant: it's not about giving the right names to beasts and flowers (although it is about finding the names already given); rather it's about finding evocations and resonances so that the world, which sometimes seems so set on neutrality, is alive to us, not dead or petrified:

> When I hand you this bunch of cornflowers
> The only other color in the room
> Illumines your eyes as you arrange them
> They are the blue reflection of whatever
> Moves in you, serene as cool water tipped
> Into crystal.

Who would have thought "whatever" to be rescued and moreover made to serve as a hinge word opening on the domestic version of fairy seas forlorn? It's the visual equivalence of resonance, of echo, nicely symbolized in the shape of flowers, whose trumpets and bells suggest sound, even as they practice silence.

Accompanying the fullness of silence is the resonance of images in "Quarantine," about the poet's mother's struggle with polio. Despicably grim as a cultural marker, what FDR—another victim— knew culturally determined as "shameful" and "ghastly," the term "quarantine" itself suggests something shelved. But there was nothing hidden about his mother's vulnerable, physically incorrect legs against the braces' steel ("the braces were hinged and ominous, / Not Mama's legs, not anything like them."). At the same time, his mother's crippling coincides with another awakening, his interest in a casually clad aunt:

> Beautiful and young, an Army nurse in the war,
> Did I dream she made us buttered toast and eggs
> Before remembering to put her clothes on?
> She died in childbirth, fifty years ago,
> And I have wondered at her all my days.

For the older poet, the wonder of that new sexuality merges directly with the elegiac pathos in that last line. Ruark has prepared for that poetic phrase, "all my days" by referencing the hovering, vulnerable ball of gnats in Keats' "To Autumn," a poem "[w]e were every one too young to understand." That understanding comes later when generations—one of the subtextual words here, give way to elegy, and a boy's interest in the sexual body learns to pursue its object not in terms of aggression, but of pity, that ancient word so close to Keats', but so foreign to our own ears. The nakedness of one and the illness of the other—sexuality and vulnerability—are linked forever as the poem ends with the mother's repose ("Only late at night could you not hear her coming."), having divested herself of the braces ("like parts of a skeleton").

A different silence pervades "Little Porch at Night," one of the loveliest villanelles in recent memory. Here silence is understood as "something...gone wrong," an absence of familiar voices that must

be retrieved and restored. The poet brings urgency to bear on this
desire to recover the neighborly and familiar voices by subtly revising
Spenser's famous wedding refrain from the provisional "until I end
my song" to the more pressing "before I end my song." This darker
refrain contrasts with the more inviting, "Pull up a porch chair next to
this chaise lounge." One line speaks to the scarcity of time remaining;
the other to time's tending toward fulfillment, its "wish" to be filled
with event and change. Both mother ("A mother should be standing
with her long / Hair tucked in a bun") and father ("For down there
in the shallows should be strung / A taut line from a father to the sea
he fishes") appear. The dead mother is addressed, suggesting two
ends of human time, while the father's image is incapable of address
because it serves, so to speak, to connect historic time with something
more remote, something that hooks us up with not only the origins
of human families, but with unaccommodated life.

   The elegy for a young painter, "Thinking of a Painting by Alex-
ander Haden" takes us to the probably unavoidable conclusion that
sight often registers after the fact, a belatedness underscored by
death ("Everything shifts and wavers until it's steadied? / By a long
late glimpse, this one without him in it..."). The poem ends in Gray's
country churchyard, and such a locale, quaint in our day and age,
ties Ruark's world both to Ireland, his spiritual and ancestral home,
and—just as importantly—to the mainline tradition of Anglo-Irish
poetry, culminating in Yeats, Kavanagh, and Heaney, a trinity of
worthies. They are the headmasters of Ruark's singing school. They
nearly also spell, one feels hesitant in adding—one of the visionary
limits of his poetic horizon. I say "nearly" because Ruark is shrewd
enough to play his other hand, as a poet who has also made his mark
as a southern poet. This is plainly suggested in "Carolina Montana
Bluebird Sonnet for Pat and the Memory of Charles" ("and Connemara rhymes with Carolina / Till we say farewell and all thanks to
the giver..."). Traveling poetically with dual passports as he does,
Ruark can lay claim not only to the hat of Auden's "transatlantic
man" but can switch easily between the space of America (see previous title) and the deep cultural time of Europe.

   The objects of attention here are woven into the redoubtable
and reliable textures of a human continuum so closely tied to the

natural one that it feels rude to mention history without noting the
continual presence of birds, the heralds, as Keats taught, of history's
insignificance. Here we find blackbirds, woodpeckers, cardinals, tit-
mice, bluebirds, and goldfinches, Ruark's affective (and perhaps ata-
vistic) connection with John Clare. It's again the recourse to natural
information that fits this poet to the mainline.

In such a cosmos of images, life proceeds by maintaining offices of
familiarity, and this maintenance is, in turn, mediated by nutritional
service (feeder for birds—pubs for people) which, on the human
side stints the communal values of church ("the Jesuits lost me to
the tender nurses") but raises the same in the public houses. One
of my favorite poems here is "Newbliss Remembered in Newquay,"
a poem that makes the publican the stage manager of Irish social
routine and the social drinker a pilgrim. In its recursive intelligence
("there's a clock on every wall, but they're all wrong")—so ably
reflected in the title, Ruark's work begins to favor that of the Larkin
of "The Whitsun Weddings," that is to say, at his most burnished and
colloquial. The pub's social advantages stand in contrast to the front-
porch, bluegrass sociability of Ruark's stateside poems. And that's
to be expected, though the poet makes no matter of it. Indeed, he
would find it unintelligible to set Connemara against Carolina—or
vice versa. But just as his friend James Wright laid claim to an Italy
standing at the end of all Ohios, Ruark has Ireland floating at the
end of all Americas, including the Anglo-Irish one whose further
career in the New World his poems in part represent. If this means
that heaven is retrospective rather than prospective, making hay of
the orientation does not commit him to Emerson's Party of Memory
against the Party of Hope. When time is steeped in custom, memory
becomes physical and hope an undiscarded platitude.

Ruark is as shrewd and observant a botanical amateur as he is
energetic in stocking his aviary. It used to be that naturalists carried
their casual Adamic expertise as easily as a knowledge of prosody.
What with *über*-massive urbanization and the sequent marginaliz-
ing of the natural world, this talent is less in view. We are lucky that
Ruark has the mojo of eld, not because it imposes on him a custodial status similar to that of the last person to speak Algonquin, but

because such knowledge for a poet links him both with discountenanced Nature and with old time. Knowing the names prevents barrenness. Reading this poet, one is aware of the presence of poetry's most serviceable virtues, but also of what it means to haul those virtues out to perform periodic service, offering skill to bear where disenchantment whispers.

On Steve Scafidi

Steve Scafidi is the author of two impressive collections, *Sparks from a Nine-Pound Hammer* and *For Love of Common Words,* both in the Southern Messenger series from LSU Press. When I tell you he is a poet of impressive reach and Elizabethan exuberance, you may take me at my word. Imaginatively adroit, formally outfitted without necessarily being formally complex, his work inhabits a large cognitive and imagistic space where ostensible subjects—snakes and weasels, a burning truck, the spruce front of a violin—grow into emanations or strands of implication. Or they are intimations of something seeming to come into view, but remaining just beyond the reach of articulation. He does this with exceptional self-possession, often with a sense of bravado and vivid pursuit. At the same time, his poems are written under the sign of formalism, and the formal strictures at work here serve to curb the self-delight of linguistic talent so that the sheer ability to be poetic doesn't run away with the show. The tendency is to hyperventilate, and Scafidi is aware of the temptation. There is throughout a Shakespearean merry war between the poet's intention to feature content and the controlled exuberance with which the content is revealed.

Since the 1970s, American poets have seemed to be of two minds about whether it is possible to articulate the "ineffable"—if indeed there is anything to articulate. On the face of it, if something is beyond speech, it is beyond the grasp of language. Might language be instrumental in another way than grasping? That's the traditional hope of poetry, and maintaining a faith in a poem's instrumental ability as it approaches the limits of language makes one the poetic equivalent of an Old Believer. This is where Scafidi comes in.

His poems not only go after (or find themselves within the precincts of) that elusive "ineffable" that is the bane and glory of lyric poetry, but they do so with the implication that it can be done—i.e., that there is something about which our language (our poetry) is interested in acquiring and that poetry is the means to bring its elusive meaning about. Scafidi's poems suggest a belief in those twinned premises. I am reminded of Wittgenstein (as I often am), who first thought—rather too famously—that our understanding of the world was directly tied to our language use. He later came to believe in the aesthetic use of language—that is, the habituation of poetic usage as itself onto something important about human life. Now, I don't know but what Scafidi has more than a passing acquaintance with that difficult philosopher, and yet his work bears out the justice of the latter view.

This is another way of saying that Scafidi's work looks to find the something like the sacred in the ordinary; it assumes that the ordinary is to be venerated as an incubator of sacred imaginings. Now it may be that the "sacred" is only what the poets say it is. Scafidi has no problem with lifting the sacred from its status as a natural thing and placing it in the category of made thing. Nor should he; in fact, the distinction no longer seems as intelligible as it may once have. Collapsing such distinctions is not catnip to the poet, as it is to the philosopher. As illustration, look at "The Egg Suckers":

To the snakes and the rats and the weasels
    who skulk and tunnel and dig underneath
the moon and the earth to find the shiny
    white ovum of their dreams laying there

warmed under the hen who coughs a little
    moving away in the darkness of the gold
hay and the dust of my chicken coop
    I say hello now from about fifty feet away

in my writing room at the beginning of Spring
    for you are the egg suckers, the midnight

takers-away, the despised and slinky
    snoopers, the geniuses of the world who

will be here when we are no more—

    The poem moves from the universal loathing of snakes to a lesser, winking disapproval of weasels and rats and that in turn to ironic identification with these beasts as, at first, ordinary consumers, then finally connoisseurs of eggs. The transformation maps the poem's thematic span, from stealthy pursuit to holy celebration as the eggs are consumed. But the holy and the aesthetic both proceed from the criminal: it takes the poem to push the one into the other. Because they are eggs (whose potentiality is eclipsed in the eating) a grandiose claim is implied—that is, in the cultivation of such a diet. The fact is not lost on Scafidi. It is precisely in finding aesthetics (a tasty meal) at the center of a morally repugnant—if natural—state of affairs (of eating unborn flesh, of consuming the options of history) that Scafidi throws light on the battle between contested areas of self-understanding.

    A well-known poem, "To Whoever Set My Truck on Fire," begins in reasonableness ("let us be friends and understand our differences") but ends in a curse ("I promise you I will lay the sharp blade deep // into your body"). The title sets the poem up so well, it replaces the need for exposition. The vandalism is reminiscent of KKK raids: night, country, idling cars, inability to ID perpetrators, the embarrassment of ambush. It's the transformation from rational behavior to seemingly justifiable (at least, understandable) violence. Again, Scafidi's customary trajectory comes into play: a transformation from one extreme of regard to another, with the result that something is learned, or intimated, or forgiven in the self's capacity for response. Here the trajectory ironically reverses what we normally take trajectories that are not physical to be: a journey from the less to the more; the bad to the good, etc. The poem doesn't just describe; by turning to a curse, it enacts the insanity of old-school racism. The truck, ironically associated with white men, is in this poem possessed by a black man (Scafidi is African-American). Again, form mediates the swell of anger and its enabling moral energy.

One of Scafidi's best poems is cleverly called "The Bee of Was." It is a marvelous, visionary poem—and it's about "the marvelous," to use Heaney's phrase. In this poem, Scafidi leaves his preferred trajectory for an *if-then* structure. It's one of those poems that try to say everything by connecting the small directly with the immense, a kind of web that catches meaning in intimations. Now whether this is nutrition by means of crumbs is up to the reader. My thinking is that connecting the dots, done right, pays a compliment to the same reader. Scafidi's poems want to involve a larger canvas than lyric has traditionally been tasked to manage. "The Bee of Was" in its cadence suggests *The Wizard of Oz* and in that, both the innocence of the myth of self-determination and the reality of deception and spin on the way to being.

> The angel in the wheel and the forest in the man
> And the old in the cold, cold bottomless Real
> Turn the world we don't understand and turn
> Dirt to roses and the tiny hands of the dead
> Grip the levers and the handles of the machine
> That lifts the lifted moon from the wide blue sea
> That says, "Enough, enough, it's never enough,"
> This chuff-chuff of want being is the gerund of...

To say language is a prison is to be somehow complicit in the fact of capturing. Running away from an engagement with the argument, however, leads toward verbal overcompensation—the danger elsewhere in Scafidi's work, less so here. But flight, when you think about it, is an argument too.

Another poem that moves among "marvelous" things is "For the Eighth Annual Celebration of St. Cecilia, the Patron Saint of Music, Purcellville, Virginia, November 1999," a title worthy of Baron Munchausen but equally bringing Dryden to mind. Dryden's "Song for St. Cecilia's Day" is a poem literally about composition, and takes the form of a creation poem for which the metaphor is replaced by literal creation by music. In Scafidi's poem, the reverse is true: the created instrument is imagined led, by apocalyptic changes, to ruin: art back to nature and nature to chaos. The image of a spruce-top

violin recurs throughout the poem, as in recent movies a metonymy
for music and as such, transcendent. By the end of the poem, the
ruin of the last violin nonetheless returns seemingly arbitrary, but
actually determined points on the globe:

> when I think of music
> so great no passage of time could ever kill it
> I think of some future day far away I hope
> when a mouse pulls some brown grass through the hole
> it gnawed in the very
> last violin lying somewhere half smashed
> in the charred ruins of the shiny ancient cities of
>
> Cleveland or Sacramento...

Yet, by virtue of his own poem, Scafidi knows that chaos cannot
be allowed the last word. No poet writes for the rats. It is another
poem of rhetorical rush, running headlong into its own demise and
imagined remembrance. This poem is also one of apocalyptic endings, but ends on a positive note, a saving note. It is not, however, a
poem of easy optimism, and I must note that its final image is given
in mind, not reality. The harmony of Scafidi's spheres is not God-
made, but internal.

In Scafidi's formalism the language is exuberant and expansive.
The use of form, however, is intended as much as anything to keep
the language from ballooning into overwriting (a weakness that
the poet is aware of). The tension between expansiveness and con-
finement, when successful—as is most often the case—results in a
poetry that is stirring in its quest for self-possession and soaring in
its literary ambition. Scafidi's poems share a similar range. They are
frequently a page long (rarely longer or short). While intimation is
his method, ordinary understatement is not. He is more allusive
than would seem to be the case at first glance. For example, "On
the Occasion of an Argument beside the River Where I Lie" begins,

> Someone says we are trapped in language, and so the sun drops
> overhead

> Through stilly pines where the river explains nothing and far away
> now
> Several men and women on the Yangtsze look up from their nets
> and
>   Point to the sky.
> Bright Chinese fish, like all my words struggle in the nets of a
> stranger.
>   And ends:
>   and it is the truth,
>   not my truth or some private certainty I tell you.

The poet glances in the direction of Hardy ("stilly"), which in turn brings up the silent ravages of chance (as related to the *Titanic*), and this in turn informs the men and women on the Yangtsze whose actions on the other side of the world, while subject to chance, are not thereby mastered by it.

Scafidi's dynamic range leads him to an interest in that old subject, the sublime. In fact he has a poem called "The Sublime." In that poem, the dream doesn't work out, and "you" become "nothing" a dog eats, then defecates. At length, you are "thrown away," and these amazing things happen to you, this continual pilgrimage through the guts of animals and of the earth itself—all shattering—are delivered with the gusto and gratitude of Hamlet's gravedigger.

Poems like "For the Last American Buffalo," where the soul is likened to a buffalo who "walks through me every night as if I was / some kind of prairie" move him in the thematic direction of the other side of the ineffable—i.e., the ineffable in one's own self:

> It is the loneliest thing I know
> to approach it slowly with my hand outstretched
> to tenderly touch the heavy skull furred and rough
> and stroke that place huge between its ears where
> what I think and what it thinks are one singing thing . . .

In the bawdily titled "Ode to the Perineum" the soul returns to suffer comparison with "that pleasurable / one millionth acre / of nerves that lies between the asshole and the valleying //gradual beginning of our sex." The poem is similar to "The Sublime." There is a sense of the phantasmagoric, of snowballing. One remembers that this rhetorical plenitude is characteristic of a strain of African-American poetry. Amusingly he contrasts the image of the perineum to the image of a hummingbird: "such a symbol for the soul / to be honest must include the microscopic blue turds //thudding lightly onto the grass." Reaching for heaven by directing his quill to that spot between his legs, the poet doesn't forget to rise for a moment just long enough to laugh.

Alan Shapiro's *Night of the Republic*

The story goes that during World War II, when the rest of France's poets were training invectives against the Nazis or writing patriotic verses to steel the determination of the Resistance, Francis Ponge scandalized his colleagues with *Le parti pris des choses* (*Taking the Side of Things,* 1942) and the first installments of *Le Savon* (*Soap,* 1967), a book-length poem about a bar of soap. He raised lowly household objects by submitting them to a scrutiny of such penetration and status-elevation that a hue and cry was sure to follow: what was Ponge thinking? Was he off his nut? By the time Neruda published *Odas Elementales* (*Elemental Odes,* 1954), the reading world, chastened by dislocation and war, was beginning to catch up. Blake had famously seen eternity in a grain of sand, and it was Blake's purpose to wake sleeping giants and point them in the general direction of the New Jerusalem. While Blake's motive was religious, Ponge's and Neruda's motives were political and philosophical. In either case, the perspectival reset was in line with the march of science, which, *pace* Blake, postulated the systematic diminution of the human. But what—as we shrank—about our new ethical size? The emphasis on things rendered us smaller in the light of contrast, but the real point was that things became, as it were, our confreres, fellow participants in existence itself. To elevate things was to get us thinking of how we took these same things for granted, and how, *in extremis,* we could come to destroy them. It was a problem made familiar by Baudelaire, as well, who foresaw how the falling away of things (as individualism swelled) left us to our own devices, with spiritual acedia and its attendant boredom as the result.

In *Night of the Republic* Alan Shapiro picks up the thread left by
Ponge and Neruda in having us spend quality time with the effects of
the quotidian, leaving ordinary things, well, not exactly to their own
devices (they have none) but to the devices of poetry, chief among
them, description. Most recently, Miss Bishop showed that, in the
proper light, just as journeys lead to pilgrimages, description leads
to vision. To use Bellow's term, Shapiro is a "first-class noticer," and
the fact, as it should, ramifies far beyond the confines of the page.
If *Night of the Republic* sounds like it brushes by *Night in the Museum*,
you may be pardoned for thinking that the resemblance is a more
than coincidental. Things seem to acquire a life of their own by
virtue of the poet's acknowledgment. Take the opening of "smoke,"
for example:

> Released a single strand of smoke straight up
> In a slender column that looked like it would go
> On stretching in a straight line to the ceiling,
>
> Though always at the same point—maybe a foot
> Or so above the ashtray—it would waver,
> And bend and branch, the branches branching too,
>
> Thinning to veins, the veins to capillaries
> Entangling and knotting up each other
> Into a bluish opalescent cloud.

Shapiro's collection amounts to a grand inventory, Whitmanian
in its delight in entering things into the register of the poems, and
yet it is also largely non-Whitmanian in form (Shapiro prefers the
short line). The inventory begins with the description of public
places ("Gas Station Rest Room," "Supermarket," "Car Dealership,"
"Downtown Strip Club," "Park Bench," "Hotel Lobby," "Race Track,"
and so forth). These spaces become even more public ("Post Office,"
"Convention Hall," "Government Center," "Court Room"). After the
pivotal, catalytic "Galaxy Formation," a long-lined, recursive and
personal poem, the flip—and yet worthy counter—of so much that
makes this volume work, the second half of *Night of the Republic* moves

into reverse, where smaller, private things, reminiscent of Neruda's odes proliferate as content: "Dryer," "Desk," "Family Pictures," "Faucet." In "Dry Cleaner," we find,

> What clings
> like memory to the crumpled-together sack-
> cloth of pant leg
> cuff or collar
> tomorrow will be churned away
> and pressed
> into forgetfulness
> till one by one the spilled on dripped on merely worn
> will rise
> in an aphasia of transparency
> to sheer raiment

This rising of the ordinary into the ideal, by way of the actual, will probably remind some readers of early Wilbur, who also sought to find the angelic in laundry. Shapiro's pinpoint deployment of the word "raiment" likewise conveys a feeling, not merely of having stumbled on the sacred, but of having created something that goes by means of its association of sacredness, by virtue of the poet's having beheld it in all its splendor—which is to say, its ability to sponsor the right language.

In "Stone Church," another poem hungry to show its Adamic muscle, he locates spirit itself in the building of belief's paradox—itself manifested in a building consecrated to the reconciliation of spirit and stone:

> there's greater
> gravity inside the
> the grace that's risen
> highest into rib
> vaults and flying
> buttresses, where
> each stone is another
> stone's resistance to
> the heaven far

```
      beneath it, that
      with all its might
      it yearns for, down
      in the very soul
      of earth where it's said
      that stone is forever
      falling into light
      that burns as it rises,
      cooling, into stone
```

"Playground" queries the prerogative of Adam, which is not only
to confer a name, but to confer the *right* name. Saussure added to
Adam's burden in showing us how really arbitrary the act of naming
was, and yet, no poet can pass by Saussure without adjusting her Ray-
Bans, for without a sense of the rightness, even within the confines
of contingency, even in the jaws of chance itself, the *mot juste* carries
the last quiddity of meaning, if only because it got there with its own
self-sustaining belief intact, fighting off competing interpretations.

```
      out in the street
      under the street light
      the inside of a ripped-open
      half of a tennis ball
      (hit or hurled?)
      is blacker than the blacktop
      it is tipped toward
      somewhere in which
      the other half is surely lying,
      tipped toward the street.
      Tipped, you could say, like an ear.
      You could say the silence
      is the sound of one ear
      listening for the other
      from the bottom of an
      interstellar hole.
      You could say sand dunes.
      Aphasic metal. The breaking
      chain links of a wave. At night,
```

in the playground,
you could say anything.

The stone arises to evoke spirit, and poetic speech retains its taste
in the cacophony of a playground. In "Gym," we see another instance
of such paradoxical comparison:

The room is a downward
and inward
exhalation, the very iron breathing
into itself and through itself
to exhalations under it,
and under that,
yielding the way everything with breath yields
finally when it's breathing out.

From the siege of contraries, Shapiro enacts an ancient struggle,
a fact of which he is perfectly aware. Hints line the poems of something mythic, as if the True Names of Things weren't vision enough:

The circulating disinfectants
make it an unearthly blue
or earth's blue seen from space,
or what pooled from the steaming
of the planet's first condensing.

On the way to these enactments he also becomes aware of the
hopelessness of it all: the impossibility of poetry, an idea that raises
its knobby head from time to time, even as the accumulation of work
belies the unsettling sense that it could be otherwise:

All night, off and on,
cool air is hurried
through the floor and ceiling vents
to keep the temperature from spiking,
and while it does
until it doesn't
fresh paper, innocent of flesh,

> on the examination table
> rustles a little
> under a phantom restlessness.

These lines appear, tellingly, in a poem called "Hospital Examination Room." If there were ever a call for poetry to renew its claim to being therapeutic, it would be now in the light of ancient claims that are called upon by reasonable skeptics to justify themselves. Why should poetry tolerate, let alone fetishize paradox? What meaning can be derived of language situated on the arbitrariness of its very means? What can be made of the fact that these means situate themselves in a world of fact, only to take leave of that world by theory, dream, and /or flight of fancy? Shapiro is not going to furnish the reader with an answer to any of these questions, as they are not at the epicenter of his discourse as a poet. But it doesn't take a theorist trained in the speculation of whimsy to see how the questions emerge and start growing out from his very premises. Indeed, just as with Ponge, Shapiro gets an ethical universal framework for his pains, and it is one built in the light of our own struggles, not one superimposed on chaos for us to deal with, training our little lights on the big (and suddenly bigger for the thinking) mysteries. There is a rightness to these poems that proceeds from the poet's sense of beautiful placement, derived from the interpenetration of absence (few people appear in the book) and presence, substance and dearth, time and the instant. Shapiro is the descendant of Hopkins and Stevens, both believers in meaning's quantum shifts, in his understanding of what I have elsewhere referred to as "ambivalence," but might just as well be named the Here-There school of Beauty and the Good:

> The unseen of seeing all at once and too
> Continuously for the eye to see
> The trackless path it traces to the eye:
>
> The finch's yellow now-there-not-there flashing
> Among the leaves, and the leaves too, their green
> Degrees, gradations, shifting moods, a green

Or yellow fire unfixed and alive
And flaring out indifferent to the sight
It woos and enters, indifferent to the bird,

The leaf, the very air it all at once
Continuously dwells in and deserts,
Awake and wakeless, light-borne, born of light?

When I got to the end of *Night in the Republic*—and it is somewhat longer than the conventional single volume, I realized that I didn't want it to end. Time and again he nailed something I had myself thought but not seen how to make manifest in a poem. I even thought that this coming upon the verity of the Here-There was his actual subject, and today I find myself thinking that again. Who knows about tomorrow? All we know is that, as the philosopher said about death, it is something about which we can have no knowledge, and yet we feel impelled to say a great deal. In Shapiro's parlance, deriving from life in suburban America, our *republic* (moreover at night), it's the on-and-off of the TV that that says this moment is unlike any other, just as it says all our moments are indistinguishable in time's continuum:

Inside the house I couldn't find extinctions
To study and by studying prepare

Myself for what I wouldn't live to see:
The way the angry little ball of fire
From a struck match would vanish when I shook it

Into a loosening skeleton of smoke;
Or how the world that watched me from the TV screen
Swallowed itself the moment I turned it off.

Anis Shivani's *My Tranquil War*

For some poets, poetry itself is either /or: there is no point in getting steamed up over insufficient options. Poets holding this elitist position do not endear themselves to poetry groups, arts councils, or people concerned with outreach. Anis Shivani has made a name for himself taking down the *fromages*, both of the tiny ecosystem that is poetry, and of the larger world of fiction. No doubt this is a good thing, both tonic and clarifying. Yet one does feel that the firepower aimed at amiable, tragedy-free poets like David Kirby and Billy Collins hit a mark past their target. I confess I am a fan of these poets, precisely because they have beheld something, idealized though it be, beyond the world's continuously self-revising wreck. Yes, they have rejected history, but not in the pupil-narrowing way that the New Critics did, in an all-encompassing strategy that indoctrinated legions of Boomers (myself included) and their revered teachers. And yet, in another sense, Shivani has a point: poetry can't, in the end, prefer idealism to reality, without suffering further erosion, leading their participants to be shriven and ineffectual in the larger culture. Many American poets, especially since the translation boom of the '60s and '70s, have pointed to the special mission of poetry as somehow truth-bearing beyond the lexical mission of words. I am thinking, for example, of the work of European and Southern American poets. For these bards, the fog of politics required a comeuppance for rhetoric, combined with a return to writing degree zero, which is where surrealism got its legs. It may be, that with the end of the Cold War, it seemed that the larger political message no longer required the same degree of study on the part of upcoming poets. Or it may simply be that it entered into poppy fields of academic discourse. But then came 9/11 and all of a sudden, Said and Foucault and their demystifying ways were cutting edge again, as we sought to analyze and understand, even at the risk of rationalizing our patrimony.

This is where Shivani comes in. He wants to, indeed he means to, connect the curricular bobbleheads of literature (Woolf, Mann, Pound, Nabokov, Rushdie), art and film (Dali, Godard, Antonioni, Cocteau, Fellini) and politics (Bush, Hitler, Gandhi, Stalin, Reagan), as well as current names (Dean Young, Billy Collins, Derek Walcott, John Ashbery) with each other to see what eventuates from the dustup. He wants to know, at bottom, that the cultural stalwarts are as hardy in the present moment as they were in their creative and productive time. He also wants implicitly to compare them to their political and historical equivalents, for whom aesthetic beauty and all that flows from it, is rarely a concern. At first you begin to wonder if the poem is the right vehicle for such a weighty (or absurd, as the case may be) solicitation. The poem, for example, frequently takes the form of direct addresses—dedications and apostrophes ("To Robert Creeley," "Letter to Jack London," "To John Cheever," "To Derek Walcott," "To Djuna Barnes, on *Nightwood*," "To Edward Upward"). But the object of the apostrophe is not just the great person, any more than an elegy is a poetic device to plump up the mighty dead. The object is the self (or its deputy, the reader):

> Creeley, I
> have to pay my accounts,
> I thrive on excess.
> ("To Robert Creeley")

Here's another that speaks, if you will, to the Jack London within, as much as to the author of adventures now left to REI members.

> You had quick worthy followers, Dreiser
> and Hemingway, Anderson and Orwell,
> and every mythmaker not a miser
> with expression who plunged into the well
> of our subconscious, and found there a hell

of our own making. Now we want a myth
the uninspired common man can live with.

("Letter to Jack London")

Like V. S. Naipaul, Shivani looks culture and its producers straight
in the face and demands they justify their role in a violent world.
And also like the Brit, he calls out the heroes whose art is suited only
for walk-ons, can be cashed in, or put to use, as with Socialist Realism, in anodyne ways. Long story short, he is a moralist whose truth-
tracking radar begins to look like an LED version of Diogenes' lantern. If the poem is in the business of finding out what will suffice,
then that goes double for culture altogether. For culture is a thing;
it is also the form-making through which that thing acquires significance in history. But the danger, as the poet knows, comes with
over-familiarity. Having lost the capacity for wonder, we arrive *tout
de suite* in the condition we know as being in-the-know. This, I take
it, is partly behind Shivani's beef against MFA programs, namely,
that we get a false sense of knowing (e.g., "craft"). But since it's one
we can wrap our heads around without too much sweat, it's gained
wide acceptance, regardless of the debased quality of the return:

It is how we read today, in that knowing wink to Eliot's

hesitation, as though we were of the Promethean genus
barreling through department doors. But we are mute as

drugged cats, draping ourselves on aristocracy's banisters:
brown-fugged, prone to politics, reading like damn whores.

Ron and Ken and John, I need this Guggenheim reference
as a cow needs mulch, so will you shovel your last doubts up

my anus? See again how the Strand fills with lissome
(still a word?) blondes from Morningside arguing over bad

Camus, as though it mattered which bed existentialism wakes
up in, as though the prophets will swoon and rest after '68.

("Juvenal's First Satire")

Shivani's hyperventilated poems seem, in their range of reference, detail mix, and startling asides, the versified outlines of Audenesque table talk. And like the ceaseless, synthetic rush that was Auden's brain, Shivani's gray matter also radiates two 18th century traits, wit and sensibility: the former, one answer to *Top Gun's* Goose's need for speed; the latter, the mental climate under which treks, land speed trials, ambles, and sometimes wrecks unfold. In the sense that both primary and secondary experience must be mashed into a Parmenidian One, all poetry measures velocity in language. In Anis Shivani's work, it's the speed of association that marks its median style, a mandarin style, with its lunges and substitutions, its strangeness of juxtapositions, its keen doggedness, not of words in their deployment alone, neither of the syllables in their atomic authority, but of words monitoring their deportment and keeping their distance from the clichéd and the jejune. It's a lot of stuff to monitor, and Shivani's poems can seem longer then they are. One is aware, at the same time, that the speedy phrasing produces its own anxious duplicity, suggesting in equal measure the jittery deer and the hair-triggered hunter. It is also speed felt in the middle of a traffic jam. Take this, for example:

Who among us has not torn up Aunt Miranda's notes
to self when she was throwing up in Daddy's bathroom?

— — — — — — — — — — — — —

I might shoehorn into my speech, for McMurtry's sake,
what made Cybill Shepard in her prime the girl
we used as waterslide, inside the confines of Main Street.
Not even Disney alludes now to fascism's seeds.
I've wondered if there's a fountain, not yet belly up,
that generates automatic writing for the eternally
blocked, its water rust free, sweet.

("When Dean Young Was Young")

Everybody remembers the scene in *Amadeus* when the Emperor Franz Joseph ventures the tepid suggestion that Mozart's music contained "a few too many notes," to which the uppity prodigy shot back, "Which few did you have in mind, Majesty?" Many litmus tests exist to exhibit the preferential divides when it comes to poetry's accommodations. But the question of how many words are required is the question of poetry's economy, this "leaving out business" which is the mirror of the assertion that, in Stevens' formulation, the poem is in the business of finding (and by implication, of delivering) what will suffice. It may be that there is no way to decide whether a verbal plenitude (or excess) is any less artistically satisfying than the most austere imagism. Is brown hair to be preferred to red? Beats me. We could disagree, and there would be therapy in that, if no further truth in the working out.

Shivani's stylistic orientation, in contrast to his sensibility, leads him in the direction of Whitman, about whom no one would say there goes a master of economy. Indeed, "mastery" is not the issue. At the same time, he seems to wish that in elsewhere resurrecting the names of olden poets, the old guard had more to guard than turf. But Whitman is a special case (remember the Pound-Whitman kerfuffle?): so wrong and yet so right; so vulgar and yet so noble, so prolix and yet the compiler of tender audits, so flaunting of rules, yet so enamored of traditions. Though somewhat atypical of the work in *My Tranquil War,* "An Address to Walt Whitman after Reading the 1955 Edition of *Leaves of Grass,*" itself a title of Whitmanian girth, is the collection's centerpiece and the one I would rank, *mutatis mutandis,* with the late Kurt Brown's "No Other Paradise" as an updating and strong revisionist reworking of Whitman's democratic vistas. It doesn't take a psychotherapist to tell us that what we don't say is what we need to say. And this is where Shivani locates the otherwise worshipful Whitman, wondering in the democratic *embarras de richesses,* if we don't know when a good thing is too much of a good thing and, if at points we may pass without knowing so, we may find that decadence lies in wait. There is a touch of accusation in his having made us believe in a mark we can no longer reach, or can reach all too well and so scorn as we move on. Or as he puts it in the final, majestic wave of a sentence, "how can you explain, bard, why we have moved so far from your vision by moving so close to it?" Naipaul is, now that I think about it, the last emanation of Whitman. At any rate, it is a fine poem and should eventually be popping up in anthologies.

At the same time, you must admit that writing to Whitman is like bouncing your résumé off Jupiter. The Whitman poem wears its rhetorical structure likewise, like a cloud projection: "you who breathed well-chosen diction, coming from the plain man / into the over-warm cockles of the professional wits." Although everybody owns Whitman, he is not therefore our bitch. Shivani writes his poem as if he were a Whitman unto the Whitman, and in the course of nailing the homage, he raises Uncle Walt all over again. It is a tour de force, the kind of resurrection Whitman dreamed of in *Song of Myself* and "Crossing Brooklyn Ferry" ("and I shall be good health to you"). Shivani knows that one of the things that characterizes decadence is its rancidness, and Whitman is as far from the toxic as a bowl of Quaker Oats. Having nothing to hide toward the spirit whose bonds used words as their ties, Shivani's homage takes pains to reveal its formal moves too.

> Tell us now that a hundred and fifty years have passed, and America
> is perhaps an aged hag with a vast burden on her shoulders, when
> Amer-ica
> is perhaps stooped and bunched and vertiginous, and might appear
> to beholders far and near like a personage who lived not wisely
> but only too well, flabby and flippant and ferocious...
>
> – – – – – – – – – – – – –
>
> do we still contain multitudes, do we still admire contradictions...?

For Shivani, the "heart-minder" is the "teacher" and "believer" whom he would ask to "tell us how it goes with you." Or, "have we disappointed you...? is this the /American you expected to find...? how can you explain this...?" Shivani wants to know, as we all do (which is to say, at all times), how culture intersects with the violence of dangerous times and the blinkered pragmatics with which we drift forward into the future. What we carry with us, both rooted and exilic, is the recurring subject of Shivani's poems, for, one bomb past, the rooted and the exilic change places:

> The *entente cordiale* declares war by plan
> prethought. As if accidents don't exist
> in the high plane generals and emperors scan.
> I still see poor kmets barely subsist.
>
> Millions have since died in Europe's trenches.
> But I don't plead. I am not the agent.
> Assassination: a word that quenches
> rebellion. When war ends, what has it meant?
>
> Europe was the tinderbox I loathed so!
> My parents taught me well not to fear fear.
> As a boy, I came to this Sarajevo
> to learn a trade—hammer blows I still hear.

("Reflections of Gavrilo Princip at Bohemia's Theresienstadt Prison,
April 1918")

That's for the old, which, though it set the stage for much we have had to emerge from, it is not longer a living misery. Rather, this is the present:

> The football field, where I used to cheer as a twelve-year-old,
> had been prepared to accept the deaths of forty murderous men,
>
> whose souls we witnessed exiting with the ease of needles
> running out of thread. It was like kicking
>
> in the style of Pelã and getting only the goal post
> on our bloody shin, and falling twisted and embarrassed to the ground,
>
> your playmates laughing over your sundered body, screaming:
> he is just like his sister, Daud pees sitting down like his sister.

("I Watched Executions Last Night with my Sister")

Religion is in one sense off the table. God may be dead, but his is a puissant ghost, for our transcendental longings demand service. This is true even in the Socialist Paradise, where Shivani finds a poem for the Samson of socialist labor, Alexey Stakhanov:

> My labor will sweeten
> whatever stands between the state's changed moods,
> ill and gloomy most of the time, and I
> alone in a statue, its inner shell,
> a being expelled from time.

("Stakhahov")

At this point, literature and art get a call-back, their avatars, from Whitman to Orwell, to Auden, trimming their pencils and cleaning their throats, before the Brooklyn Eagle and the BBC microphones, to say nothing of soapboxes around the corner: *The Paris Review, Encounter, The New Yorker,* and *The New York Review of Books.* If our heroes of aesthetic labor no longer fail to impress or meet their quotas, then what? Is it then just George Bush and al Qaeda all the way down? Shivani's ultimate concern in these poems is that—God et al. to the side—the artistic legacy, which is an image of the metaphysical legacy, must uphold, direct, and inspire. Moreover, it has to do so, in a Shelleyan sense, with the clout and consequence of the other guys. Otherwise, it's not worth the bother.

> In Ch'ang-an, the winehouses gave me a special name
> I both abhorered and loved at the same time:
>
> Banished Immortal, meaning he who imagines life
> as a continuation of the mountain's other side.

("The Death of Li Po")

It's no wonder, on the one hand, and yet a felicitous state of affairs on the other, that Shivani departs from his day job as writer—and moreover a free-verse poet—to work in forms: sonnet, villanelle, sestina, ghazal. He is adept at all of these, as if to say he's working with a full hand, and the poetic culture he so frequently puts in the

witness box is the same one by which he frames his questions. It's
in the forms where Shivani finds a cadence to soothe the spikiness
of history. For given free rein, that spikiness will file away at your
receptors, until all experience (from the most violent to the most
humane) becomes averaged and leveled, seeing beige, and singing
only in B-flat: smooth, yes, but not therefore calming or becalmed.
The sound that inheres in closed form comes closest to proposing
alternatives by showing their image, while history sits it out in brack-
ets, like a hockey player watching from the penalty box.

> My mates on the dinginauka sing old Tagore,
> his odes to the breath and gloom of stalwarts
> building the nation, while I question this lore
> for only sampling how the watery grave hurts.
>
> Our ancestors came this way and were content,
> we are told, stitching frayed nets and fixing
> the leaks in the boats, their future already lent
> to the moon that preys on love, any odd mixing.

("Small Time Fishing in the Bay of Bengal, 1970")

Sometimes history is itself sung, as in this villanelle:

> The strap on the shoulder could be a child.
> Or a bomb. How can a pacifist tell?
> The weather this month is serenely mild.
>
> The AP correspondent had just filed
> his last ever story before he fell.
> The strap on the shoulder wasn't a child.

———————————

> What need exit strategy when we smiled
> as the whisper of doubt turned to a yell?
> The strap on the shoulder will be a child.
> The weather this month is serenely mild.

("The War in Iraq Poses Irreducible Problems of Identification")

As a reviewer, I sometimes suspect that there's a certain circularity to making a critical point, that the conclusion is just the premise, so to speak, in drag. You're just reasoning poorly, you say? Rather, disregarding a certain circularity may be a serviceable way to dampen contradiction, for without that handicap, it's doubtful any robust criticism can get started. You may assert meanwhile that all criticism begins in contradiction, and, in a sense it does, of course. So the reviewer finds himself on the horns of a dilemma: on the one hand he wants to evaluate the beauty of the verse, but in doing so, he finds his criteria tied up in premises he doesn't fundamentally buy. On the other hand, if he praises the prescience of theme and subject, he hears the music calling, like the nightingale in Keats, who says the individual doesn't matter, just the song. If that's so, then there is no tragedy, and the reviewer likewise meets a dwindled mojo, while history, as Delmore Schwartz reminds us, is unappeased. Shivani is quite aware of these issues, and to his credit, he doesn't back down from the moralist's dry creed, although his capacity for grace and ease and beauty itself is undiminished:

> The Viceroy's niece reveals a studious gift of gab, which she uses
> to plot sending down old colonels to their grief in the plains,
> and the reporter for the *Times* is too changed to notice.
> The munshis and darogahs pretend to no loyalty
> they do not have. The chill wind bears a redeemable ill-will.
> The parties go on so late at night the bachelors yawn,
> with all of empire's terrible boredom, its magnificent sin:
> These will be the days least written about, least recalled.
>
> ("At the Simla Hill Station June 1910")

The moralist fears anomie and casual cowardice as much as clearly profiled enemies with their machinations and failings ("Who among the prisoners will make so bold / as strike the sheriff who frees the haters?" ["After the End of Books"]). Thus art that tries to take wing against historical grounding produces anxiety as if fearing, in doing what some think it does best, instead of thrilling, merely goes AWOL. On of the things that Shivani's poems do is show us the two-edged blade that art is. Yes, it inspires, edifies, and corrects. It also repudiates the history to which it owes its birth. Perhaps the problem with sweet airs, with music, generally and with all made beauty—is that it keeps us from the meeting. And instead of asking like Gary Snyder, echoing Herzen, what is to be done, it makes us cry to dream again.

Judith Skillman's *Heat Lightning*

Poetic intelligence comes in three varieties. There's the self-delighting *joie* of Eliot's "words alone" (which, in the Possum's formulation, means something like "words without the moral assistance of..."). Then there's the intelligence of perception, of seeing into reality to a deeper extent than is the normal experience. Finally there's the intelligence that understands the rule of paradox as a (if not *the*) key principle of our significance-gathering-and-disseminating engines: Czeslaw Milosz was the great recent exemplar here. Of course, the categories overlap, and they should. You might more usefully think of them as medieval humors: we are composed of all three, but the balance determines the character that results.

Judith Skillman is a poet assigned by her Muse to the second category, with considerable shading from the first. Martin Amis observed that writers with the most élan are those who take possession of the intelligence's will to penetrate, by which he means to look both into and beyond simultaneously, to (really) notice, remember sequentially, interpret, synthesize, and judge. This means too that Williams' command, "no ideas but in things," is under no obligation to pay a compliment either to things or to ideas, but does so to the imagination that makes of the two a felicity. Consider this:

> From the prison of a week awake
> I walked, feeling my way
> past the silent doves,
> the uniforms, the counsel of friends,
> birthdays, seasons, and cancers.
> Birth in the sheen of ugliness.
> Death in the conversation of an old man's hand.

Sidney Bloom, who gestured, upon being told
he'd meet his dead wife in heaven,
enough already.

("Silk")

Is it enough to "see" what's going on? Can seeing itself, in that wider sense, powered by concentration and curiosity, produce the "insight" necessary to lead on to a realization of what will suffice? May a sufficiency consist in no more than this? Skillman's poems argue for the advantages of such a cultivation. They are descriptions of a usually imperfect domestic world, where it is possible for the poet and her readers to rise to an appreciation of how enhancements to the ordinary, both positive and negative, become the new. In this dynamic, we participate as co-seers. Just how description gives way to vision is a mystery: surely all the borders that separate the two are in constant flux. Yet it is in following the leads brought up by the descriptive will (or re-descriptive will: the will to tell back to ourselves as a way of understanding) that we trigger something we had not met with before. In that "ah-ha!" moment, inadequate levees, long taken for granted, buckle, and we realize we're on to something. And as in my analogy, it may not be something good, either, but it is something worth our study. Take this, for instance:

Any person may be regarded as noble
more or less honored depending upon
how far they stand
from the bowl of salt placed like a child's allowance
in the middle of the table.

("Silk")

It was Dickinson who recommended that the truth be told slant. It is certainly tempting, reading these poems, to argue that slanting favors the figure, if not the accessibility, of the truth anyway. It's not just a matter of coming up behind and flushing the shy truth from its cover. The "angling" that these poems accomplish relishes in its own craft and novel point of view. Consider this from "Magpie Eyes":

One by one my charms grew legs:
quartz elephant, horse, owl, turtle
moving slowly as the earth.
That's when I took my butterfly net
and walked on up the ridge.
I can't tell you what I caught there.
It was rare
but not popular enough to keep.

The slanting tacitly recognizes the provisional and on-off nature of all our ordinary truths. I don't mean to come off as a relativist, either, in suggesting that truths of the sort that we most frequently encounter in poems are merely greeting kisses bestowed on facts. But they are something that responds to just the sort of collaborative appreciation that poems invite, even as poems exist also to generate such truths. In "Ornamental Plum," Skillman writes that "to be beautiful is the same, / but not quite, as forgiven." In that "not quite" is both a *terra incognita* beckoning the explorer (and colonizer) and the daylight needed to spy the requisite word opportunities. At the same time that Skillman's poems perform their watch on the quotidian, the momentary, and the provisional, they also exhibit a welcome finish. I was reminded of the poetry of Maxine Kumin, whose work also displays these qualities in just about the same proportion. The title poem, about a high-heeled woman witnessed by children looking through their blinds as she goes about her *affaires de cour* by the intermittent flashes of heat lightning, is seen not only by the dramatic flickers in the humid night, but through the linguistically adjusted lens that allows us to make of heat lightning an image of a metonymic weather:

So what if she never needed to tell the truth,
which was, after all, nothing more
than a blur, a white lie
leftover from a series of days
above ninety degrees.

("Heat Lightning")

Elsewhere, she makes a bitter tea of the frustrations generations
of women have felt:

> Cursing like Hecuba
> I fill the mouths
> of machines with clothes
> and dishes. My chores
> give rhythm and pace
> to this life grown cold and childless.
> And no man, wearing a carnival hat
> and carrot cigarette,
> will come from the snow
> fearing a wooden instrument,
> my French violin strung
> with lost desire.

("House of Moon")

While much of her subject matter comes from such familiar *topoi*
as the sputtering of marriage, the drag of children—of home life
generally, on ambition, on housework, crafts, and gardening as time-
tested schemes of sublimation, she also feels how the larger theme of
cultural origins both fashions and derives from these same domestic
parameters. Two poems about her ancestors focus on aspects of Jewish determinism. In one, her father's recurrent "cussing" is seen as
redeemably Jewish in its blasphemous vigor, which, as the camera
pulls back, also reveals the quizzical humanity (and animality) surrounding the man:

> there was never a man as kind
> as my father, who said *shit*.
> That word *shit* he held onto like a lifeboat
> in bad weather. A hatless fellow,
> a short Jewish man, hissing.

("Sad Breed")

The other poems brings to the occupation of a relative, presumably a grandfather, all the associations latent in the image of that

guilded occupation, tailoring: the steady, manual toil as antidote to
the heavens' empty promises of freedom, the occupational abase-
ment, the remunerative modesty, but also the secret craft, the innocence of association with the Fates:

> The halves of his life,
> quartered, come into my own,
> and I turn to my cousin,
> saying how beautiful it is
> to live in the service
> of Venus, and we wonder
> what the four years
> meant to him, all those
> fancy men and women
> stylish in the face of his dullness,
> the scissors eking it out,
> the blunt sun rising
> in a sky sewn shut.

("The Cutter")

While earth is a pale reflection of heaven, it can hardly be denied
that heaven could even more profitably go to school to an earthling.
This is the message of many poets, as Skillman acknowledges in
"Dante's Nest":

> This afternoon thirty-three cantos
> tell me what Paradise is—
> an incomprehensible, ecstatic light
> piled on asphalt and dirt,
> dim reflections
> from a pall of ice.

Skillman is expert in resizing the modest to meet the expectations
of readers hoping to see the outlines of larger things. Her expansive
imagination squares with insight, and in the end both seem aspects
of a single unified sensibility. I like the feel of these poems, their
commitment to attention and naturalizing of nuance, and reading
them with care and a similar commitment to their worked contours,

I sense that something of her enterprise is now something of mine.
Readers will experience a like return on their investments, if for no
other reason than this:

> Maybe the only way to tell
> is to keep on walking,
> talking to God
> who leant his name
> to every living thing
> and then withdrew it,
> come winter, leaving
> only the objects—
> lamp and spoon—haloed
> holding the mandolin string
> down with your third finger,
> ringless. You know the book
> by now—whomever you call on
> will have also turned inward.

("Marked")

And Then Something Like This Happens

On the Poetry of John Skoyles

The phrase, "a poet's poet," is a sure-fire way to draw a yawn. And making superfine, hair-splitting discriminations at the tiptop of virtuosity was ever a boring pastime for the masses. Yet the epithet is meant to indicate something beyond someone's approval (presumably someone you don't know): the acknowledgment of a grace potential, an ability to fine-tune the instrument to fit the still sad music of humanity to the Music of the Spheres—an activity denied humble artisans who proceed merely by way of craft. It also helps if your *oeuvre* is spare. It's the kind of talent that leads you to reflect that you didn't see that coming, not with these simple means, nor with such a natural sense of inevitability, as if *tout le monde* should have seen it coming, but somehow missed it. Skoyles' poems are full of such moments, and it might be that in his years of working and reworking familiar terrain, he might be able to walk away with the sobriquet and, and far from looking even more peculiar than an ordinarily accomplished poet, might lend it some of the same fairy dust it supposedly empties on the recipient. It seems to be the case, at any rate, that in each of his four collections, he lays out the perimeter of a personal terrain and then stays there until each recorded moment is a complete shining one or gray blank, whatever the case may be.

Two things stand out in the first collection, *A Little Faith* (1981), a book that works the '70s Iowa poetry vibe to a fare-the-well. The first thing is the trying out of off-the-shelf rhetorical strategies. I'll give but one example:

I don't care at all who died today.
There's not a single reason
to list the deaths today.
Maybe my father opens the sports page,
or my mother a mystery novel
in New York this afternoon,
a place where on another day
I could follow death like a woman
into the subway, where death
is just a headline, where boys
light freezing derelicts on fire.

This kind of thing—stylish though it is, close as it is to provocation—puts a drag on invention by insisting on a kind of inescapable logic ("there's not a single reason...") which, once pushed, reveals itself sheepishly as a device. But Skoyles is too fine a tailor to buy off-the-shelf for himself. The search for the right devices, however, did yield a gem.

I once had a poem taken by *Ironweed*, a literary magazine notoriously difficult to get into. I was elated when the editor, Michael Cuddihy, accepted my poem and enclosed a note saying that, except for one line, it was "a perfect poem." Although his compliment set my face in a smile, I never figured out which was the offending line. But the idea of drawing razor-thin aesthetic distinctions was something that, as a young poet, I was drawn to and hence sought to acquire. I mention this because Skoyles did manage to write, as far as I can see, a perfect *poem*, one that has graced the refrigerators of several of my poet friends over the years. And this is no mean feat. Mark Strand once remarked to me that the whole point of composing poems is to write "an immortal line." I thought, well, there it is. All of our compulsions meet, in Larkin's phrase, in such a thought, and the emotional and psychological "compulsion" in Skoyles' poem trumps the compulsion of form used to secure it. Here's the poem:

No Thank You

Who'll be the lover of that woman on the bench?
If she wants to hurt someone, she can use me.

Did she mean it, or was she trying to be unforgettable?
If she wants to use someone, she can hurt me.

I'll use my manners to stay in one piece,
but I end up believing every excuse that I make.

I always sigh when I see a woman like this,
I don't know where it comes from and I don't know where it goes.

I thought I'd enjoy a beautiful day like today.
I took a walk in the park and then something like this happens.

To our Millennial ears, so attuned to deflections of *whatever* and
as if, it comes as a refreshing message from the past that the forked
nakedness of our hearts owns its determinations, even as it embraces
its own intolerable (and unbreakable) lease. Grounded in the terms
of subjectivity, the speaker is able to fold an immense amount of
implication into his apparently hapless discourse. The duality of the
stanzaic layout matches the "I thought... but then..." self-correcting
(and self-truing) rhetorical structure, even as its fantasy grows into
the mystery of failure and the hinted compensations that seem to
arise at each of the impediments to fulfillment. When I said that the
poem is a site where our compulsions all meet, I mean to suggest
that the poem's worth lies in its ability to spread and carve a delta
of significance, something of endless complexity, although it is also,
from another, more skeptical duck-blind, just a theme-and-variation
maneuver. The questions it raises are self-perpetuating: why do we
desire? Why are we disappointed? Why doesn't disappointment kill
us, or conversely, why is disappointment, on another level, a desirable thing, perhaps even the real desideratum? And if the latter is
the case, does the poem, in hugging its failure Stephen Crane-like,
not lead us to a Frost-like direction, drawing us into the justice of
failure and the complicity with our undoing? If that is so, then the
only contrary movement is toward precise utterance—the perfect
poem, the immortal line—to record, like the streak of a quark in
an X-ray, our profound allegiance to the *néant*, which seems to have
been hooked by what was once the thought of a dalliance, someone

on a bench, just as momentary as we ourselves. And the reception, the reading, of the immortal line is likewise ephemeral. Let's face it, it only has to last a nanosecond longer than you do to clinch that immortality. Perhaps that is a question of (poetic) justice too.

The stance also—vulnerable, alienated, yet fraternal—radiates a sense that his willingness to get down into the muck will establish solidarity with the ordinary. And yet the fact that he wrote a "perfect" poem that expresses that solidarity shows him parting company with the ordinary. Say what you will, the very fact of writing a poem about anything establishes ipso facto an advantage—but of what? Perhaps just something as simple as a trace of a freedom that once was intended to be made manifest here, in the life always already leaving us. In a later poem, "Uncle Grossman," the uncle in question is given to delivering such riddling bromides as this: "Pain makes a world that would not exist / except for pain." You might say the same for love. Or desire, which makes up, then reflects over its own incompletion. Unless we are all poets (a premise worth pondering if only for a New York minute), the poet is the exception to every other human type, and his pledges of allegiance notwithstanding, his is less a report than a representation, less a *cri* than a metaphor. He insists on authenticity, neglecting to recuse himself from his own fabrications. The inescapable self-awareness accompanying this difference in a poet, in every hue from narcissism to self-castigation, is the hallmark of both modernism and postmodernism, as has been noted by everybody.

I find it noteworthy that with his first collection, Skoyles' literary intelligence quotient is already sufficiently high that it works in terms of emotional exploration, a domain traditionally gender-fogged. These early poems seem interested in exploring personal relationships, their meaning, and their ability to make meaning. It was once a truism that young men didn't think about relationships as such, and if they did, they didn't commit their thoughts to paper. As a young man, Skoyles did both, which puts him at the head of the class, where, as he puts it in "Hard Work," such "sullen men" as keep their secrets to themselves find their luck at cards "makes them experts at bluffing." Just as the poet adjusts to the ordinary to seem a part, so the taciturn players conceal their lack of expressiveness and opt for bluffing, as if to fear that the lack of expression—the general condition—would draw attention to their difference, instead of to the prevalence of their malaise.

A Little Faith is in many ways an apprentice work, as busy looking over its own shoulder as it is looking into the—dare I call it this?—heart. It's also parochial, deferential to its Catholic roots, nostalgic for the Queens bona fides, where as an only child, he learned about being old by taking on the fierce equity of the young. Was he a *senex puer*? Probably. It's not that he had a lousy childhood; on the contrary, it seems to have been of a self-sufficient nuclearity, as well as lovingly interconnected, but that everything he experienced passed through the temporal membrane into what we perhaps too-broadly call personal myth. The original templates at his disposal, the Iowa-neo-surrealism-lite he quickly discarded. They handle anecdote, but they don't encourage verbal ambition.

Ten years separated *A Little Faith* from *Permanent Change*, and the latter title suggests a thematic connection—not to say bookend—to the earlier volume. It is more specifically about the poet as member of a time, a city, a religion, even a borough. The poem as memory, often of loss or imminent loss, typically comes to uneasy but fateful rest on a paradox. The clarity of detail in the poems of this collection—indeed, of all four of Skoyles' volumes—seem threads leading to lost worlds. He mentions that his grandmother, working in fabrics, "restitched a hat / for Guy Lombardo's wife," and it should be remembered that Guy Lombardo and His Royal Canadians gave the world New Year's Eve as surely as did Robbie Burns. But just as probably, the poet remembered how Lombardo also romanced the post-war generations of newlyweds in Levittown through summers when he played in the Jones Beach Theater built by his powerful (and unmusical) friend, master-builder Robert Moses. All that is also stitched into the image. Similar images await unpacking. But wait, you say, isn't this the case with any poet's images? Doesn't a paper-clip on Mars rewrite the Martian chronicles? Success in Skoylesian moments makes you rethink the career of images you have read in other poets: some are truly original and fetching in their strangeness, others hackneyed and predictable, without being inevitable. Or inevitable-seeming (the same thing). It doesn't take many repetitions (just one) to equal a cliché. There are no clichés in Skoyles' work.

The poet, as do all poets, sides with the underdog—here including the losers and bums, but he is never naive or sentimental in this identification. Rather, the emotional dynamic range seems to go from not-so-bad-as-that to you-need-to-get-over-it. He trims the extremes ("the way I was taught to see things") and recognizes in that confession how much is left out of the account. You had, so to speak, to be there—but that is the case with all our destinies (and destiny in Skoyles, reassuringly lowercase, seems more fitting than the conventional "life"). A certain disappointment, therefore, haunts *Permanent Change*: parents, loving though they were, are gone, whose own lives show what's family in a family resemblance, including an affirming stoicism. The family resemblance stretches its democracy to include acquaintances and even strangers. Thus we are verged on permanent change, which is, among other things, a virtuous vantage point, even as it is also an oxymoron.

Skoyles' poems depict the world of his parents' generation, and ours. In this way, generations of New Yorkers link up as contiguously, as causally and as aesthetically as the cultures they generate. The approach is often spectatorial—the poet observes the scene he depicts:

> It was easier to see yourself
> than the street outside
> from behind dull windows
> of the candy store.

("43rd Avenue")

As the scenes are now gone, except as they appear in verbal images—which is to say they are metaphysical, Skoyles imagines them in terms of memory's climate—fair or foul, baking or freezing, each memory standing in its own weather, and weather, and we experience that too, as if no image were pure:

This is what the climate
of memory must be:
to breeze through untouched
like a boy in a museum
who moves his fingers
along a death mask's chilled lacquer,
then spins away,
into the neither comprehending
nor indifferent heat.

The weather of memory, its emotional envelope, stands so to speak apart from the objects of memory and establishes their irreducible mystery. The emotional range doesn't veer off into dazzle or burst into ecstasy. Dazzle can't be harnessed and ecstasy won't do: the *lacrimae rerum* are more a philosophical sigh than a drench of tragic resignation. As he opens "Dark Card," "Grief that lingers begins to mock." Skoyles doesn't mind using modifiers to adjust the focus on details. It is one of his talents to add the qualifier whose freshening allows the reader to pause and run her hand over the new construction. Had its currency rendered it a cliché, I would be tempted to say that he allows (and knows that he allows) readers to "savor" the details, like wine snobs drawn to the bouquet of a particularly fine Malbec:

I started to feel extravagant scorn
for the sluggish chat brought on
by flowers splayed like open hands,
her fundamental rouge, and the cold
that trailed everyone's coat
through the putty-like air
of the small funeral home.
I missed the quick encapsulating glee
with which she spoke,
rushing everything together
in the energetic tongue
of those who live alone.

("Dark Card")

Like the moralist poet in a poem by Zbigniew Herbert who plays his music by banging stick to board, Skoyles likes the tunes that can be played on the two strings of attributive modifier and noun. Note how he works two directions with

> The commuters are slightly incognito,
> spies from past holidays,
> wearing useful gifts against the cold.

("On the Train")

Saying "slightly incognito" is like saying slightly famous or slightly suicidal: the phrase slips past its congruency marker to arrive at a condition irrationally precise. And "wearing useful gifts" leads us directly to the pathetically practical gifts that seem to condition our patience with Christmas as surely as the unwrapping of fruitcake. Moreover, we know the wretches forced to wear the ugly scarf, the pathetic sweater, and our embarrassment is laced with gratitude, as Philip Levine notes in a poem about absurd socks that in Detroit winter wring gratitude out of the wearer.

Skoyles wants us to think of him as a passerby—a spectator before a diorama of players. But he is a *flaneur,* curious and in-the-know, a sampler. The thing about a *flaneur* is this: the wandering curiosity and the *savoir-faire* are the mirror image of the Blakean, open, even agreeable, wonderment, but they are not willing to cease shading the brightness. He seems to know intuitively or outright, that the sense of wonder is at odds with intelligence, which when you come from Queens, is a survival skill. Wonder is not.

Skoyles is the kind of person who takes note of deaths rather than births. That is merely to say that he also prefers departures to arrivals, to associating with the last, instead of the first. The past, rather than the future, gets his attention:

> My book of astrophysics fanned out charts
> to prove man
> a nothing in the cosmic fray,

and it was for a nothing,
a death, that I climbed the train.

("Visit Home")

Never have our neighbors been so stranded
in their past. One tries to get to work
and the sound of his footfalls
is surprisingly loud
like pagers turned in waiting rooms.

("Snowfall")

The act of reading, Skoyles knows, can be found in just this way.
Reading—and by extension, the poem—and metonymically, literature itself—even at the level of the haiku or a whimper—broadcasts
its status as surely as if James Earl Jones were in the house. In this
case, the house is a waiting room (a doctor's waiting room?). With
that thought comes all the rage of poetry as a kind of "therapy"
(Keats-style, not Mary Oliver). The waiting room calls up another set
of meanings when Skoyles undertakes his most recent volumes, *Definition of the Soul* and *The Situation*, as we wait to hear the judgment of
the experts: physicians—men of science—come to heal, but also to
pass sentence like judges. The physician, the master of the physical
is no less judge than Hizzoner, who sends you to the slammer for a
myriad of violations. And as we write about the paramount events of
our lives, Skoyles takes his illness—and the body itself as text. "The
Repairman" hints of a new kind of case examination and judgment:

I can't help compare myself
to this man, Mr. Moore:
his prizing of age
to a precious degree;
the frank manhandling
with which he divides
the redeemable from the junk.

In poems like "Holy Cross Church," "The Repairman," and "Front Street," Skoyles comes back to familiar bookends: the starting out, followed in due course by the disappointment of wheel-spinning, followed by the silence and one's wish to wring out a few drops of consolation, even when *requiescat in pace* is superseded by the more utilitarian *pro forma*.

The poet in Skoyles haunts the graveyards of New York, the kind that are staples of mob movies, where the bereaved wear the same razor-black as the cars and it's always autumn, when the leaves try to become metaphors. What better time to talk about worth, than to be that disenchanted figure at the funeral, the one who stands between the yews in dark glasses and vanishes before having to undergo perfunctory consolations with persons, also in black, also in sunglasses? That mystery man makes an elegy and puts the world as he has felt it into it. Such a self-portrait ("every elegy is a self-portrait") joins the big (death, meaning...) with the small (the demise of ordinary individuals, their quick irrevocable demotion to nothingness). In keeping with Skoyles' squeezing of bandwidth, removing like the old Dolby system the high hissing and mushy low moaning—both verging on and bleeding into noise. It's measured as classical in this way, but restraint in the face of dying family is not the same as restraint in the fact of an actual, personal, physical pain of one's own. Uncle Grossman was right: there was no world there until pain came along to make it. But world-making is like that, while memory, death, and pain, plus elegy itself, conspire to make a world that wouldn't be otherwise.

The compressing of the range moves in inverse proportion to the poet's ego, and so it should hardly come as a surprise that Skoyles is a poet of modesty (not a modest poet), whose lack of pretension would seem to stand somewhat at odds with the bite of his diction; it's one part Dalmatian, one part Doberman. *The Situation* (1998) begins with a version of a poem by Pasternak:

> The attempt to separate my soul from yours
> is like the creaking of a lamppost
> against a sapling in the wind.
> Soon someone will come
> and hack through the more fragile one.

The fragile one is, by suggestion, the more loving, as Auden noted. This is as far as a poet of Skoyles' dignity will allow; there is no emotion creep. The humility of the poet extends to the modesty of his subjects, and it is not without sympathy that sex for some is a chunky experience, best encountered first through the ear:

> Sex for them was a burly thud
> that sacked the women
> and bound the men
> to their friends at Elmhurst Lanes
> and the thermos factory.

> ("Ancestors")

Baudelaire, in a sardonic, if sober aside, reminds us that sex is the "lyric for the masses," the body singing electric, though when heard from the exterior perspective—you have to then proceed with a little faith. And he does. The spot-on language isn't a covering for tenderness: it is that tenderness itself. It is perfected language fitted to the dignity of the imperfect. It is an exaltation (you have to go through a lot of language before you get to a "burly thud"). But even with the exalted in language, you have to refine powers of discernment. As he says in "Elegy for Munro Moore": "A friend in a dream / Is not a friend but a dream . . ." The dignity arises out of an incompleteness—of ambition, of resources, of desire. Skoyles achieves what a poem can do so well, when it does it at all, and that is construct the praiseworthy. For what was praiseworthy before there was a poet to articulate its terms? Oscar Wilde says in *De Profundis* that "Every thing to be true must become a religion." Skoyles, who has spent ample ink repudiating the religion of his birth, manages grudging (and sometimes more than grudging) respect for the incense and saints, while aware of the dead end of superstition:

> So for a time, the train existed
> only in the mind of my dreamer,
> until I woke
> to the name of my hometown,
> and rushed off

into an open-air station
straddled by cathedrals.
Sun touched the brass locks on luggage
as if torching them open,
and an overwhelming church bell
tolled a soul from its body.

The poetry, not the religion, verges on magical realism here ("as if torching the brass locks on luggage /as if torching them open") that reminds one of the James Wright, who saw "the droppings of last year's horses / blaze up into golden stones." While there is a solemnity to the soul's response to its summons, it is "overwhelming," and hence not subject to choice. At the same time, the image is visionary, a moment of beholding that begins at once to breed multiple implications. For this reason alone, understatement never goes out of style. When it comes to matters of the spirit, Skoyles is a friendly, though he steers well clear of any unfounded hooey:

We stand and kneel and sing
under the steeple where god
is nothing more than god,
but man is more than man
because he talks to those not there.

("St. Bartholomew's Church")

From my perspective, this distance extends his authority: it's the classical tack, to turn back from the shoals, but leave fellow travelers in mind of the land mass behind them. Skoyles' credo, typically posed as a question, not a statement of belief, can be found in "History":

If we take too much care,
fearful of the god
whose footfalls we hear approaching,
we go nowhere,
caught in the song
of our age,

the flickering storm of ash
from the raked leaves,
and in the flurry,
a black butterfly
bats the air
as it dips through the cinders.
Which one's on fire?
Which has a home in this world?

Skoyles' most recent collection, *The Situation*, raises an issue: what, in fact, is the situation? To which the poet answers, using rhetorical thrust-reversers, with a series of questions:

It's tough, isn't it, star,
to be harangued
by every strain
of brimming heart?

It's hard, isn't it, moon,
when crowds fidget
with their swizzle sticks
as you brighten the bay?

And head, doesn't it hurt
when love ignites
its pesky orbit
and all logic strays?

("The Situation")

That logic strays usually signals the onset of logistical hardship, but here, it's emotional pain. We make a sort of category mistake, he suggests, bringing logic's rage for order to the heart, and the idealism that fuels the heart's red-pencil agenda falls similarly to a "tough" lot, being harangued by what it should be fed by. The situation, in other words, arises when our best selves meet to find commerce with our starkest needs: category mistake indeed! It's human fate to be incongruous, he seems to imply, and yet it is our ill-fitting condition that is the very one that fits. As the late Russell Edson put it, "and of all the things that could have happened, this is the very thing that happens." That is "the situation." Another thing that happens on the way to our desire is illness, and Skoyles' experience in that dour realm brings out the Frost in him, which is to say the human face of Realpolitik. The regnant tone is now fastened to the language that clears up our most desired misconceptions, including the trust that things will work out. Of course they won't, but that's not the point—at least not the main point. Rather, the diction is bright, the cadences—rarely straying farther in space than the tetrameter line—in proper order, neither rushed, nor tempted by the call of the wool-gatherer:

> A girl pats her forehead
> with a powder puff
> as if dotting the letter i

> ("The Wish Mind")

The Situation could be Skoyles' testament. There is something in virtually every poem I would like to point to with admiration, often that thing of a moment's notice that Yeats reminds us took years to get. It's a book that I've added to the essential collections of my generation: I think that now makes half a dozen. There is brilliance in what it refrains from doing (because it does it with panache), though brilliance is exactly the kind of imported word that doesn't get what makes Skoyles' work so impressive. He is the protégé of Alan Dugan ("Uncle Dugan" is felicitous), his forerunners Frost and Larkin. He is in turn, an emanation from the 17th century, who would have been right at home with the religious Metaphysicals. He likewise harmonizes with the musical Elizabethans like Fulke Greville and Thomas Campion. Looking at other languages, I sense poets as varied as Montale, Cavafy, and Vallejo, whose variations are reconciled in the kind of plain Modernism most familiar in art: Morandi, rather than Picasso. At the end of the day, however, he has made his own music and so leaves questions of derivation moot. They are poems of a high poetic intelligence, managing in modest verbal circumstances a meeting of occasion and formal precision that I don't see in his more flamboyant peers. Call me elitist, but I am moved by this very intelligence because its manifestation is a man whose use of language honors both the subject and the language itself, which, until he came along, didn't unify, esteem, lament, or laugh this particular way:

> I stand back
> and perform that cruel gymnastic
> for the soul:
> I take a good look at myself.
> And I begin to laugh
> until I am whole again
> until I know it's not funny.

("Fishing")

On Jordan Smith

Driving through Utica, New York one spring evening back in the 1970s, a colleague who was with me remarked that Utica had never recovered from the Depression—of 1893. That remarks comes to mind when I read the work of Jordan Smith: our wounds are old, the sutures still visible under the sleeve. But just as economics undergoes a metamorphosis to history, so scar tissue, it is always said, forms more tightly than unblemished skin. It is both a reminder, pointing to the disorders out of which we arise, and an earnest against the future.

Smith writes three kinds of poems: meditative lyric poems about upstate New York, poems about music (mostly) and art, and dramatic monologues that update Browning by way of Richard Howard (one of his teachers at Johns Hopkins). Sometimes, the three merge. Even when music is the thing exalted, the song is muted, and the speaker as likely to muse on the wonder of its eternal relevance as if he would, in the next moment, burst into song himself. Let me hasten to secure the very word *song* inside quotation marks, for music in language is a thing to be referenced sooner than undertaken, say what you will. Unfortunately, the temptation to think that referencing music is enough to give a poem its dash of song has led to all sorts of mediocrity, has led to the approval of "chopped prose" in Kinnell's apt phrase. Smith is well aware of the trap, and to say that this poems are "quiet" is not to say that they are deficient in music. Rather, it is to say that they acknowledge the chasm between the music of jostling consonants and vowels, syllables scannable on the flatness of the page in forms' deployments, and the effect of actual notes that may or may not bear linguistic content for a Mozart or Doc

Watson. And thus one could make the case, as Smith seems some-times about to do, that poetry stands in an elegiac relationship to the music it refers to and the music it implies. And this in turn puts us in mind of all the elegiac bestowals that commence when means come up short and the ineffable seems to loom in the beyond in dreams and memories, to say nothing of the desire to experience beauty with a capital B and perhaps there discover what goes beyond the pallia-tive and therapeutic, where so much of our daily poetry founders.

All three of these types imply memory and its cultural territory. They are backwards-looking, not a party to the "hope" that Emer-son identified as the proper stance toward what is not-yet. They are equally about the legacies of imagination and the art and artifice of the towns that dot the riversides of the Hudson and Mohawk. Are they transplanted immigrant communities? Do they converge to share a destiny many years on? What is it like to confront and, in some sense, to take on the old? Smith frequently lets the reader know what's on his mind: "But I was thinking of what it meant to be / In the evening of things…"("Sitting Alone in the Moonlight"). At what point does our desire to take on the olden things so depart from curiosity, growing to become custodial in the way that *caritas* is custodial? It is as if in investigating how these communities managed to cling to the past, the poet is on a quest to find something defini-tive about our relationship to time itself. The search is not simple, as it ramifies in ways that mix public and private. It has become an old canard, for instance, that America is a country minus a deep past, such as European countries can claim. And yet, many regions in the country bear the stamp of the Old Country and thus smuggle the past—and time—into the present. In its old-fashioned and some-times odd municipalities, its deep ethnic loyalties and Horatian ties to the land, *temps perdu* joins the quotidian.

For all that, Smith, like all good poets who have educated and aestheticized themselves beyond the prerequisites for townsperson citizenship, acknowledges an unavoidable alienation from things to which he is also drawn, a melancholy paradox appropriate for the artist who escapes:

I'm too disheveled for suburban
Church-going, too uneasy
In my stride for the country, and
That's just the beginning of how
I don't fit ...

("Grooms Corners", *Three Grange Halls*)

But we are to understand this as less a resistance to commit to a
common fate, than an allegiance to the impersonal knowingness
that goes with love of place. It is in turn a submission to native disposition, though it does not imply belonging:

Listen, you upstate hillsides
Which I have loved
So loyally, you woodlots
and trailers and old farm houses,
Your satellite dishes...

("Money Musk")

Naïveté is not available, but neither is the full-on irony of down-
state natives. Smith's seeming antiquarianism is in fact something
that places him, on the one hand, beside the clapboard participation of Hayden Carruth, and on the other, beside the childhood
snapshots of John Ashbery. It is his sense that so much of the upstate
narrative melts, like the dirty snow of mud season, long after the
season of the suburbanites has arrived in its self-important glory.
These sensibilities feel right at home in surroundings that, they suspect, would have been superannuated, except for the mystery of the
past which, as John Gardner knew, holds the imagination in funny
but tenacious ways: Palmyra, Utica, Rochester, Buffalo. And notice
that we're not talking about Lake George and Saratoga Springs, the
watering-holes of the rich, but of Onondaga and Troy. Then there
are the little towns—Oriskany and Glenn's Falls, the towns of far-
off beginnings, Russia, Paris, Rome, and Poland, hamlets tethered
to whole cultures. With the world of Jordan Smith you get upstate
New York, with its stop-time look, littered town squares, and grange

halls, string bands and plaid-shirts. The nineteenth century is also present, sitting in the back. You get as well a grudging respect for the prejudices of place, of the disqualifying (and yet somehow satisfying or at minimum, wistful) sense that one doesn't belong.

But meditation is a covering and runs the danger of a stultifying reliance on stasis: the object of meditation has nowhere to go, and the subject's only action is mulling, its go-to only verb—"is." Left in the absence of dynamism, yet claiming the privilege of the bestower of blessings, however turned into prose by time and circumstance, Smith often reaches for music and art to expand the view. Music, including opera and the dance, runs through Smith's work like a key vein through the limb of a woodland animal, and like a vein, it has its own pulse that it manifests, even as it also represents stylized movement. Just as Smith's poems have been a meditation on upstate life ("just to catch a glimpse of you as you once were"), with its intrinsic nostalgias, so the love of music coordinates, indeed *orchestrates* a soundtrack of representations that invoke music's ability to compensate for meditation's stillness.

Is the meditator, then, a rhapsode? But of course! When Smith says, "the landscape grows deeper," as he does in "Vine Valley," you had better watch out. You are likely to wind up remembering that "all we are given are the steps of a mower / coming home in the evening along the sheaves," and thereby hangs a sight, in fact a manifold of vision, where, of the heron, we

> can only watch her pass, blue and dun pinions
>   spread, until the scuddings of pines and river
>   are netted in her flight, forgotten . . .

And of the old hymns, another kind of custom:

> Remember, I asked myself,
> that pause before the hymn's last chord,
> how the tenor draws one long breath and turns
> for a moment toward the pews,

filled with the pride his voice is given, sure
that gift is beyond his measure.

("Apology for Loving the Old Hymns")

If the word "beyond" shows its trip wires, you're on the right path. As he remarks in "For Dulcumer & Doubled Voice, " "…we know our lives in the fall / and swell of strings…" Our capacities sometimes stop short of comprehension, that is, pull up at experience and sense something important in the impossibility of wrapping the mind around the very thing we undergo, be it of the moment, or of deep time. Acknowledging this as "something important," a phrase itself that perhaps moves us an inch closer to the fusion of knowledge and felt experience, leaves Smith beholden to the various arts he evokes, none moreso than music, since its relationship to language is rarely desperate. Moreover, its ability to gesture restores the poet's sense that the numinous can, after all, borrow raiment sufficient to reveal itself to us without dragging religion in its wake—almost as if to suggest that religion is music played in the wrong key.

Louis D. Rubin, Jr., the eminent Southern critic and one of my professors at Chapel Hill, wrote: "There were no Good Old Days; my father's generation knew that very well. Yet we are our memory, and we exist in Time. What we can know is the distance we have traveled, and where we have been." And yet, Smith's recourse to dramatic monologue suggests that we can imagine, with some plausibility, places that are a part of only the common memory:

> Your loyalty was to the older sadness
> Of mingled song: pavans danced
> with courtly airs, grief mixed with gladness,
> With elegance.
> This was art's token,
> Which you wore gladly. But now our consorts, broken,
> Play tunes of common madness;
>
> There is no cure.

("A Sad Pavan for These Distracted Times")

There is no cure for the decimation of the old loyalties. The poem remembers one man's quip at the death of Charles I's court composer William Lawes: "Will. Lawes was slain by such whose wills were laws." That is, the rational will always seeks to unseat the song and the dream, supersede the first with its successor, the second, override poetry with criticism. Smith is not unaware that the period of history in which he lives and writes is one more attuned to Cromwell than to Lawes. I used to set as a theme topic the following question: Which would you rather be, the last of the old or the first of the new? By sizable majorities my students would choose the latter. But Yeats was of the opinion that the last brought one the benefits of both nuance and beauty, which required time to craft, just as he understood the labor it would take to secure the powers of artifice.

But then Smith avers in one of his key poems,

> ... if I had hoped to kneel at last
>   On fallen cattails, drink
> And be absolved of my pettiness, minor
>   Fears, minor affections,
> I might tell this more simply.

("Cedar Shoals")

What then is the effect of meditation? If the object is what escapes articulation and can only perhaps be adumbrated in sister arts, what is its status and relevance, such that a poet of accomplishment would be interested? In the same poem, whose meditative title suggests that, imaginatively speaking, we are in a marginal way, Smith writes,

> ... How can I tell you what I felt then,
>   When I had lost myself
> In that trace of spirit—fleet, unspent, common—
>   And found at last nothing
> More than insistent, untranslatable stone.

The stone, as Yeats' catalytic image, returns us to the question of intelligibility, where, in the same poem, fearless Whitman ("the smallest sprout shows / There is really no death") provides no comfort, urging

> ...denial
> Of what lies so deep in
> Longing and grief, is so unanswerable,
> It filled my mouth like stone.

In the midst of elegy or on the trail of a natural analogue, the fear is of incoherence, although the fact would be a given in a tragic world. It may be that Smith has stumbled on the post-tragic, for beyond intelligibility there is the question of belief and whether desire itself counts as a kind of belief:

> Listen,
> If I said such desire seems a kind of love,
> Would you take that on faith,
> Or want to? I sat by those cliffs a long time.

The question of faith exists (or persists) alongside that of coherence (i.e., what is "so unanswerable"). Phrases like "For once I would speak plainly / About what I have loved well." ("Remains") and "I knew that my death meant nothing, /Although there were no words to appease my wonder at it" ("The Dream of Horses") show that the threat of chaos always underlies the discourses of coherence and form and momentary stays. It's not really to show we're adroit with abstractions that we stalk the questions we do. Each question for Smith joins up with a memory of a scene, its *exemplum*. Perhaps, in the spirit of truth-tracking, these meditations enact what they seek, moments of equilibrium, for these things are not, finally, derivative from nature:

> Nothing speaks
> Of the stillness in the scattered
> Shade of the rafters.
> Only a shrilling of crickets and peepers,
> And the redwings
> Crying from the marsh,
>
> Flushing and darting—what peace
> Could I have take from these...

> ("Remains")

Good question, especially when you consider both the abundance of natural upstate charms and the poet's predisposition to consider that they might have something to offer, something connected to "peace." But it is to his credit that he doesn't stop there with the questionable notion of closure (or the more fatal—and romantic— closure of a quietus). Rather, he seems to find what he's willing to accept, even if it isn't what, precisely, he's seeking:

> The memory of loss, which
> Is also the fear of it, let each
> Step alongside this blossoming be
> An accomplishment of the moment's
> Graceful resolution of labor and praise.

("Grooms Corners" from *Three Grange Halls*)

Praise and grace go together here, and they share an arbitrary nature, not unlike chaos. But maybe this is why priests place so much emphasis on the gratuitous nature of grace. It not a bad place to be. At least it's a place we can live with:

> I drive to work in that diminishment
> Of light that comes from staring at the sun.
> The world's not over yet, but it's done.

("AM Classical")

Central to Smith's output, bringing as it does all his themes and moves to the fore are *Three Grange Halls*, originally a chapbook. A grange hall is itself just such a slightly mysterious, fuddy-duddy, yet benign and communitarian, structure fit to provide for an equally mysterious membership. You might say the same for the poems, demotic, yet mysterious in their all-purpose iambic tetrameter and pentameter garb, that set out to describe them. The grange at "Grooms Corners," the first of the halls is "a sometime / Church now," but that fact does not diminish the look of skepticism upon the arrival of the speaker, "without even /A dog for an excuse." While his arrival may invite a cool response, he is anything but unsympathetic to the new iteration of the grange: "I'm thinking of how the word- /Made-flesh is everywhere evident." And yet, as he imagines his encounter, his thoughts bend to an alternative, a working farm:

> Pollen and pitch, buds and seed husks,
> A tractor jouncing slowly between
> The orchard rows. Better work
> Than praise, although my own mind's
> Labor on this day is this self-conscious
> Forgetting of forgetting which becomes
> Almost a prayer.

This grange hall, ironically sacralized, presents its own tempta-tions—of closure, of "the vocative in the place /Of mere presence..." The poem concludes with characteristically nuanced equipoise:

> The hymn
> Dwindles to its blessing, and I get on
> With my walk, the congregation with the sermon,
> Each a text shadowed by the mind's
> Disaffection from this
> Unclarified, unintended plenitude...

If the fullness baffles the unwelcome mind, in "Brunswick Center," the speaker finds difficulty locating the grange hall for a dance and frets over the naming of the granges and of the towns themselves:

> (East, West,
> North, Center) as if speech mapped
> another form of scarcity. The grangers
> Hated the railroads and tight money.
> They wanted a community like
> Water...

Now lost, he imagines he might more profitably be anywhere than where he is, in space or time,

> Maybe I
> Should be in North Brunswick or
> Down the Hudson in East
> Greenbush where Melville taught
> School, already caught in the lifelong
> Habit of being didactic about
> What he knew to be frankly
> Unknowable.

Here we come up against an "opacity" against which only labor, with its rhythms and largely predictable risks, works, reconfiguring time in the plebian image. What's "unknowable" speaks not just to the quality of our questionings, but to our willingness to acquiesce to knowing (and hence to ignorance), at the expense of other equal, if not superior, commitments of mind and being. Once more, the speaker finds himself moving into position to locate, while not in space or time, Yeatsian paradox of thought versus embodiment.

> From one side of the grange hall
> To the other, as if beyond all
> Opacity were an argument
> For light's commonality with dust.

If the image speaks for itself, it's a testimony to our terminal nature, energized by Darwin, but drained by the author of *Moby Dick*. The place of dance, so hard to find, so lacking in tragedy ("That's the thing about a dance. It isn't tragic."—"Elektra") becomes the place of Yeatsian questioning:

> Each road, plainspoken on the map, pointing
> To where the dance goes on, somewhere
> You can't get from here.

The final grange hall, "Malta," finds us among ruins. The poem opens with a time-lapse of dilapidation ("A dozer and backhoe parked in the lot"). But the speaker counters the disappearance of his subject with a freewheeling specificity that moves from do-it-yourself renewal to the draw of music:

> But the clapboard
> Grange hall at the junction of Route
> 67 and East Line Road has stood empty
> Too long on a road given over to useful
> Occupations (a lumber yard, gas
> Station, feed store, and nursery).
> I could get a chain for the saw and pressure-
> Treated timbers for a retaining wall,
> And if there's time, stop on the way
> Back at the mall for another Bill
> Monroe tape...

This burst of activity, part civic-spirited, part deeply private, questions our allegiance to particulars of space and time, "On a road that's just one mile / After another, one mini-mart / To the next." Surely categorical fidelity ironizes itself in the midst of such ubiquitous tackiness. Near the end of the trio, the speaker exclaims,

> How tenuous is our hold, and on
> What, that we can be dispossessed
> So easily?

It is as close to a *cri de ceour* as Smith, whose expressive register is most commonly gentle and unforced, gets. And it's not surprising that he walks it back:

> No
> Wonder I'm off to the hardware store
> For tools to make this endless
> Work of loss seem like something
> I intend...

I believe in the energetic travel of this red plaid shirt of a poem, if that is what it is. The damage control, here as elsewhere, is fine, and that, I realize, is a funny thing to say about damage control. But if loss is dispossession—which is a less robust form of *depriving*—can we argue that we are dispossessed only, and somehow not double-shackled by (conventional) symptoms like depression and despair?

The final line of "Malta," tells us that where we are is, in some sense, what we intend, a notion raised elsewhere but not brought forward as a proposition. But here, with the note of finality ("If there were anywhere else to go.") goes the note of necessity. It is at this point that art returns: to sing, draw, to praise, to write. These things mirror necessity, except that they favor us.

In poems now appearing, Smith writes about the insane but terribly lucid John Clare, who knew better than any poet how to play the lot he was dealt, how to erect the retaining wall, how to do "whatever you do when you've done enough." In "A Chinese Landscape," he considers, again in a manner not unbecoming an Irish poet, how the lyric subsumes dispossession and necessity without resorting to abstraction. It's the art that puts us on equal footing with and within history:

> If I could draw,
> I'd praise those shapes—as elemental, as uncanny
> As the Maine woods that made Thoreau cry out
> *Who are we, what are we?*—with just a few lines,
> Sharp and suggestive at once, and if I could sing, well,
> I'd find a banjo-tuned mountain ballad to take all
> Loneliness into a few broken high notes.

The Final Vocabulary of Gerald Stern

It was Kafka who remarked that in the last analysis, when all is said and done, life isn't ironic. Sadly, I think it was an intuition of this sort that fueled the greatly gifted David Foster Wallace's wariness of his own talent for the ironic turn and of his generation's interest in recentering literature. What I mean is that there has been a perceptible wish to reach for the reset button and refashion serious literature as a species of authenticity (a thesis), rather than let it be one more ironic "take" on some prior and illusory authenticity (an antithesis). In a larger sense—and it is always in the larger sense that the truth of Kafka's aside takes hold—American literature (including poetry) has been seen as having succumbed too long to the tractor-pull of irony. And yet why not let that tractor do its work? Irony is, after all, a defense against the fear that we may be finally incapable of tragedy. At the same time, as ironists have aimed dart after dart at literature's many presumptions, those who allow the occasional nod toward the old belief system have been stigmatized as traditionalists in the bad sense, as benighted Sad Sacks of the cultural right. Gerald Stern's example rejects the injustice of such a claim on its face; as for the assigning of poets into the camp of the right—preposterous!

In Richard Rorty's terms the loss of irony is tantamount to writing in one's "final vocabulary," that end-point of expressiveness where there is no way to pass the buck along: things are as they are, a situation that would have delighted Tolstoy, for whom rhetorical shenanigans were a kind of moral failing, a refusal to insist things be what they were, rather a push that they stand for other things (and as for the leftovers: under the rug!). In the final vocabulary, we are surrounded only with what we hold to be true, with what we really believe: hence, no irony, since irony is just passing the buck of meaning. It is as if Stern's poems are all written in his final vocabulary: they are what they are, and you cannot imagine that they could be something else. That's why he's able to get away with nostalgias another poet couldn't presume to express without inviting knowing jeers. I wonder, reading much contemporary poetry, how much of it could have been otherwise (often, how much of it *should* have been otherwise). When I read Gerald Stern I don't wish any of it could have been otherwise, although I am occasionally, mildly vexed that some of his poems seem pieces ticking toward one grand, baggy symphony that we can't yet see, what with our being, so to speak, on the inside.

Having situated his poems in the context of final vocabularies, I should turn around and point out that perhaps even this is the very illusion—the illusion that poetry deals in final vocabularies—such poetry seeks to overcome. Why? Because once Gerald Stern transposes himself to the page, he becomes "Gerald Stern," a larger-than-life character weeping, trembling, decrying the unjust, the cruelty and coarseness of existence, but praising the natural, the beautiful, the cultured, the steadfast. His are also the intellectual heroes, as if culture is for him one of those key threads that link otherwise temporally and geographically discrete human purposes: individual threads, yes, but rope all the way down. We have seen such self-branding in terms of absurd expansiveness in Whitman, but we have also seen it in terms of more *buffo* limitations with poets such as Paul Zimmer. The virtue of creating a character of oneself is that one no longer has to maintain a respectable relationship to fact. After all, "fact" is just a state of affairs uncomplemented by the warmer breezes of truth, and so not being tied down to that is no biggie. On the other hand, the temptation, as with any persona, is to commend oneself to the clouds. This Stern avoids, while indulging in effusiveness, sentimentality, excessive pity, all the good stuff on whose ridiculous petards lesser poets are more or less continually hoisted. How many times do we find him trembling and weeping, clutching his and others' sorrows? Or launching apostrophes to the air? How many times do we find Stern dutifully observing his own movements, as if the registration of his passage in space and time were of significance in addition to—or beyond—the sanctions of history and place? C. K. Williams, in a fine observation, mentioned how ordinary our collective passage was before Stern's poems came along to "exalt" it. And the fact is that in most cases the effects of these exaltations are bumps: we are goosed into momentarily waking from the dream of subjectivity long enough to see Pittsburgh. Yet Pittsburgh is Pittsburgh, quite apart from anyone's benediction or nostalgia. O'Hara spoke of a kind of versifying he called the "I-do-this, I-do-that-poem." For O'Hara, the designation was self-deprecating; for Stern it is reenactment, and reenactments rewrite time in a way that favors the protagonist-actor-poet at the expense of history. For though it (history) has shot its bolt, yet it curiously returns to take a bow in Stern's poems. The figure of the poet absent of irony dignifies the time that lurches forward as much as the time that goes nowhere— which is much of the time. Thus it would require a persona drenched in nostalgias to make sense of the times in which it set about doing this-and-that. At the same time, time renders the person, as well as the persona. Stern comes from that long line of Romantic seers, the smell of Eden still fresh in their shirts, who know to train the political eye into the not-yet, into what occurs after the book.

As he tells us in a lovely poem about W. H. Auden, Stern suffered from years of neglect, but it was a particular kind of suffering:

> ...I would have to wait for ten more years
> or maybe twenty more years for the first riches
> to come my way, and knowing that the stick
> of that old Prospero would never rest
> on my poor head...

("In Memory of W. H. Auden")

Perhaps poets place too much significance in the laying-on of hands, but even in the absence of a benediction, there is something to commend invisibility, something touching the growth of feelings, provided it be temporary:

> I think of Gilbert all the time now, what
> we said on our long walks in Pittsburgh, how

> lucky we were to live in New York, how strange
> his great fame and my obscurity…
>
> ("The Red Coal")

Many people have noted a similarity of project between the Stern and Whitman personas, and Stern has cautioned readers not to make too much of the similarity. He is right to do so. Whereas Uncle Walt is a census-taker, filling up a roster with what he dreams our democracy will be, Stern is a hoarder of memories who suggests that, notwithstanding the fact that all sweetness is snatched untimely from life, there is a beauty that continues after-the-fact. And this beauty must stand to evoke forgotten bliss and overwritten pain— the bliss of love and family; the pain of war, separation, and death. While both are rhetorically sweeping, one beauty sways outward, the other inward: one is centrifugal, the other centripetal.

To be true, fullness of the human must encompass weakness and failure, loss, pain and incapacity. This is but one reason why a poet is the opposite of a general, who in many other marshaling respects (s)he may resemble. These conditions are also remote to the ironist, whose preferred road leads to nihilism. Embracing the powers of the weak is one of Stern's specialties. It allows him to maintain an often inflated persona because the character that "Stern" is becomes larger-than-life by carrying all of life, things insignificant or regrettable, as well as laudable and traditionally important. As a result, he finds his own mind reflected not in empirical models with which most are familiar: the blank sheet, the scientific theory, the ratiocinations that lead inexorably to powerful conclusions at the expense of freedom, imagination, and love. Thus the discarded, the invisible, and the minor provide him with a more fully human image than an idealism that would allow him to go "from strength to strength." In "I Remember Galileo," he refuses to identify with the master power-strategies of knowledge, preferring an image of the confused and weak, at whose expense such knowledge is mounted:

> I remember Galileo describing the mind
> as a piece of paper blown around by the wind,
> and I loved the sight of it sticking to a tree

or jumping into the backseat of a car...
but yesterday I saw the mind was a squirrel caught
    crossing
Route 80 between the wheels of a giant truck,
dancing back and forth like a thin leaf,
or a frightened string, for only two seconds living
on the white concrete before he got away,
his life shortened by all that terror, his head
jerking, his yellow teeth ground down to dust.

Having found the image of his mind, a thing closer to the animal than to a machine for abstract procedures, the speaker has a "eureka" moment and breaks, as he often does, into apostrophe, which is tantamount not only to having discovered something to say, but something to present to his "wild God" as acknowledgment of his—and our—humanity:

O philosophical mind, O mind of paper, I need
    a squirrel
finishing his wild dash across the highway,
rushing up his green ungoverned hillside.

As Blake knew, animals are a part of our humanity as much as humans are a part of the general creaturehood. In fact, it makes more sense to turn "humanity" into a big tent than to extol virtues of creatureliness among humans. Only people fail in offices of love and moral deportment: animals, we recall, were exempt from the effects of the Fall. Meanwhile, when it comes to being brutes, no one scores like good old *homo sapiens*. Upon this thought, Stern has excelled in reinstituting the force of pity, that old-fashioned and yet not superannuated word.

You who knelt on the frozen leaves,
you know how dark it got under the ice;
you know how hard it was to live
with hatred, how long it took to convert
death and sadness into beautiful singing.

("Singing")

When Stern arrived on the national scene in 1977, it was almost as
if, in spite of Wright, Levine, Hugo, Simpson, and their confréres, no
none had ever trained American poetry continuously on defenseless-
ness, not as per victimhood, but as per virtue and beauty. Hence the
rich title of his most-anthologized poem, the road-kill masterpiece,
"Behaving like a Jew":

> —I am going to be unappeased at the opossum's death.
> I am going to behave like a Jew
> and touch his face, and stare into his eyes,
> and pull him off the road.

The unforgettable final image of "the little dancing feet" identi-
fies the lowly opossum's suddenly stilled movement with the possibility implicit in the "dancing" squirrel of the mind in "I Remember Galileo." The bodies of animals figure prominently in Stern's
poems, but none more hauntingly than "The Dog," which is itself
a haunting, the canine in question speaking posthumously to the
same reader that would witness the shock of the squirrel and the
mute opossum pulled from the "greasy highways." This is a lot of
disbelief to suspend, but that overhead is, you might say, the degree
of difficulty whose overcoming will win something not at all unlike
belief to accompany appreciation (for appreciation in this kind of
poetry will not suffice). The poem is also "Behaving Like a Jew" written from the non-human point of view:

> What I was doing with my white teeth exposed
> like that on the side of the road I don't know,
> and I don't know why I lay beside the sewer
> so that lover of dead things could come back
> with his pencil sharpened...

The dog's—and Stern's—sly reference to the poet as a "lover
of dead things" paints elegy with the same quizzical brush as any
deathly activity. It is not that we die, but that we know we do, that
brings our fallen experience close to the tragic, which becomes a
possible ground, both for self-understanding and for love, even if

these things are never realized. The dog's slightly different understanding of mortality throws the poet, the object of the dog's observations, into relief:

> I think his pencil must be jerking and the terror
> of smell—and sight—is overtaking him;
> I know he has that terrified faraway look
> that death brings—he is contemplating.

The speaker then tips his hand (or paw) in one of those cascades of emotion for which Stern is famous:

> Great heart,
> great human heart, keep loving me as you lift me,
> give me your tears, great loving stranger, remember
> the death of dogs, forgive the yapping, forgive
> the shitting, let there be pity, give me your pity.
> How could there be enough?

The dog instructs the teacher, the poet, in a way that suggests, in relating the lesser to the greater, the relationship of the human to the divine. We may be a dog's divinity, but as our creature, the dog is ours by virtue of having given up his wildness. Yet he stands to teach us about our condition, and that teaching is greater than the "little tricks" and domestication for which we congratulate ourselves and our new dependents:

> I have exchanged my wildness—little tricks
> with the mouth and feet, with the tail, my tongue is a parrot's.
> I am a rampant horse, am a lion,
> I wait for the cookie, I snap my teeth—
> as you have taught me, oh distant and brilliant and lonely.

The final image, from the perspective of the ground (and soon, the ditch), finds the poet isolated in the tower of his inquisitions, and it is questionable whether he can understand the meaning of the dog's soliloquy. Be that as it may, we are made to understand that our relationship to death is special in one sense, just as it is utterly ordinary in another. The special sense—that elevates us—is also the one that leaves us distant and, above all, lonely.

The format for many of Stern's poems is syllogistic: if A, then B. This thought-template, if you will, takes two forms in Stern's work. In "The Dog" and "Behaving Like a Jew," his speakers suggest that if, say, roads must be built at the expense of innocence, then the poet is going to be forced to resort to ancient stereotypes, themselves the enemy of bourgeois conformity: in the one case, a curious poet; in the other, a Jew. Elsewhere, the syllogism takes an even more denuded form:

> If you know about the Babylonian Jews
> coming back to their stone houses in Jerusalem,
> and if you know how Ben Franklin fretted
> after the fire on Arch Street,
> and if you yourself go crazy when you walk through the old shell
> on Stout's Valley Road,
> then you must know how I felt when I saw Stanley's Cafeteria
> boarded up and the sale sign out…

("Straus Park")

While these syllogistic wind-ups are sometimes gnomic, they always put forward the suggestion that intellect is an honorable thing, something learned by means of which we can conduct our lives. They also set about establishing a complicit air in which poet and reader are assumed to be part of the same significance grid and participate in a process during which the reader completes the logical circuit. And so it is with every poem, you say. Yes, but Stern's repetitions, like a bolero, are designed to pull the reader tighter, to get in the reader's face:

> If you saw me walking one more time on the island
> you would know how much the end of August meant to me;
> and if you saw me singing as I slid over the wet stones
> you would know I was carrying the secret of life in my hip pocket…

("If You Saw Me Walking")

It is the tightness of that grip that lets you know you are in the arms of someone who not only wants to impart information about himself, about how it is with him, but about how it is within the zone of his affections. And that, as we see with the animals, is an altogether larger matter.

As with his nostalgia for the texture and feel of culture, particularly in its lost mode, luminescent minds also populate the place where his imagination and memory cross. Readers are not surprised to find heroes of the mind and art as varied as Brahms, Bach, Beethoven, Coleridge, Dostoyevsky, Schoenberg, Wagner, Stieglitz, Casals, Debs, Luxemburg—the list is long. In "Fritz," he offers another explanation for this proliferation of cultural naming. Remembering having seen violinist Fritz Kreisler in Pittsburgh in the 1940s, he wonders,

> What have we lost?
> Does Kreisler belong to the dead? Was that a world
> of rapture that we lived in? In what year
> did he fix his imagination. Will there be strings
> two hundred years from now? Will there be winds?

The questions are hardly academic, for what is the sense of culture if sense itself, starting from our forebears and ourselves, changes into unrelatable forms from which we are unintelligible to humans of the future? But the ace up Stern's sleeve concerns what it is that is rapturous about any world—lost, present, or to come. Passion is the key because passion is the cure for cold thought. He plays that ace just when it seems wistfulness and nostalgia will cover the memory of Kreisler in unlikely Pittsburgh, Stern's home town:

> I love him
> because he strayed from the art, because he finished
> his formal training at twelve, because he was whimsical
> and full of secret humors.
> To this the speaker counters,
> I began
> my journey in 1947. I wrote
> four hours a day, I read five books a week.

I had to read five books, I never knew
the right hand was raised like that. I never knew
how trapped the body was. I didn't believe
you gave yourself to the fire like that.

But, like Kreisler ("who knew both Schoenberg and Brahms") he
realized that,

after
awhile—if the brain was in the fingers—the heart
was all that made the sound, whatever I mean
by "sound," and that we have to start with feeling—
we poor machines—which stood me in good stead
for ten or twenty years, that and Marlowe's
tears, and Coleridge's soft flight, and Dostoyevski's
rack—it was the fire that moved me.

Dedication to art can be its own religion, and one often senses
that such is the case with Stern. For him it is a religion that dovetails
with Christ and the Jews and exhortations to pity, not by-and-by,
but at all points. In "Soap," the poet who has pulled us so close that
we share his breath, both at the necessary intake and the artificed
expression, now takes us on a tour of ultimate inhumanity, but does
so by holding the item—soap—both dear and familiar. This little
commodity, by which we make ourselves clean, was, as everyone
on earth now sadly knows, perverted into one of the last century's
most shocking atrocities. Indeed, turning humans to soap is a kind
of inverted triumph of ingenuity, the likes of which evil has been
waiting centuries full of dull tortures to invent.

I buy a black Romanian for my shelf.
I use him for hair and beard,
and even for teeth when things get bitter and sad.
He had one dream, this piece of soap,
if I'm getting it right,
he wanted to live in Wien
and sit behind a hedge on Sunday afternoon
listening to music and eating a tender schnitzel.

There is enough tenderness in the "tender schnitzel" to make it stand for a whole lament. Unfortunately the schnitzel exists in the imagination only, not in Wien and not in the mouth of the Romanian, but it becomes all the more desirable and delicious to the extent that the Romanian has been transmogrified.

> I write this poem, for my little brother, if I
> should call him that—maybe he is the ghost
> that lives in a place I have forgotten, that dear one
> that died instead of me—oh ghost, forgive me!—
> Maybe he stayed so I could leave—oh live forever!
> forever!

There is no one I know who comes close to the real tenderness of Stern's poems. All that is lost is what is within reach. His poems ask over and over: what is tenderness worth? Why does pity fail? When does moaning become music? Surrounded by the dead, he is like those few other poets who have imagined the underworld and the clamoring desire of the dead to seize the opportunity of their visitor's presence. They would hear news of the future and to be remembered, to have their limbs rejoined, and their lives resumed. His greatest blessing: live forever! Notice that it comes straight after "forgive me." But then "forgive me" means something akin to "bring me back to life." But in this case it's the dead who are being asked to forgive the living, to bring the living back to life. Stern, who punctured the end-stopped subjectivity of the 'Seventies by titling his breakthrough book *Lucky Life,* finds life lucky in just this respect: the honor of requesting forgiveness from the dead means too that he writes to the dead. And that is the best way to instruct the future in its obligation not to disappear among in its own tempting lotus-eaters, its own unknowable nihilism.

Gerald Stern's *Save the Last Dance*

If you've read *American Sonnets* and *Everything Is Burning*, the previous collections, then you know the kind of poem you can expect from *Save the Last Dance,* Gerald Stern's latest. Like Picasso, Stern, now in his 80s, has moved into a phase that mediates between immutable fact and implacable desire by adjusting the succession of content and image upward (a feat for the verbally robust Stern) while adjusting the level of form downward. Some people I know don't go for late Picasso, those kinetic paintings done sometimes three and four a day. I find them, however, full of righteous impatience and imaginative candor. They're impatient with our sense of time as luxury and at the same time never fail to keep desire working at high pressure. Did someone just think that Gerald Stern must be in a state of contradiction? So he contradicts himself, but age explodes the containers which are, in some sense, a kind of formal set of markings that let us discriminate between one work and the next, rather than giving us license to think of the whole as more worthy of our contemplation than the parts. Stern has always seemed to be writing one long Representative Man poem (albeit a Man of startlingly large humanity and feelings), and the short poems of recent memory both continue and fill in while giving a means to let waves of perception and memory take their place.

For most, the years become a brake the mind taps, sometimes without its being aware, but for others, fit though few, the mind speeds up in age. Stern is, as Flannery O'Connor would say, "one of the latters." In recent years he has developed a stylistic advance that departs from his familiar ebullience by appearing to be less anaphoristic than free-associational:

Diogenes for me and sleeping in a bathtub
and stealing the key to the genealogy room
close to the fake Praxiteles and ripping
a book up since the wrath had taken me
over the edge again and you understand
as no one else how when the light is lit
I have to do something.

("Diogenes")

Their relentless insistence on flow and overflow, of juxtaposition and chance dealing of emotions and things, reminds me just how language is another thing to put beside our emotional, moral, experiential life-kit. When you realize that it is a thing of "marks and noises" (and here, I was about to add *just* marks and noises), you begin to see with what facility it can accommodate rapid-fire thought. Brodsky remarked that poetry is thought running at maximum velocity. While it's true that a great poet's multitasking is a redoubtable thing, you don't always notice the fact of that velocity. With Stern you are rarely allowed to notice otherwise. Take, for example, "Traveling Backward," a poem that snaps from backward to forward like a pinball off a loaded cushion:

Traveling backwards in time is almost nothing
for here is the brain and with it I have relived
one thing after another but I am wavering
at only reliving though what is hard is being there—

From here it's not clear where the poet must go, or that his going there will seal the deal of meaning, but something happens that is satisfying, even if its level of indeterminacy looks almost like caprice:

I don't know what the Germans called it, existing,
non-existing, both at once, there is a rose
explaining it, or it's a table;
imagine that, from one tree and its branches
once it was rooted, once the leaves were glabrous
and coruscating, then came everything.

And sure enough, once "glabrous" and "coruscating" enter as terms and instruments of judgment, then, as Wittgenstein promised of Moore's "proof" that he had a hand, you can have all the rest. As he gets older, you notice even more, if more were necessary, the degree to which Stern is a master at evoking the sensory world through everything he says. Words themselves almost become living things. And then at the far end of the mind, those pesky Germans—like the difference between sense and nonsense, determinism and chance, Leica and Luger—occupy a space between profundity and atrocity; they are "both at once." Perhaps the larger point is that the accumulation of experiential stuff supersedes the organization and deployment of all stuff whatsoever because the mind wants it all ("such is my mind") and beyond even that, emotion cries out to the mind to submit to its service. Thus organization—as per Germans, as per order versus time—often bends the note sourly:

> and what did
> I need the dried-out grapes for and the wet
> leaves and one harmonica under a rusted
> burst-out water-pipe and even a mangled
> sparrow under the porch the way my brain works.

("Dream III")

Stern is one of those poets who wants you to go along with him, to become a co-conspirator. He gets an amiable salesman's foot in the door with outlandish emotional or whimsical charm, then works these into trust—which is just as well, as underlying his poems is not only the sense of wonder that brightens the surfaces but the continual pall, first of history, then of reflections on history, then of desire *mit* shuttering fall of the real, then of nature and our common destiny in time and "dirt." Not for nothing do several of the new poems deal in the foot, in the shodding of Americans ("Thom McCann") who might otherwise believe their heads and the products of their heads were paramount.

It is in such a collaborative spirit that the last, and most surprising (and satisfying) poem unfolds: "The Preacher," a chapbook-length

reflection on *Ecclesiastes*, especially, as he notes, in view of Alicia
Ostriker's essay (which appeared in *The American Poetry Review*)
on the Hebraic and linguistic nuances of that book, in which the
"vanity" of "all is vanity" is sourced to more elemental meanings of
"wind," "mist," and "spirit." An interlocutor, the poet Peter Richards,
and Stern discuss this most-quoted and least-understood book of the
Bible in terms of the ambivalence inherent in "holes," of which lacunae, graves, buckets, Pascalian abysses, mole holes, empty thoughts,
historical and national omissions qualify as specimens. The dialogue that ensues between Stern and Richards builds a text of great
cumulative power, micro to macro, *urbi et orbi* that, as a repository, is
itself a hole and at the same time the very opposite of a hole, being
fuller and fuller as we read.

> "What made you think
> of a hole the way you did?" he [i.e., Peter] asks.
>
>   "My figures
> always start with the literal and the spreading
> is like blood spreading," I say, "and as for the wound it
> comes from growing up with coal, the murder
> of everything green, rivers burning, cities
> emptied, humans herded, the vile thinking
> of World War I and II, the hole in England,
> the hole in Germany, and what we can't en-
> dure, the hole in Japan..."

That coal, which goes from black to red in the poet's *oeuvre*,
no longer needs a gloss to underscore its special significance re:
Pittsburgh, fame, inspiration, friendship; neither does the movement toward questions of judgment, often political, need continual
support:

>   "It's justice you want,
> isnt it? quoth Peter.
>
>   "I'll tell you what,
> (I say) when I see a hairy vine encircle a

tree and make its red mark on the life sap
gushing desperately into the forementioned leaves I
even sigh then..."

The question of form that I mentioned in relation to the poems
in the first sections of the book is addressed in "The Preacher," too,
as is form's ambivalent nature. Peter begins a telling exchange:

                    ...form was a bucket, it stood there
tilting a little on a rock, it was
inside the bucket, and sloshing, give it three days
and it would evaporate, it would return
as form always does, to air.
                    I was still struggling
to free the poem," I said, "to free the poet,
buckets sound good to me, Immanuel Kant sounds
good, Schiller sounds better. I shouldn't be spending my
time doing this, the only point is releasing
the tongue...

The ambivalence is that the hole, what we might call the receptiv-
ity receptacle, is, in its other aspect, a drum. Peter notes that this
key image, in moving from hole to drum, also moves from mere air
(the "vanity" of *Ecclesiastes*) to the membrane of presence, the music-
maker's instrument:

                    ...but if I turn the bucket over
I have a drum, and I can start with
fingers or palms, I hold it between my knees
it's always held like that—and it was tilted,
as everything is tilted.

This is good, but Stern is not content to leave it there. In his rejoin-
der, he laments,

                    ...what I
long for more than anything else is speech
not tilted, it breaks my heart that I
grew up in darkness so.

We're left to wonder if that tilting in darkness isn't also a kind of tilting in rhetoric, of the sort that Dickinson recommended for its "slant" but that for the very same reason Tolstoy was moved to condemnation. It is no easy thing, the releasing of the tongue.

"The Preacher," in its sturdy, yet nuanced approach to language, spirit, vanity and air, reminds me of another long poem (one of *Two Long Poems*, 1990), one that didn't make into the 1998 volume, *This Time: New & Selected Poems*. But I remember well its final poignant admonition, one that resounds in a universe where lamentations are rich in love, and love, rich in lamentation. The dance of these two—the "last dance," whose binary motion both embodies ambivalence and celebrates the "wild God" of his imagination is as close as we can get to an unwobbling pivot of a great poet's mind: "That's right," the speaker says when confronted with inept meddlers and facile Prometheuses: "No fucking with the stars!"

A. Van Jordan's *Quantum Lyrics*

David Wagoner is not the only poet looking down from his summit of seniority to lament that the chief fault bedeviling younger poets is their willingness to accept work not fully imagined. Surely it befits our ADHD epoch that this curse has sometimes come to be accorded the status of a virtue. But the contrasting figures cut by some 40-ish poets, educated in the same workshops Wagoner implicitly faults and whose reputations have arisen post-millennium, show an inclination to keep what we might call the verities of poetry under review. Though irony is still a staple, the heady whiff of nihilism is not there. It's just such a regard that distinguishes a poet like A. Van Jordan. In fact, in his new book, *Quantum Lyrics*, there is sometimes a sense that the overtopping of imaginative fill is the norm that he practices and, in practicing, implicitly recommends. Early on in this book, whose title alone shows its eagerness to blind us with science, comes a lecture by Richard Feynman that shows just such a fullness of imagination:

> Love begins in the streets with vibration and ends behind closed doors in jealousy. Creation and destruction. What do we pray for but the equation that helps us make sense of what happens in our daily lives? What do we believe in if not that which tells us we're alive? Sex, laughter, sweat, and equations elegant enough to figure on our fingers. Math is spirit and spirit is faith in numbers: both take us to the edge but no further than we can imagine.

("Richard P. Feynman Lecture: Intro to Symmetry")

The scientific lens, one that poets of my generation have sometimes applied as cognate to their own work, quickly brings to focus what is, at bottom, of interest to Van Jordan in this volume: race, history, popular culture, science as a generator of language and grammar. He is also keenly drawn to melodrama figured in terms of dualities: necessity versus chance, access to knowledge versus secrets, and identity versus freedom from identity's burdens. You can collapse some of these by argument and make others vanish by changing the subject: the mechanism, the working out, of many of the poems in this volume shows how. Others you cannot. Knowing the difference is all.

Although Einstein's inner life provides the massive centerpiece for this collection, it is bookended by poems delivered in the voice of Feynman bearing on the question of symmetry, which is to say, the question that addresses what aspects of a system remain unchanged as transformations get in gear. Like other borrowings from physics in this book—relativity, quantum mechanics, the uncertainty principle, string theory—the emphasis is on the application to existential and psychological facts about people. These borrowings carry with them the same cautions as with, say, Social Darwinism—that is, it may be science over there, but it's metaphor in here. That said, Van Jordan's appropriation of concepts that physicists would prefer remain locked inside their disciplines and terminologies, reminds me of the easy tactical use of Ptolemaic schemes in poems of the 17th century. And while no less an Einstein-and-Feynman-level egg-head—Ludwig Wittgenstein—pointedly warned against large-scale vocabulary switching as delusional, its use in poetry is clear, as the very terms come *tout compris* with their handy metaphorical menus already charted out.

What makes the question of symmetry first and foremost is the question of whether culture itself can continue in some fashion "unchanged" by hungry generations without or faulty memory within. An early poem, "Que Sera Sera" tells the story of the young poet, already understandably transitioned from Doris Day to Sly Stone, who is pulled over in small-town North Carolina and is about to receive a driving-while-black citation when the mirror-shaded officer is nonplussed to find that the driver is a professor and poet at the local college. Adjusting his dignity, he lets his prey go. This poem's counter-lyric, "R & B," the final poem in the collection, takes place years later when the speaker finds himself contemplating the fates of two young Arby's employees whom he at first mistakes for young men locked in the monotony of gangsta rap, who surprisingly call upon him to adjudicate a question on the strange similarity between the falsettos of Al Green and Ron Isley. Feeling generational already, as his father has just died, the speaker finds consolation in the notion that such questions still matter, although he has himself—in the eyes of the young employees (and in the eyes of the reader)—moved from the on-deck circle to the plate:

> Here I insert a caesura, while I ponder this cogent point:
> You know, I say, you've got a point.
> I never thought about it before, but it's true.
> If you listen to Ron Isley, and didn't know the song,
>
> one might mistake him for Al Green. At this moment,
> I laugh with these brothers louder than I've laughed
> since my father's death.

Albert Einstein is so much the icon-in-chief in this book, as he is in pop culture and Andy Warhol, that he can be made to bear a raft of meanings, even as the facts of his life—his affairs, marriages, and emotional detours—are not in dispute. He can also be made into a kind of cartoon figure, just as, later in the collection, a second-string DC Comics hero is promoted to the status of a person. This willingness to let historical figures and cartoon characters exchange hats matches the further emanations of relativity, in which the subjective lays a wreath at the tomb of objectivity—all of which is standard operating procedure for lyric poetry anyway:

> This is relativity.
> Journalists ask for a definition,
> but the answers are all around:
> a woman loves you for a lifetime
> and it feels like a day; she tells you
> she's leaving, breaking it off,
> and that day feels like a lifetime ...

("Einstein Ruminates on Relativity")

Van Jordan further warms the Einsteinian pop-cultural credentials by writing in the form of an imagined screenplay. It brought
John Collier to my mind, whose own *Paradise Lost: A Screenplay for
the Mind* wed Milton to *Star Wars*. Van Jordan's Einstein sometimes
comes across as a League of Justice worthy—one of those whose
powers embody, even as they conceal, yearnings and anxieties. Van
Jordan's Einstein goes the distance in uncovering the relativity of
private life, and one senses that it is the private life and the shifting
waveform of its perspective that is a manifold topic for the poet too:

> It's much harder
> to comprehend what men and women
> share than the universe's infinity
> which is more difficult to grasp

("My dear, naughty little sweetheart")

One of the key issues of this private, domestic relativity is the place
of intimacy and indeed, in a wider sense, of irrationality's claim on
a man supposedly inspired by the grail of rationality. But this is the
same man whose science leads him back to the interplay of desire
and chance, the very spot from which, in a sense, he took flight. Van
Jordan also expresses this as the difference between chance and
necessity. As Schrödinger observes:

> We're born
> with no lovers on the horizon; we go along like Einstein
> trying to find our purpose and then we look up and wonder
> how we got here. We don't know
> if we willed it, or if we fell in with the body next to us.

("Erwin Schrödinger")

What Schrödinger realizes, in his capacity as a specimen of *homo
sapiens*, is that chance is itself what is necessary. Well might he put
the matter thus because it's the quantum nature—that is to say, the
fundamentally unknowable nature of love—that sets his colleague

Einstein on and that invites reciprocation from Einstein's first wife, Mileva. Here, Einstein is talking,

> Everything we do in life comes down to experiments
> with love and curiosities. Lives should be experienced as two
> children masquerading as adults. Although the public reads
> the work of scientists and poets, this they don't understand.

("Collaboration: Albert and Mileva")

Elsewhere the relative nature of love is as reversible as the lovely nature of relatives (the Shrödinger poem follows upon the death of Einstein's second wife, his cousin Elsa):

> That love is born not out of deceit but from the quest for light,
> makes me shake my head. No man has held wife and lover both,
> not even Einstein, and not been changed, indelible with wonder.

("Erwin Shrödinger")

These are indeed the vexations of a man, albeit a supernerd, but therefore all the more vulnerable to hints of unpredictability, even as he (Einstein) wants to ground all in a unified field theory, even up to the moment of his death.

Van Jordan dramatizes Einstein's—i.e., ironically Everyman's—push-pull relationship to certainty in terms of knowledge of the outside world, of self, love, and fidelity. He also contextualizes Einstein's subjectivity with reports of other scientists who also, as it were, collaborated in the undoing of the Newtonian template, but also from a more consciously dramatizing and racially aware social and artistic world. Here the names themselves take on importance: Charlie Chaplin, W. E. B. DuBois, Paul Robeson, Marian Anderson, figures for whom margins and centers were of abiding interest. Van Jordan also makes the point that Einstein's work involved some heavy collaboration with first wife Mileva, subsequently omitted in the record ("Your little urchin experimented / with the math, unveiling mysteries with you in the shadows."). Whitman knew how to flourish with

contradiction, and Hopkins knew that dappled things were another
way of talking about Schrödinger's cat, but it took science another
fifty years to sign on to the quantum nature of reality (a nature that
left Einstein himself most unhappy).

Van Jordan's accomplishment is to show us ways into this new
world, brave or otherwise, unauthorized by official history, but sanctioned, like biography itself, by plausibility. Take this encounter with
Chaplin:

> Two men with charisma.
> A world begins with an embryo
>
> of ideas, motion, velocity,
> and ends with comic tragedy,
> and thought experiments and proofs,
> with flirtation, marriage and divorce.
> Whatever we need to know
>
> can be learned by watching a tramp
>
> ("Society Page Review of *City Lights*")

Just as Chaplin's triumph was to create a character whose dignity
grows in inverse proportion to his worldly successes, so Einstein is
the intellectual magician whose famous theory becomes the more
baffling as it approaches real life. The difference between them is
also expressed in terms of their perceived differences:

> The world sees Chaplin and sees
> the human condition; they see
> Einstein and ask, Dr.,
> where is your mind leading us?
>
> ("Society Page Review of *City Lights*")

The key here, the structuring idea that keeps the montage from
drifting off involves, of course, all the equivocations and variations
that can be wrung from the Einstein keywords. Each poem in the

montage is a cut-to or flashback, and the implicit invitation to think
of the sequence as a movie is, I think, an attractive one. Smuggling
tricks of cinema into poems is hardly a new idea anyway (see Yan-
nis Ritsos), and as a matter of fact, it did make me briefly entertain
the notion that I was reading a screenplay for a movie tracking the
parallel tasks of science and marital fidelity.

This is a book of extensions and proliferations followed by inver-
sions and unwindings. The initial promise of objective clarity (in
science and poetry) gives way to the *longueurs* of subjective misalli-
ance as the years pass (i.e., private life). The book's architecture also
replicates this exchange of energies as the cartoon section inverts
the Einstein section. Here, a microscopic cartoon hero takes center
stage, all earnestness and struggle, not the halo-haired, just, mystery-
encumbered, larger-than-life icon. Of the Lilliputian Atom, toonpe-
dia.com mentions his "'atom-size' schticks, such as launching himself through a window by grabbing hold of a shade cord." This hero,
himself a scientist, plays the foil to humanize Herr Professor Einstein who, at length, certainly needed no additional humanization,
especially from a cartoon. Indeed, the whole section exists to show
just how human genius is. Certainly the montage, for all its charms,
makes this plain. Yet, the Atom's adventures inversely parallel the
Nobel scientist's, and his ground-up trajectory mirrors Einstein's
entropic coming-to-terms with the contradictions, inconsistencies,
and equivocations down on 112 Mercer Street in Princeton.

The value of a book like this is that it offers new ways to get at
notions of fame and with it, the use of equivocating tools—words—
in a universe supposedly ruled by the no-nonsense hand of math-
ematics within the no-nonsense framework of physics. The irony of
fame is that it lies somewhere between gossip and public knowledge:
it falls upon our ears with downy contingency, but over time it may
come more and more to resemble something we ought to know—or
something we think we do know.

There being two sides, etc., equivocation permeates the sense of
Quantum Lyrics—and therein lies its irony. When Einstein writes W.
E. B. DuBois, he might as well be subbing for Eliot: "There exists no
erasure for race," the physicist intones. Van Jordan's Einstein—and

his amatory accomplices—are as in love with the sounds of words as
they are with each other and with numbers and symbols. One unsettling thought is that the equivocal nature of our communications
tools mirrors the relativity that rules the physical realm. If that's
so, then one could argue that reality itself is somehow grounded in
aesthetics, a thought that swings all by itself between alarming and
charming. There's no point in arguing that reality is "constructed"
in language: the former already comes ready to be understood any
of a number of ways—all subjective. This is a rich and accessible collection, enjoyable, and knowledgeable: it must be the first poetry collection in memory to feature not only endnotes, but a bibliography.
It is tightly structured, so the whole feels informed by symmetries
that pass beyond the obvious, yet the voice is capable of operating
in numerous registers, sometimes simultaneously, just as that voice's
resonance invites the partnership of memory and judgment, all too
often forced apart, from the reader.

Walser/Pantano: *Oppressive Light*

Like the *fort-da* of Freud, the "I" of a poem both proclaims and conceals. Swiss-born Robert Walser, the novelist, short-story writer, poet and member of the generation that included Kafka, Trakl, and Hesse, wrote small poems of uncanny subjectivity, a trait he shared with the knowing, endlessly alienated, endlessly accommodating imaginations of his peers. But no one would confuse the limpid style of his poems with that of anyone else. Fancy, if you will, a balloon and let that balloon represent the speaker in Walser's poems. The surface of the balloon manages almost to cast back something of the environment in which it floats, while simultaneously registering the movements of the mime-like creature within that creases and distends the surface. Walser is both the speaker who describes—in a roundabout way—his surroundings and records, often in ways that feel like inverse sculpturing, the man who makes his pilgrimage. This man both is and isn't Everyman: you may hear your thoughts in accents other than you are used to, but at the end of the day, you will find Walser has composed in that "final vocabulary" where meanings stop their spin, and the balloon surface becomes, finally, a mirror.

Daniele Pantano, himself a Swiss poet who has previously translated Dürrenmatt and Trakl, does a superb job in making the English speak in German, even as it speaks in English, so that I found myself lifting my eyes from the text, saying, wait a minute: this is not in English: it's in German! Only then does "this" refer to the original, which is indeed not here. It is usually the case that a translation becomes at once an elegy for the poem that isn't there: the striver's sense of linguistic duty that emanates from the translation only reminds one of the fact. Pantano's renderings are free of that sense of the loss of meaning. *Oppressive Light* also comes with handy references and an afterword, and the introduction by Carolyn Forché is superb in placing Walser's poetry, not only within his *oeuvre*, but within the several phases of his life, the years of peregrinations between Switzerland and Germany, only to end in an asylum. It was there he famously averred, "I'm not here to write. I'm here to be mad!" Those who visited him there did not find him mad, but the poems preceding his arrival locate him, in Forché's words, writing "his way toward a liminal state of non-attachment and hovering, weightless acceptance."

> There is a little tree in the meadowland
> and many more good little trees there too.
> A little leaf freezes in the frosty wind
> and many lone little leaves there too.

("A Little Landscape")

The "non-attachment" takes several forms in *Oppressive Light*. In a contingent world, such as the previous quote implies is the case, there is the declining of commitment on the part of the *flaneur*, a creature of Baudelarian dimensions, urban, urbane, pursued by ennui, but determined to give it the slip by indulging in odd appreciations. One thinks of Baudelaire (minus the inverted Catholic zeal), of poets as distinct as Verlaine, Prévert, and Reverdy and in our own language, of writers as never-before appearing in the same sentence as Bruce Chatwin and James Schuyler. Note that my examples are heavily tilted toward the French. It was the French who invented the type, though by the time Hans Castorp appeared in German Literature, it had become a virtually iconic European character: he passes by (or in Castorp's case, he perches) and observes, in the course of which observations he becomes, for closer or farther, the focus of his own discourse. The sound of this character goes like this:

> Here I live like a child, enchanted
> by the idea that I've been forgotten.

....

Of course, people forget each other quickly,
but I believe everyone's
to blame for the fact
that those who were forgotten
were forgetful themselves.

("The Comfort of Complaining")

As Walter Benjamin, for one, suggests, the line between interior and exterior worlds becomes blurred for the *flaneur*, and so the attempts to coordinate features between self and external world become a kind of poetic feature, an enactment of metaphor:

Cowardice, are you still here?
and Lie, you, too?
I hear a dim, Yes:
Misfortune is still here,
and I'm still in the room,
as always.

("As Always")

Much of Walser's poetry seems a journey adjusted downward to a stroll. And just as a stroll implies no commitment on the part of the stroller, neither does it imply a response to Forster's famous plea to "connect." Walser's poems are not about human relationships, and one could say that the investigation of parts prior to reaching for that ever-elusive Other (the self is the other) takes precedence in so subjective a poet. There is a kind of naturalness in bringing up the important topic of forgetfulness, as he often does: never having registered in ways that would matter, what matter forgetting? To remember is to recall a presence that once did register. Forgetting, on the other hand, is either an endorsement of indifference, or, conversely, it is an act of love because it retires old business in the name of fairness and honor.

> Music is being played somewhere
> in a garden, we take a stroll, eat
> and drink and walk and sleep,
> and everyone who claims to be
> a member of society is used to
> restaurants, jobs and other business.
> That which we see as movement
> and so on resembles sleep. Do we
> all forget each other, one after another,
> in life's strange bright hall?

("Sleep")

Something of Walser's power as a poet stems from a lightly borne contrarianism that looks for all the world like the picture of a lover seeking to be spurned in order to become a poet. No less a bard than Yeats recommended this egregious act. In "Self-Reflection," he writes,

> They abandoned me, so I learned to forget myself,
> which allowed me to bathe in my inspired soul.
>
> …
>
> No one who's content with himself ever needed help,
> unless he happened to be in a accident and needed to be carried to
> the hospital.

We don't learn who "they" are, and in a sense, it doesn't matter. *They* equals *not-me*. Walser is not making social commentary. At the same time, the speaker of these poems often loosens the noose of self-reflection long enough to feel the pang of desire, of which he never seems completely free. Unfortunately, desire often gives way to the fantasy of fulfillment and becomes, simply, misery:

> I've waited so long for sweet
> talk and greetings, only one sound.
> Now I"m afraid no talk or sound,

only fog setting in excess.
Whatever was singing and hiding in the dark:
Misery, sweeten now my grave path.

("Afraid")

and

I carry that longing that will
never die, like that meadow dies
stiff and dead from the mist.
You do see me crossing it, full of dread?

("Do You See")

This in turn, as the perspective widens, invites the *Weltanshaung* of
the title poem:

How small life is here
and how big nothingness.

("Oppressive Light")

But there is *something* having to do with brevity that keeps the scope
of nothingness from playing the heavy, and the poet, in the studious-
ness of his self-involvement, his *smallness*, somehow derives a kind of
happiness that is all the more joyous for being framed in the chilled
language of Kafka:

The vast evening gray
is not just the sky.
A vast evening gray
covers the entire world.
The snow is silent as evening.
The green is beautiful as evening,
the trees, too,
and houses, too.
And smoke rises from

the houses into evening air
filled with happiness for me.

("Evening (II)")

It's the brevity of Follain and Prévert, and its general air of understatement and reliance on generic modifiers that leaves plenty of
room for readerly projection—which may be the point. Walser
doesn't so much actively engage the reader as provide a screen upon
which his or her own subjectivity comes into play and completes the
circuit. But just as it seems the poem magically appears via intersubjective consensus, the poet disappears again behind serviceable but
blanket images. And just as his disappearance throws some doubt on
the reliability of our own subjective response, our ability to organize
the experience of others with our own rules, so it returns us to the
push-pull of the poems' mechanisms. Walser sometimes plays with
his own experience as if it were hearsay, as in "And Left":

He quietly waved his hat
and left, they say of the wayfarer.
It tore the leaves off the tree
and left they say of the harsh autumn.
Smiling, she shared her mercy
and left, they say of her Majesty.
At night it knocked on the door
and left, they say of heartbreak.
Crying, he pointed at his heart
and left, they say of the poor man.

Submerged and yet in motion, Walser seems sometimes content
to pool his resources in both generalities and rumor, generic rather
than specific, a straw man rather than the specific person. He even
resorts to the hoary "He who..." format, beloved of nobody since
the Bible but Woody Allen:

Presumably no one minds
that the woods are greening again,
that meadows are full of grass,

that birds are singing in the trees,
that violets are blooming from the dirt.
Hundreds and thousands of green leaves!
Spring is a field marshal
who conquers the world,
and no one holds a grudge.

....

Only he
who truly loves achieves a song.
Kissing and dreaming.—Nearby,
with a sinister face, life's gravity
is standing by a wall; and whoever
walks past it, must tremble.

("Spring (1)")

And yet, the sense of detachment that goes along with such rhetorical tactics allows him to weather a host of emotional atmospheres, ranging from delight to dread. In "Faint-Hearted," his short-lined quatrains come across like an austere Dickinson:

Silent grief
visited me,
I lowered myself
into its chill,

I felt there
not fear, not haste,
only a heavy burden.
Grief led me

further on
through a dark sorrow,
until this striding
returned to the light

I bade softly:
keep me—
but it moved on
to a new journey.

The diffident *comme ci, comme ça* is also a defense: it keeps self-destruction at arm's length because—as he might have said—he who wants it, also doesn't. Grief appeals to the evenly divided heart just half of the time, but a poem, where time is in abeyance, glows in the light of contradiction. In "After Drawings by Daumier," he writes,

A man sits in a pleasure boat, when
suddenly a steamer heads towards him,
he shouts, "Oh dear, je suis perdu."
Many have believed themselves lost
but luckily in the end they were not."

These contradictions also go by the name of paradox and ambivalence. Situating the poem within their contraries, the poet when challenged is in a position to say, with Blake and Whitman, that only repetition is a fit reply. But there is that saving element, that carrying of opposed energies, past-and-present, presence-and-absence, worth-and-futility, that somehow justifies the man in his picking and choosing. If something can be both chosen and not-chosen, then the perennial death-where-is-thy-sting boast is a real proposition. Art takes that idea and with it, enters into its own commerce with time. In "October," he writes,

Flowers must indeed wither,
people too grow older,
and that's how it should be,
yet I think, and you may be
thinking the same,
that there exists a new bloom,
and a former bloom, that follows
you through past experiences
and never dwindles, because it
lies behind you.

Walser's sly complicity ("you may be thinking the same") is his replacement for readerly intimacy, perhaps. It also gives him tacit permission to stay within the borders of subjectivity that his other poems have specified or implied. In "Gloss," he writes, "When you're in the midst of the essential, where else can you go? I don't miss out on the basics, even when I'm being a bit trivial." Those "basics" may strike some as special pleading, but in fact they most assuredly include the paradoxes he took to his bosom, as he seemed to do that Christmas day in 1956, when he was discovered, eyes open, lying face up in a snowy field. What he saw before the cold world closed over him was the subject of this book.

Michael Water's *Darling Vulgarity*

The collapse of metaphysics may have turned philosophers to Prozac, preachers to an even shriller falsetto, and scientists to peacock glory, but for diverse writers the spilt religion regathered in poems finds its subject in the grossest of materialisms: sex and all that comes with it (including, as Baudelaire knew, imagination) and the larger grind of generation—and all that comes with that (as Keats feared). Waters is not the first, nor is he the best-known, but he is surely one of the most naturally inclined when it comes to connecting the dots between sex with some intimation of divinity. Or what passes for divinity these days, where high and low no longer avoid each other, but have each other in sight. The title itself—*Darling Vulgarity*—with its edgy charm, shows the way. Thus, in "Erotic Roman Antiquities," we find,

> ...glass cases lit like store windows
> displaying their goods: penises
> with bells hanging from them, penises
> with legs, penises with wings and, in one instance,
> a penis with bells, legs, and wings.

Here, the presence of erotic possibility maps aesthetics too, in a manner that reminds one of the late masters of that coincidence—Yehuda Amichai, in its earthy directness, and of Jack Gilbert, in its Mediterranean inflection—where Waters' fancy also finds its objective correlative, one seemingly congenial as well to his New York City origins, though without the mildew of standard "old country" associations.

A poet with a distinguished catalog of work, Waters covers ground common to his immediate predecessors—Logan, Poulin, Carver— as well as his slightly more distant heroes—Lowell and Pavese. That is, his poems have always found grounding in a subjectivity that, far from finding itself destabilized by time or eroded by the shifting standards of the age, has grown more capable with each book. Capable of what? Well, capable of outlasting the attacks on the privilege of subjectivity, for one thing. It is an irony that a poet of such subjective muscle and intention finds himself having survived the ongoing war on the subjective, Romantic project. Be that as it may, his career is as good an example as I know of the rewards that come of persistence over enlistment. That same war has produced one of his pet loves: punk rock music (see "Sonnet for Strummer"), which upended the faux sensitivity in which the '60s fizzled by violating every personal and public space, as well as every orthodoxy, with one exception: the creed of all-out resistance.

Waters underscores the body itself as a place of artistic transfiguration. In one of several poems that hook up with the sister arts (painting, sculpture, music, dance), he directs attention to such transfigurations:

> look: they've taken both my breasts.
> Yes, I reply, but listen: hasn't God replaced them
> with such glorious music?

("Miserere")

We are given access to the world where cancer and Gorecki may sign for each other's deliveries, which is to say the world we recognize with its odd affiliations bound not by lining up to the straight lines of orthodoxy but by the private and often impolitic wanderings of love. As he reminds us in "Black Olives," history takes place on the level of the body. The body could then be said to be incorporated by its time:

> Always
> I'd select a half-kilo of the most misshapen,
> wrinkled and blackest olives

sprung from the sacred rubble below Mt. Athos, then
had to shout, "fuck Kissinger!"
three times before the proprietor would allow me
to make my purchase.

Because fled gods inhabit those shadows, it is enough to glimpse,
as Cavafy knew, a wing disappearing into the hills to certify that the
world is thick with rough, immanent splendor—and not of another
world only, but of other ways of construing the onrush of time and
space of simultaneous worlds. Waters limns the presence of such
another world in the midst of this one:

> We had been arguing, slightly drunk,
> about ex-lovers with flirtatious
> gestures, about low murmurs in corners—
> suddenly they appeared.

> ("Fauns Fleeing before an Automobile")

The layering of the natural and the supernatural, of the natural
within the natural, is often figured as a trick of the light. This trick
enforces the ambivalent nature of interpretation and so tempers
judgment. Rather, it is the feeling that characterizes the poet's concern: how it felt, not what it was.

> Our rampant voices stilled then—
> that awestruck hush,
> creation's tentative pause—
> then only the tick of wipers urging our arrival
> home, the undressing, the desperate
> confusions of flesh...

In "Poinciana" the speaker recounts "The man who offered one
hundred dollars / to watch my wife undress." The poem's wide-
eyed setup reminds one of Christopher Walken in its confused-but-
deliberate hyperreality and of Raymond Carver in its moral bargain-
hunting. Its seeming bedroom nihilism has another purpose:

> I tapped one finger along the ivory
> keys of her spine, not knowing what came next,
> or how to strike our shame
> before money exchanged hands
> or when waking next morning wild with thirst.

Waters has never thrown a punchline, and it's clear in this poem why timing is crucial. That thirst—for clarity, for bodily renewal—stands as the default position for much of Waters' poetry. Because the thirst is ultimately metaphysical, it can never be quenched, and thus the poems achieve the impression of being given additional power by a supplemental engine. It raises the inconvenient question of whether the body itself isn't in some sense ultimately metaphysical, too, the acceptance of which would go a ways toward getting rid of confusions attending the connections of the body to sex, divinity, and textuality.

Rare among contemporary poets whose aesthetics were honed at Iowa (but not among those few who read their John Logan), Waters is what might be called an organic formalist. The heightened rhetoric, the poetic language so often associated with formalism, has never been his interest. The distance between high and low, as we have seen, operates within a more demotically tweaked bandwidth so that heightened language is so as a result of quiddities and *ad hoc* moments, and wears its knowingness conspicuously, if lightly. He has written a number of poems in syllabics, for instance, a form that often doesn't announce its presence. Within that form, he brings the master craftsman's ground-level intelligence. Take this passage from "American Eel":

> Suddenly my daughter let loose a shrill *ewwww*! —we heard
> below that sour pitch, a dim
> sorption like soapsuds sieving through a wooden bucket:
> eels stranded in low tide …

The syllabic alternations enact the "flaccid /intimations" of their "doubling back," and "the sorption like soapsuds sieving," with their serpentine hiss and rising vowels, remind us why the daughter's cry

is so instinctual: when we look at eels, we see snakes. By the end of
the first, erotically charged section, sex has become a word. The
daughter's use of the F-word produces her father's double response:

> "Bad word," I wagged my finger [.....]
> "but," I couldn't help myself, "you used it correctly."

"Eddie's Parrot" is a good poem to start off the post-erotic section, as it goes to the question of substitutions and the ways in which
wording underwrites the body. The parrot's insistent "Where's
Eddie? Where's Eddie?" continues after Eddie dies, until his widow
"snapped and stormed that Catskill comic's /stage." Echoing an early
poem of Gregory Orr (who himself follows the classical Horatian
example), Waters shows that when the word is gone, you are, well,
also gone.

The parrot is followed by the poet's own ventriloquism in "Family
Outing," both a family tale and a wide parody of "tough-guy" writing. The poet's off-duty police grandfather "nabbed the thug" who
seems a cartoon of sexual abuse:

> Soon a buddy cop huffed up
> to cuff the creep who leaned in close to whisper some filth
> into my grandmother's ear.

Here, each keyword is an indictment in the dream of rough
peace and rougher justice. No problem with water-boarding in this
poem. It mirrors our insecurities in a former age when good people,
the prey to "creeps," are collared and dealt a summary justice, the
techniques of which receive tacit approval of women, the intended
victims.

A middle section of prose pieces is reminiscent of Lowell's famous
prose bridge ("92 Revere Street") in the seminal *Life Studies*. The
similarity is not just fortuitous: Lowell figures as a character in one of
the pieces. This section shows that it is not true that poets who affect
concentration at verse fail at prose. In the first piece, the young poet
is afraid his bike will be stolen if he spends too much time in confession, and the anxiety over having to choose between this world and

the other world builds to a crisis. The second piece recounts the young poet's meeting with the scandalous Allen Ginsberg just when his mother has discovered that he is attempting to become a writer by scribbling piecework porn. The third prose piece describes an encounter with Robert Lowell in England, just when it was thought necessary for British dons to discountenance "confessional poetry." The final piece ("The Soul") plays a good riff on the *poét maudit* theme. A neighbor offers to pray for the poet who is on the way to have ear-fluid unclogged, presumably in order the better to hear Blink-182. This quaint gesture is received with patience, but later the poet wonders, in fact, about whether the soul isn't saved in some sense by its damnation. It concludes:

> I have a colleague who asked my creative writing students if they thought I was going to hell. Waters? On skis, one laughed, and when they told me, I reminded them that "skiing" might be the only word in the English language to employ the double i. Hawaii, one said. English, I repeated, racing downhill, the slope all to myself.

This would be a good place to end another collection, but one of the virtues of Waters' talent is its recursive intelligence: careers like his evolve because the poet takes another look. In "The Tether,"

> Some almost-shapes drift by.
> Awe. A distant knocking.
> —Then the long haul.

"Commerce" takes as its occasion the faking of miraculous survivals at that epicenter of honeymoon kitsch, Niagara Falls. In the "commerce" with time and circumstance, desire trumps credibility: the entrepreneurial intelligence knows this, just as it knows that casual cruelty is the American key (and if the blind torture the blind—all the better):

> Then one cat was found, eyeless, legs broken,
> so for the next decade tramps tortured strays
> to sell them to tourists, farm boys, and Poles
> as The Cat Swept Over Niagara Falls...

Several poems juxtapose the slacker urgency of indie and punk with classical artifacts, and yet what hints at eccentric accommodations turns out to be the diurnal pendulum of process. In "Ossuary,"

> The widow hawking postcards hustles us
> toward sunlight—we've breathed centuries enough
> of mold & spore & crumbling fibulae.
> We've witnessed enough. These schoolgirls want more.
> Let them follow each other—a scraggly
> crusade of backpacks & pierced lips & brows—
> till they flame to spirit down the noon glare.
> Let us all unburden ourselves before
> the next plague...

His love of music situates him among those for whom the distant past has not yet established a grip, and yet, being a poet, he finds one foot here, the other in that past. Moreover, he declines the attempt to reconcile the contradiction and stands as poets since Whitman have been invited to do, highlighting his own ambivalence. This is a healing ambivalence because it references the violence of exclusive choice, preferring the "weak" position of indecision to the "strong" one of judgment. Likewise, in "The Crusades," the "martyrdom" of the Notorious B.I.G. is the thematic overlay to French sarcophagi. The ambivalence, the declining to judge, is on display here too. Between hip-hop and solemn reliquary art: no choice. As the poet who knows the name Jean D'Alluye is aware, hip-hop (and popular culture generally) is a kind of crusade to liberate us from the necrotic reach of the unreasonable past.

A poem about student days ("Backrub") finds the speaker accepting the siren-song of an obese woman who haunted the campus like "a wet dream of Christo, a draped tornado / clanging its ceramics, her bracelets & earrings," who beckons "with a wheedling tongue, / wanting someone please to touch her." What must have started with gallant self-sacrifice ends with, "So one morning, why not, I volunteered." But while the possibilities for recognition and contrition are numerous, the poet doesn't go there. Instead, he finds that he is "losing myself in the laborious process of creation." Acceptance, seemingly so arbitrary is seen—in that same arbitrariness—as participating in "the process of creation," though nothing is created that would count as a "product."

The process of creation is touched upon again in "Making Love at the Frost Place," here contrasted with the Good Gray Poet's process of creating poems, in particular, "After Apple-Picking," which manages to tame the *timor mortis*. Now, as an unintended consequence, it provides a master-auspice to the lovers.

There is much to admire and much to love in *Darling Vulgarity*, not least of which is the sense of experience as a worthwhile congeries of unsortables and exuberances. The plain fact is that we age, and in aging try to figure out whether experience is a fit substitute for love. Yeats wondered it, and said no. Waters, whose poems are vibrant embodiments, would agree, except that he would equally agree with Miles Davis, the subject of "Junkie Tempo," that time is the thing: "*always time and time again relentless time: / time, Miles used to smile, like a motherfucker.*"

C.K. Williams' *Wait*

Williams gained wide notice and admiration using the long line and publishing the wide book. It seemed quintessentially American, yet what that national adjective comes to stand for has never been for a moment uncontested. As proof of his bona fides, Williams sees to it that his claims on the modifier come complete with their own antitheses: what he affirms is undone in the unconscious, in the night, in the secrets of our dual natures, most especially in our idealism's clash with convention, the Imp of the Perverse's tussle with the Deathmaster from Germany at one moment, with the steely orthodoxy of a Dante at the other. But wait! Such dualisms are reserved for the old guys, aren't they? No, Williams seems to say: they are up-to-date as are the vexed contents of our psyches.

It's no accident that the poem "Shrapnel" and the poem "Assumptions," poems about, respectively, violence and religion, share a form: the long-limbed, Whitmanian line with its bills of lading, its whiplash, even its *longeurs*, grouped into stanzaic phalanxes. After all, it was this form that Williams used to reload after venting his spleen on all things Nixonian (did he make the "Enemies List"? he should have...) in the falling-down 'Seventies. In "Shrapnel," Williams adopts a straight face and clinician's language to lace up his outrage at the violence to which flesh in warfare is visited:

> In the case of insufficiently resistant materials, the shards of shrapnel
>   can cause "significant damage";
> In human tissue, for instance, rupturing flesh and blood vessels and
>   shattering and splintering bone.

Similarly, in "Assumptions," the poet rises to a dry, high-church register to hold religion's (and God's—known here as "the entity") grip on History up for ridicule and to reveal its necessary ties to violence:

> That inherent in these interpretations was the thesis that the now
>   silent entity intended its legitimacy
> To be transferred to various social institutions, which, though in no
>   obvious relation to it itself
> would have the prerogative to enact its name anything necessary for
>   the perpetuation of their dominion.
>
> That what is often specified by the inheritors of those thrice-removed
>   sanctifications, that certain other groups,
> By virtue of being in even potential disagreement with the entity's even
>   tacit wishes, become offensive,
> And must be amputated, slaughtered, has been deduced correctly
>   from these syllogistic tangles.

It's as though Williams has thrown in his lot with the "Brights," who don't need an inexplicable, transcendental loom to keep rainbows from unweaving. But Williams' beef with religion is not directed at spirituality as such, but at the clerical and political power freaks who invariably show up to co-opt its authority and bend it to nefarious ends. Ultimately he is more nearly a Kierkegaardian, for it is the struggle that yields art, and therefore we like, in some way, that struggle. The result is the scar carved upon the given smoothness, the figure on the ground, after the struggle abates to a ceasefire. If Emerson's term "alienated majesty" still has application, it applies to the poetry of Williams. As he writes in "Brain,"

> I began to wonder in dismay if the conclusion I'd long ago come to
>   that there can be nothing
> That might reasonably be postulated as the soul apart from body and
>   mind was entirely valid.

For him it's not a question about an external scheme that validates and underwrites the workings of consciousness. It's a realization that

wonder (and it's flip side, cruelty) are both in some sense privatized
in the process of our knowingness:

> this sensitive bit
> of cosmos that streams
>
> towards us, like filing
> to magnet, then shyness,
>
> timidity, then, sometimes,
> deep reasonless
>
> fear, a rankling,
> even, absurdly
>
> like anger, soon cooled,
> then knowing,
>
> *knowing*, without
> knowing how

("The Glance")

As Iago says, "you know what you know." And that means our knowing—without wonder's Wonderbra-style ethical uplift—that evolution
does not mete out goodness to tip the scale toward our ideals:

> One branch, I read, of a species of chimpanzees has something like
>   territorial wars,
> And when the…Army, I suppose you'd call it, of one tribe prevails
>   andcaptures an enemy,
> *"several males hold a hand or foot of the rival so the victim can be damaged*
>   *at will"*

("Apes")

Or as Eliot, who plays apogee to Williams' perigee in just about
every other orbit, famously wrote, "with such knowledge, what forgiveness"? One wonders if even forgiveness quite gets Williams'

mature dismay or helps ease the improvisational overtime of his own idealism. That very idealism is the issue that permeates *Wait*, and the obstacles looming in its way constitute the most interesting subject matter. I am reminded of Solzhenitsyn's self-representation as the rebel calf butting heads with the Soviet oak. In "Wasp," Williams has his own version:

> That invisible barrier between you and the world,
> between you and your truth.... Stinger blunted,
> wings frayed, only the battering, battered brain,
> only the hammer, hammer, hammer gain.

As all of Modernism has taught, you don't do this with the expectation of knocking over the tree. Nor is it all the empty heroism of Sisyphus. As Williams tells us in 'The Foundation" (and as has been the case with other poets), his pantheon consists of agonists like himself ("Watch me again now, because I'm not alone in my dancing"):

> But Vallejo was there all along, and my Sidney and Shelley,
> my Coleridge and Hopkins, there all along with their music,
> which is why I can whirl through the rubble of everything else,
> the philosophizing and theories, the thesis and anti- and syn-,
> all I believed must be what meanings were made of,
> when really it was the singing, the choiring, the cadence,
> the lull of the vowels, the chromatical consonant clatter...
>
> Watch me again, I haven't landed, I'm hovering here
> over the fragments...

But the wages of improvisation are often either zealotry or a too-facile equanimity. Williams acknowledges both, but succumbs to neither. Perhaps of all the poets I have reviewed in the last few years who exhibit signs of a lingering duality (and while philosophers are keen to do away with it, it remains in just about every poet's kit bag) as an enabling ambivalence, none surpasses Williams for in his uncanny characterization of the B-side: the shiny ambivalence that papers over a lack of commitment, a lack of empathy—often of non-human beings, our biological others:

On the sidewalk in front
of a hairdresser's supply store
lay the head of a fish,
largish, pointy, perhaps a pike's.

It must recently have been left there;
its scales shone and its visible eye
had enough light left in it
so it looked as they will for a while

astonished and disconsolate
to have been brought to such a pass.

("Fish")

Such mental travel makes skepticism raise its head. The classic version for poets is the one told by Issa, whose emperor dreamed he was a butterfly who woke up and couldn't decide if he was really an emperor—or a butterfly. In Williams' version, he asks,

Will I be myself again
now. Must I always
forever and ever
be me? Without wings?
O butterfly, without Issa?
Without wings?

("Butterfly")

That the here-not-here of skeptical wondering might not be available one day is a question for this poet. As the poem suggests, it might leave him wingless, and no poet is down with that. There's that big alienation Emerson spoke of again in the "Must I..." of self-inquisition, which we can also translate as "why can't I be a poet of a better age"?

But it would not do for Williams to succumb to ordinary skeptical moves, finally, for, as Jordan Smith neatly put it, poetry is "a believer's art." It's just that that belief needn't connect up with orthodoxies,

for, as Coleridge knew, poetry was a further—possibly the furthest—
emanation of belief's program: it conditions consciousness itself.
Williams is a poet of the complication of consciousness (and its look-
alike *conscience*) chief among which is the issue self-consciousness. It's
that split-focus and the dualism inhering thereto that feeds the skeptical muse. We have Baudelaire to thank for that (Williams mentions
him as a master), but no poetic antecedent is necessary to account
for the battle royale between the minatory *I* whose bluster is a dead
giveaway for trouble and his scofflaw counterpart, the Other. In fact,
Williams practically bangs the gong for his subject in "Gaffe," which
also happens to open the volume. In this poem, the poet recalls a
faux pas that occurred in his childhood and finds it emblematic of
his later career's chief themes:

> I'm a child then, yet already I've composed this conscience-beast, who
>   harries me:
> is there anything else I can say with certainty about who I was, except
>   that I, that he,
>
> could already draw from infinitesimal transgressions complex chords
>   of remorse,
> and orchestrate every-undiminishing retribution from the hapless rest
>   of myself?

The gently rolling polysyllables of these Latinate lines run
aground at the realization that the ego is not in control:

> We're joking around, and words come to mind, which to my amazement
>   are said.
> *How do you know when you can laugh when somebody dies, when your brother*
>   *dies?*
>
> is what's said, and the others go quiet, the backyard goes quiet,
>   everyone stares,
> and I want to know why that someone in me who's me yet not me let
>   me say it.

In "Light," the poet reprocesses the duality of self-perception,
combining that with a test involving another species:

I think of a troop of the blissful blessed approaching Dante,
"a hundred spheres shining," he rhapsodizes, "the purest pearls…"

then of the frightening, brilliant, myriad gleam in my lamp
of the eyes of the vast swarm of bats I found once in a cave…

Dante again,
this time the way he'll refer to a figure he meets as "the life of…"

not the soul, or person, the *life*, and once more the bat, and I,
our lives in that moment together, our lives, our *lives*,

his with no vision of celestial splendor, no poem
mine with no flight, no unblundering dash through the dark,

his without realizing it would, so soon, no longer exist,
mine having to know for us both that everything ends,

world, after-world, even their memory, steamed away
like the film of uncertain vapor of the last of the luscious rain.

The question of competing narratives is not only a hallmark of the
skeptic, it's key to understanding what we mean by authenticity—a
quality to which poetry has traditionally clung and one which underwrites the art's claims to prestige. It used to be that philosophers
and poets parted company over the question of what constituted
the truth of content—was it words verbatim or words generally? In
other words, is truth subject to paraphrase? For the philosophers,
meaning was capable of being translated whole, while for the poets,
there was nothing that passed for paraphrase. It was an early argument for measuring worth and what's what:

Ten times an hour, it feels like, I arrive in my brooding,
 my fretting, my grumbling , at enormous generalizations,
ideations, intellections, speculations, which before
they're even wholly here I know I'll soon disprove.
Yet knowing I'll refute them, knowing I'm not qualified
to judge them, still I need them, still forgive me, cherish them.

("Rash")

Death and memory also bring up these considerations: is memory a kind of presence, or does death disqualify presence altogether? Are we left only with images, representations, and symbols? This was, again, Yeats' subject: how does representation intersect with presence? It's another variation on the old, "is that all there is?" In "Peggy" we find,

> But now, the false-mullioned windows,
> the developer's scrawny maples, the lawns—
> I don't know what to do with it all,
> it just ached, like forgetting someone
> you love is dead, and wanting to call them,
> and then you remember, and they're dead again.

But regardless of his forays and probings, he circles back in a motion whose recursive loops enact and reenact the doublings of consciousness, often verging on paralysis, the avatar of Prufrock and his Edwardian curlicues:

> I want to act not because I've coerced myself to,
> but because I'll have responded from the part of myself
> that precedes will, residing in intrinsic not projected virtue.
>
> I have no wish to be good, or pure—inconceivable that—
> but I wish not to have to consider who I am or might be
> before I project myself into quandaries or conflicts.
>
> All this that I crave, which I know my craving impedes,
> the absurdity of which might diminish further who I am
> and what I stand for, if that's the term, to myself—
>
> (can one stand for something to oneself? can one not?)
> I've never found a shred of evidence for in myself…

("Ethics")

Williams rightly turns to the example of Paul Celan, for if there is one way to entertain a modern notion of authenticity it is to consider the centrality of the margins, and what more marginally emblematic person can there be than a Jew in the Holocaust?

> Celan was so sick of the *Deathfugue* he'd no longer let it be printed.
> In the tape of him reading, his voice is songful and fervent, like a cantor's.
> When he presented his poem to some artists, they hated the way he recited.

("Jew on Bridge")

But artists find a way to take such loathing as approbation, and Williams was long ago admitted to their crew. After all, he's one of those guys who will say anything. For all that, we also know and feel that what sets his art apart is not his Baudelairian mental scouring, his political and moral outrages, nor his philosophical plate-spinning, but his capacity for tenderness, which is the real measure of his—of anyone's—humanity. I say this with the realization that I risk turning an omnivorous poet into a quiet vegetarian. The title meanwhile directs our attention in two directions. There is the sense of wanting to stay ("Stay, thou art so fair!"), of the times, the poet's age and mortality, and of our—the reader's—time. There is also the sense of expectation and eventuality, of hope that somehow, as none other than Yeats fantasied, it might still be otherwise—and we be souls rising in spite of ourselves to some heaven of our imagining that rises in turn to meet us. And we might be, even though we aren't. And it might be, even though it isn't.

Eleanor Wilner's *Tourist in Hell*

Eleanor Wilner specializes in a medium-sized poem made to seem the larger by a finely-tooled rhetorical control switch. She is one of those poets who often sounds happier in literary English than in the patois that is all of our inheritance (and in which, notwithstanding, she seems to find no aesthetic issues in using). It would not be obvious to first-time readers, but to those of us who have followed her career, it's nice to be reminded just how wide, flexible, and variegated her range is. And yet it's no wonder to find that the language agreeable to her Muse often comes from the more literary side of the spectrum, marking her affiliation with a more senior generation and netting much of what is implied by that affiliation. Often too, her cargo seems to travel a long distance, coming from myth to moment. The far end of those psychic and biological caves, where our narrative paths began to emerge like turtle's footsteps providing forensic evidence of our origins are now more evidently remote than ever, the way back choked with distractions. For Wilner, the classical stories retain their ability to speak to us, thanks to the fact that their ambiguities—by no means diminished by modern utterance—push against, but are contained by, the outlines, the configurations of their principle images, their figures—whether footstep or profile.

When they are not being only abandoned or superseded perspectives, the classical promises us the lure of the most ancient questions in some fashion close to their original formulations. Pursuing them presents us with binary options: the then and the now. The *then* is dim and must by metamorphoses such as those poems specialize in acquire the luminance of proximity, of the *now*. George Seferis, another poet obsessed with linking origins to present moments, writes of the name of an obscure king, bound for Troy, whose cata-strophic destiny, like a solar flare, projects this merest piece of iden-tity (his name in the catalog of ships), this true representation of authenticity, into the present. At length, though, as the narrators—tourists—lose steam and interest, it again submerges and recedes into the roster of those who came to offer their lives to war in the hope that chance would find them at last on the side of right, if not of victory. What is suggested then, is that we are Baudelairean *lecteurs* of just such calamities, whose responsibility it is to hold off "all oblivi-ous enmity" one more time, by one more thread (or in Ariadne's words, a "clew"), be it ever so thin:

> ...I am only   the echo of a voice
> Husk of power   king of cobwebs   cast off shell of the cicada
> the singing insect   long since flown   memory   a spectral
> thread
> broken   line   across the centuries   perforations
> a place to tear   open again the rift in time...

("Minos")

This is from a section called "Voices from the Labyrinth" that recalls the myth of Minos, Daedalus, the Minotaur, Theseus and Ari-adne. Wilner knows that the poet aspires to the status of Daedalus, but confesses that "we were ourselves the labyrinth / and the clew" ("Ariadne"). Part of the labyrinth's gift to amazement lies with the realization that these players aren't people, but masks and personi-fications, and that it would be nearer to the truth to say that we are the labyrinth itself—a construct—than to insist that we are sealed identities, persons of robust authenticity. And so it is that we are also the thread out of ourselves: the clew, our clue. Wilner's approach is to take up classical myth and fit those transformations to the present (all myth, in a sense, being present, just as the past and memory are).

In "Thinking about Unamuno's "San Manual Bueno, Martir," Wil-ner meditates on Unamuno's great story of an unbelieving Spanish priest who refuses to come clean so as not to disillusion his simple parishioners. Maintaining what is in effect a lie, he reaches toward what he considers a higher truth. In Wilner's retelling,

Late in the story we learn
he did not believe in the hope
he kept alive   believing as he did
(like his author) in the sustaining power
of fiction.

To which we might add, believing "like this author." If history is hell, then a lie—the right lie—does not offend it. The point is not that a fiction is a "lie," but that "fiction" is always an equivocating term, as the Shakespearean Wilner recognizes. It is in exploring the fissure that divides a fiction as a falsehood from a fiction that constructs that Wilner's poems take hold and illuminate. In "The Show Must Go On," she references drama as a famous vehicle of such equivocations:

The play had been staged as long as we could remember,
a sordid drama in which truth kept changing sides,
the name of the enemy was never the same;
sometimes the players poured over the edge
of the proscenium, spilling into the audience,
who ran terrified from the house
that had become a scene of massacre; sometimes
the drama played at a distance relaxingly remote,
caught and burnished in the bright little
dollhouse screen, so far away it was no more
than fireflies in a bottle, mere hiccups of light—
the carpet bombing, the village, torched.

For all that she likes the sustaining power of fiction, the desensitizing effects of aesthetic distance do not go unnoticed because, as Kafka (another master of the labyrinth and the Lie) knew, at the end of the day, there is no longer a meaningful distinction to be made between the aesthetic and the moral.

So at one end you have the existential person, entirely wrapped up by and in language—moreover, language that is aware of its status as linguistic construction. At the other, you have the last emanation of a person's being—a word, a name. Or it could even be a word that no longer signifies a person but is merely a placeholder for a human

singularity. Horace boasted that the linguistic animal could monu-
mentalize itself, and Shakespeare (one of Wilner's household gods)
promised that, as death-defying inventions went, the poem was a
good bargain as a destiny, albeit a cold one. Yeats followed in this.
It has been traditional to see the Horatian/Shakespearean boast as
art's coping mechanism for responding to our natural discontinuity.
In "Ariadne," Wilner brings the classic within the scope of the boast:

> Daedalus   serves a new god
> and I   a foreign figure
> in a greek story
> the Greek key is a maze
> it is their design   fit
> for the walls of their temples of stone
> finding us weak
> they took what they say we gave
> I shall free myself
> from that fiction
> as soon   as I find
> the right turn
> a way out
> of these
> lines

At the center of "these lines" is a word; Seferis, whose work haunts
about the edges of Wilner's poems, says it is a name. If that is so,
then the name, the final registry of people, the final placeholder,
lies at the center of the labyrinthine destiny. Given a clew (thread),
one might reverse the direction, or if that isn't possible, represent a
reversal in much the same way that formal, recursive art "reverses"
time—or at the least, rewrites it in a way that favors us more. What
makes Seferis a point of reference here is the suggestion that Wilner shares a belief in the scope of poetry (or at least the scope of a
certain kind of formally strict, rhetorically-powered poem favored
by literary cognoscenti) as having some ongoing business with the
facts of names, be they ever so remote. Meanwhile, she never loses
sight of the fact that the poem, too, is cast into, or upon, the future,

even as it immediately begins receding into the past. Readers will not be surprised to find her cautioning against a too-fond belief in art's abracadabra. For example, in "Encounter in the Local Pub," she is

> like a man who wants to hang a hammock
> in his yard, to let its bright net cradle him, but only
> has one tree, so he—wild and aware of it—knew
> he had lost the order he required, and with, it, rest...

By contrast, in "Restored to Blue," what we would, we are,

> So look away, or look: today the sky
> is cloudless as a canvas used exclusively for blue
> and filling in the blanks seems nothing more
> than sport, a game to leave behind, a way to keep
> the mind from knowing that the blanks, though
> time and time filled in, return: a cloudless sky
> we're meant to read as happiness, and so we do.

Although a formalist, she relishes the elasticity of form in a way reminiscent of May Swenson, who also made her way by syllabic path-finding. In "Meditation on Lines from Shakespeare's Sonnet 73," an elegy for Julia Randall, Wilner considers the endlessly readable " When yellow leaves, or none, or few, do hang." In such a sequence (like the sequence of seasons, of which it is a parody—and yet no parody) we discover,

> But most of all, I love this line because
> I hear by heart, when that "do hang"
> rings at line's end, the deeper sound...

What better way of writing an elegy for a friend than of employing Shakespeare as intermediary and intercessor? The dead poet (Randall) is described as the "fierce critic / of the failed melodies of mediocrity..." In the Shakespeare sonnet, "where late the sweet birds sang" establishes birdsong itself as melody. Rhythm, by contrast, is a traffic barricade. Song—not meaning—is the thing. Or rather, song is the meaning. Hence birdsong is central (not Eliot's "jug jug to dirty ears"), and hence the appearance of the critic who practiced criticism on the basis of such "meaningless" melody. Also like Randall and May Swenson, the neo-formalist Wilner has an interest in not simply adhering to classical principles of containment but in following more idiosyncratic paths, in moving ahead, where others would fold. In "Colony Collapse Disorder (CCD),"

> when the beekeepers arrive to see to their bees
> in the spring, the colonies have collapsed,
> the dead bees tumble out like pieces from
> an old game, the dried comb crumbles
> at a touch, no milk and honey left to spill...
> in the rutted rows of stumps, the olive grove
> (what were we thinking?) cut down, the hum,
> a wind in the ghostly trees,
> grown louder now—dead bees
> in the phosphorescent flowers
> tossed in an open tomb.

The poem itself is about ecological closure, and I take it as a mark of her poetic intelligence that her own investigations of closure depart from the expected, if only, as Larkin memorably put it, "that so many dead lie around." Among the voices not heard and yet heard with the inner ear here are poets as diverse as Virgil, Milosz, Linda Gregg and Robert Hass, poets whose imaginations find Mediterranean light agreeable. Wilner brings these poets along, not in imitation, but in a more remote camaraderie of aims.

In "The Gyre," she imagines the custodial ennui of the historian/ cartographer, whose world, recreated in book and map become "the world unmade." The Yeatsian title tilts us into the direction of the widening spiral of scholarship and intellectual mastery, until "syntax and sense" come to seem synonymous with comprehension:

> as centuries and cities fall, cascade
> into the landfill of history... worlds born
> on the waste of those that came before.
> As a glowing cloud of smoke will hang
> over a burning dump at night, and the bears

and raccoons come out, eyes shining in the dark,
to paw through the smoldering heaps—
just so the historian sits, sifting and sifting
entrails, cornices, motives, bones—all
that is left to be indexed and filed,
rearranged, given syntax and sense...

("The Gyre")

Similarly, in "Wreck and Rise Above," she considers the contrast between fact (wreck) and interpretation (rise above), finding the vocabulary of transcendence, the "vertical direction of virtue," illusional and yet, as with magic tricks, not without "wonder" in view of

all those bodies not exempt from gravity,
beneath our notice as we ride
above it all, like froth on a wave
that will be water falling by the ton,
soon, when the tide turns.

Such a tsunami of souls takes us to Keats's paradoxes, of unsung melodies and frozen harps:

But for those of us who stayed, the absence
of the trees grew larger, and with it,
the sky, which began its vast retreat
into the past, light years away...

("Larger to Those Who Stay")

Here, vividness itself is situated on irony, and to the extent that it is, is a kind of "reverse art." Is there affirmation in private irony? There are analogues in the classical world—which is both absent and fictive—and therefore rich with implications (and complications). It raises the question: does implication have (can it have) the force of assertion? This is in turn another way of asking whether secondary utterance, i.e., criticism, can have the force of art. Such writing invites a sigh of Stoic fatalism, a mid-course correction to the long bloody slide. However, the darker sense comes through without the usual hints of doom that, like too much acting, can sink a poem.

As with Hamlet, it is possible to track the play's development by reading the soliloquies, so with *Tourist in Hell*, it's possible to do the same thing by reading the sequence of section epigraphs. Beginning with Hegel's "Man learns from history that man learns nothing from history," we move to the irony of the infamous "Mission Accomplished" of Bush/Cheney, to Ovid's "then all but failed to find his own way out again," to Milosz's "I was left behind with the immensity of existing things." As a thematic arc (and it is an arc), the book travels a Romantic distance, spiraling back upon itself, but with evidence of its own chastening, and on a higher plane. Wilner is not a poet much enamored of redemptive promise, but neither does she throw up her hands. There is about as much redemption as a clear focus bestows on a picture, and isn't that enough? Speaking of epigraphs, it is Hayden Carruth who supplies *Tourist in Hell's* lintel-piece: "What do you think hell is if it isn't history?" How to move the mind (if not the body) around, given this sobering malediction is the question that this collection poses. Michel Tournier has remarked that "writing can only ever be rewriting, not just the rewriting of key myths but also conscious and unconscious inter-textuality." Myth, then, does not try to circumvent history, but to provide historical creatures formal narrative opportunities—nothing resembling closure, mind you, although poems are closed, aesthetic wholes. But even form's enclosing arms embrace commensurable events in human life: we identify, sympathize, and imagine in ways so often an outrage to the aesthetic sense. And what is an effrontery to the aesthetic sense is an affront to the moral sense too.

This is a big, moving and intellectually satisfying collection by one of our most humane, wise, and intelligent poets. I was recently aghast to read the syllabus for a graduate-level contemporary poetry course at a local university. For one thing, there was nothing of the real diversity of our national poetry hinted there, although the tone of self-congratulation on this score was evident. But what most struck me was that poets of Wilner's stature, of which there are only a handful, were themselves completely absent. And it occurred to me that I didn't know whether a book working at this level would stand to redress such an omission. But I do know the students are thereby impoverished, and not withstanding the fact that graduate students are bellwethers of nothing, such a narrow and partisan readership as that syllabus showed can only imply that the split between academic and literary culture works to the advantage of neither.

Carolyne Wright's *A Change of Maps*

Carolyne Wright starts her new collection of (mostly) first-person, autobiographical poems with a humdinger about studying with Elizabeth Bishop when the latter found herself forced to seek employment teaching at the University of Washington, her prelude to a series of gradual declensions ending in her death ("the dropped telephone at Lewis Wharf"). Asthmatic, alcoholic ("she staggered past me, unseeing, one April afternoon"), she appears in implicit contrast to the ghost of the equally alcoholic, huffing Theodore Roethke, in the environment of whose "mythic maniacal / dolor" she toils, "a scarf of pure froth floating at the throat of her / Bonwit Teller suit." Bishop's hallmark good sense is not to be found here: "One Art" is still a ways in the future.

Wright, by composing a poem that draws attention to the indirect, often slippery nature of literary pedagogy, unobtrusively assumes a place in the line of succession, after the demise of these great talents—and great egos (something her work betrays little sign of). Not for Wright the Roethkean dolor or Bishopian *Weltanschang*: "Still / Zen's empty bowl runneth over. Awful? Yes! But cheerful!" Yet the lack of ego's torque probably goes some distance in explaining the occasionally solicitous posture of these poems, as they move through event and memory, balancing homage with gentle self-assertion. Don't get me wrong: this poet has radar for the boundaries of immodesty and never strives (*pace* Bloom) agonistically. That wouldn't do. When the poems get into the zone—and a great many do—they require no solicitude.

"Studies with Miss Bishop" provides a foundational shot, as it both applies Bishop's lessons and brings up the subjects that will be Wright's own: the past, the present coordinates, how divergence is the shape of time, and the importance of origins. It also brings into focus a still-rippling question: how it is possible for an American poet, lodged between classical inclinations but reared on rock and roll, the Sixties, and Bad Boys, to make a *gradus ad parnassum* so that doing so does not result in just another homemade American destiny, privatized into anonymity? A standard reading suggests that the poet hunkers down for some long winter, her work packed with irony's insulation from the very demotic energies that initially propelled it and that constitute one of her topic areas. This would put her in a continuum where it is fair to say many poets have submitted their life's works in the hopes that they will have flown under the radar while everything else that used to be art falls under culture's commodifying, totalitarian blade. The question is whether the poet participates in and attempts to modify (in her favor) the irony that taste and vision automatically meet in their journey across the U. S. of A.

Bishop's ambition found its objective correlative in her master metaphor—cartography, that is, knowledge derived from coordinates. The cartographic imagination can also move readily to the moral, as well as the aesthetic sphere. Here, one may note Stevens' ghostly demarcations and Keats' sensations beside Bishop's gridlines, although Sevens' sensibility would find little difference between the aesthetic and the moral. By contrast, Lowell devalued the poetry of fact in deference to that based on imagination, and in doing so was rephrasing a distinction made familiar by Keats, who wished, contra Lowell, for a life of "sensations rather than thoughts" and why not? Such a life would never have the need to raise, as Wright has it, "basilisk-lidded grey eyes to the dazed / clutch of undergraduates clustered in the same Parrington Hall / classroom where Roethke had blazed..." Wright sides with Keats over Lowell: life rather than (merely!) something imagined. And yet her imagination, like Bishop's, redresses facts and their rebarbative edges, shape-shifting through art's chastening forms—and therefore providing a kind of compensation with the way life evolves, while memory devolves into discontinuities of meaning. As for Bishop, defensiveness and denial after the clink and heigh-ho of old money become another way of life, a come-down grudgingly accepted,

> First of all, I don't like teaching, but the trust
> fund ran out—exhausted—so we'll make the best
> go of it we can.

Just so, we might say. The book's title signals both adoption of purpose and a departure from the teacher. This theme is again taken up in the title poem, one that references one of Bishop's key poems, "The Map." "A Change of Maps" manages to exchange Bishop's Baedecker for Wright's own, the learned from the invented:

> Early fall looks both ways
> into the year—how we will outsmart
> the distance

Outsmarting that distance is in effect to outsmart both our notions of fate and our reliance on debased versions of ourselves.

> Where now? We want to know of landscape—
> houses and poplars and children the maps
> and master planners have no idea of.
> Our arrival will coincide with the true
> colors of our going.

Notwithstanding the fact that Wright is adept at ambiguity, clinging to it is not her style. On the one hand, poets want, in some sense, for their inventions to escape classification, although the facts from which they take their departure work to limit their free play. On the other—better—hand, they want the recognition of having striven on the grid—another reason maps are useful.

Speaking of maps, any poet knows you can talk about time in terms of space, and you can talk about space in terms of other space. But you can't talk easily about space in terms of time. Does this mean, one wonders, that space is superior to time in terms of its usefulness to *homo sapiens*? If so, then the cultural brain-pan of the Emersonian American is larger than that of the Old World aesthete. Poetry's win-win is that it can talk the talk of both and has access to both in terms of technique. American poetic developments often come about in terms of space (think of "field composition," Black Mountain aesthetics, the "deep image," Whitman's tropes of space). Meter and rhyme are hooked forever to time—or should I say Time, but issues with time are not over and done with just because they originated in the *vieux monde*. Wright is one of those poets who wants to make sense of both, and yet at the same time this sense can't be made once for all. It remains slippery, subject to our evolution as poets and readers to contingencies of many sorts.

Such contingencies are at the source of our vast interest in the never-repeatable private sphere. "Love Affair in a Small Town" locates Wright in reflection upon a geographical place, bearing the imprint of intimacy and time, and it always turns out that the latter is an ironizing agent for the former: "That was the winter we clung to each other," when "[y]ou played songs from the days / we believed music had the answers." The wised-up disillusionment is sometimes too wised-up—one might say lyrically enhanced, but at the same time it's gentle, not destructive, not finally distancing.

Recollections of intimate life, for all their significance, can't take us to origins. Family, on the other hand, does. In "Return to Seattle: Bastille Day," the poet begins by musing rhetorically,

> How could I go back
> to where I first took my age
> between my hands like a lover's face
> and said, "This far, no farther"?

But in the face of the changed daughter's encounter with her past life's sudden immediacy, rhetoric gives way to biography's status quo:

> My mother, 1945, stepping from
> the Armistice Day prop plane
> with her unchanged face,
> light off the Cascade rain fronts

troubling her memory with its danger,
years before she could blame
herself for everything.

Ambivalence toward home is the right of all, and anxiety about origins can further mute the neutral tones of place with the shade of self-awareness. The destinies of families certainly look fixed: the mother's universal acceptance of blame takes place in a culture and time unlike that of the daughter. Her sacrifice seems at once limited and overwhelming, not fitting—except by forced thought—the time or the imagination. But if family is destiny, then return is a trap. Everybody in the family is in the process of manufacturing avoidance: father's sleepwalking, sister's vanishing, mother's vague-but-vast self-recriminations. It is not the place to find restoration; neither is it a hell of dysfunction.

Likewise, in "A Reply to Storms in New Orleans," the poet remembers those evenings of resounding climatic threats whose outcomes could go either way. The memory is brought back, mythically enlarged, by that city's image of the seasonal deluge:

> No nightly pyrotechnics,
> no Voudoun-Thor hurling his thunderbolts
> upside the sky, great swags of rain-laurel
> slapping the jalousies. Never the dull
> pressing-down of cloud cover, breezeways
> in heat-stunned swelter, saltwater
> glaze on the skin. Not the river
> twelve feet above the city, the levee
> that cradles the current in its arms
> rolling slow as thunder. No monsoon's
> straight-down drench, Creole sweetness
> and crepuscule making an evening of afternoon.

Our vulnerability exists both as danger and opportunity, to say nothing of the sense of menace, becoming hard to distinguish from victimization, indifference, or for that matter, baptism. Chalk the confusion up to sub-tropic swelter, and you've understood how ambivalence imparts its regime on memory itself, whose own daughter was the Muse. In the end, the poet remembers how her mother ("younger than she'd ever be again") once soothed her brother over the *Stürm und Drang* of another kind of wild weather—that of the Northwest, precursors of wilder metaphysical storms surely to come.

In the echolalic "Unfinished Country," Wright imagines emotion as space,

> "How high the moon?" we talked around ourselves
> as air and ocean switched polarities
> over the heart's unfinished country.

The image-complex includes not only geographic space, but outer space ("solar wind") and moon. As if in response to her seemingly disingenuous question, the poet's Diogenes' quest for truth falters under its own circularity:

> Hands recall their bruising rhythms
> that linger like multiple entendres
> over the darkening bluffs.

And so, as is so often the move Wright executes, there is little reductive truth to take home, but plenty of emotional experience left to make a claim:

> The truth—
> we hesitated, lost ourselves in lamplight
> while nighthawks circled, crying for direction.

The prospect of "the heart's unfinished country," neither to be easily discovered or divulged, is a few pages later raised anew to form an answer in the form of a question: "the heart's / subzero weather?" ("Celebration for the Cold Snap"). Say what you will: a poet like this saves string and is not without resources.

"*Bildungsgedicht*," as the full-mouthed title suggests, examines adolescent temptations, here set in cheap cityscapes, almost as if it were a poet's duty to cruise to the beat of adolescent rock, back in the day

when low was low and high, invisible. Of course this is but another
variant of the Bishopian theme enunciated by Robinson Crusoe
("homemade, homemade' but aren't we all!"). The requisite boyfriend
who in his bathos is lame enough to say "ta" instead of goodbye, is also
a full-blown male chauvinist ("your mascara's smeared"). He pens a
song for her ("Hey you're gonna dig this song"); he follows this not
long after with casual betrayal: "he brought blonde Suzie / to the
Food Court, I sobbed by the Orange Julius machine." But what upsets
her more than this boorish display is the failure of imagination:

> His tenor was smokey and nasal
> like Dylan in "A Hard Rain's Gonna Fall."
> "Well?" he looked me up and down. "Symbolical,"
> I breathed, not yet knowing the word cliché
> or bright moments of love's throwaways.

But Shakespeare-the-Fixer puts all to rights when the poet turns
to her part in a local production of "The Tempest" ("'Clear, concise,
poetic,' the reviewer wrote of my part"):

> I went home and tore up Johnny's song, wrote one
> and tore it up. If I couldn't be with him
> I wouldn't be him. I opened the Cambridge edition
> of Shakespeare, and told my mother the truth.
> I'm starting a poem.

No less a diva than Akhmatova noted in what trashy neighborhoods our masterpieces have their origins. One of the ironies that
emerges from *A Change of Maps* is how the poet's natural nobility
reflects not merely on the insufficient and self-involved, but on the
class pretensions that emanate from and limit such an iconic, sacro-
sanct figure as Bishop.

Similarly, in "Cult Hero" another poet figure—this one
unnamed—contrasts parodically with the poet as cultural custodian, his male grooviness combining the effortless cheese of the
rock wannabe with the winsomeness of the lover. As anonymous and
yet ubiquitous as Pan, this person "vanishes" and in a way that is his

truth—leaving us with our disillusionment. The poet suggests that our first mature literary steps are situated upon just such disillusionment, and that fact is persuasive ("our best rhetoric"). Is instruction, then, somehow modeled by a fickle lover's abandonment? Leaving us with "nothing" (the culmination, you might suppose, of love's "nothings") may only lead to the negative space of opportunity: it is purposeful enough? Does it leave a clear enough space? Still, like his more famous poet/teacher, something of the lessons of poetry cash out the same way—in different denominations, to be sure, but according to the same script (scrip?): faith, disillusion, departure, revision.

Knowing that no knowledge ever arrived without its emotional weather system, Wright gives us the lover as deflated demon in "After All Is Said and Done": "I ride past your house, my body / heavy with total recall." Like a meteorologist (whose likeness to a cartographer would be noted here monitoring the course of systems), Wright monitors the divergence that occurs between lovers, whose persons change readily into cyphers.

> We were too alone for the long haul,
> we hadn't yet learned
> doubt's forwarding addresses.

As Clare noted, those we love the best are stranger than any others; thus maturation, whether for the emotional being or the artistic one, is often antithetical to one's motives in seeking love in the first place. Look how far the once-beloved travels:

> You've sat in the medicine circles
> between shamans who carved
> the spirit poles: ravens and seals
> under the rain spell, cured
> of the vision called forever.
> I live with shopping malls.

Which is better? The question of the difference between high and low art is perennial, never more so than for poets who passed from the 60s through the theory-correcting late 70s and 80s to the whatever 90s and beyond, assimilating and synthesizing, cherry-picking inspirations from the downlow to the transcendently high-brow. Shopping malls don't make the shamans look any better by contrast. In fact, as a comparable destiny, the shopping mall makes the shaman look, well, diminished.

There are too many good poems here to discuss, but I will mention just a few for their combination of formal felicities, savvy diction, and controlled voice. "Darwin's House at Downe (Closed Fridays)" looks at the ever-changing nature of memory—with poems, like specimens, overseeing and managing the freight of detail like the great naturalist's taxonomies. "Another Look at 'Albion on the Rock': Plate 38 of Blake's *Milton*," one of several sestinas (I haven't seen such a commitment to the form since Marilyn Hacker's debut over three decades ago) considers the waves and emanations from Blake's great vision to the contemporary poet's vision that "love is our wealth. It holds nothing in its hands." "As I Drive over an Irrigation Ditch at the End of Summer, I Think of Small-Town American Preacher" is a dead-on parody of James Wright's mid-America evocation of lonely Chinese questers updated to millennial evangelism in the context of Y2K, OPEC and nuclear silos.

Carolyne Wright's journey through nearly four decades shows that the past is often a world that resists disclosure, and yet the fact is less a fact about the past than a fact about our ability to find signposts among contingent scenarios. Wright has this ability; which is less a concession to the spell of technique (which she owns) than a kind of knowledge about poetry's secret sway and coterie wisdom and therefore of abiding interest to poetry's serious readers—be they ever so few—who know that the intramural is what we used to call the universal, but know also that that is no come-down but a field promotion fitting for the lean hereafter.

Acknowledgments

Gratitude goes to *The Cortland Review* (www.cortlandreview.com), where most of these pieces and all of the reviews first appeared. Thanks to the editor Ginger Murchison for her continual support and encouragement, as well as he editorial suggestions and corrections. Thanks to publisher Guy Shahar, *without which not.* Also thanks to Phong Bui, Editor of *The Brooklyn Rail*, Kevin Craft, editor of *Poetry Northwest,* John Lawson, editor of a *Precisely There: A Festschrift for Ron Bayes* (Palisade Press, 2010), and the late Ralph Cohen, editor of *New Literary History (Remembering Richard Rorty,* Volume 39, number 1). "Preface to *Margaret Rabb: Greatest Hits 1987-2009,*" Kattywompus Press, 2009. Diane Goettel has offered wise and gentle encouragement of this collection, and my gratitude to her is deep. Angela Leroux-Lindsey has likewise trained a keen and candid eye on this book, and it has benefitted from her expertise.

Works discussed:

Betty Adcock: *Slantwise,* LSU Press, 2008 (*Cortland Review,* Issue 55)

David Baker: *Never-Ending Birds,* W. W. Norton, 2009 (*Cortland Review,* Issue 47)

John Balaban: *Path, Crooked Path,* Copper Canyon Press, 2006 (*Cortland Review,* Spring 2007 Feature)

Laure-Anne Bosselaar: *A New Hunger,* Ausable Press, 2007 (*Cortland Review,* Issue 36)

Kurt Brown: *No Other Paradise,* Red Hen Press, 2010 (*Cortland Review,* Issue 48)

Michael Burkard: *Lucky Coat Anywhere,* Nightboat Books, 2010 (*Cortland Review,* Issue 52)

Jane Cooper, *The Flashboat: Poems Collected and Reclaimed*, W.W Norton &
    Co., 2000 (*The Brooklyn Rail*, May-June 2001)
Mary Cornish: *Red Studio*, Oberlin College Press, (*Cortland Review*, Issue
    35)
Stephen Dobyns: *Winter's Journey*, Copper Canyon Press, 2010 (*Cortland
    Review*, Issue 49)
Stephen Dunn: *Here and Now*, W. W. Norton, 2011 (*Cortland Review*, Win-
    ter 2010 Feature)
Claudia Emerson: *Secure the Shadow*, LSU Press, 2012 (*Cortland Review*,
    Spring 2012 Feature)
Tess Gallagher: *Midnight Lantern*, Graywolf Press, 2010 (*Cortland Review*,
    Issue 53)
Linda Gregg: *All of It Singing: New and Selected Poems*, Graywolf Press,
    2008 (*Cortland Review*, Issue 41)
John Kinsella: *Divine Comedy*, W. W. Norton, 2008 (*Cortland Review*, Issue
    44)
Carolyn Kizer: *Cool Calm and Collected*, Copper Canyon Press 2000 (*Poetry
    Northwest*, Spring-Summer 2011)
Dorianne Laux: *Superman: The Chapbook*, Red Dragonfly Press, 2008
    (*Cortland Review*, Spring 2009 Feature)
Philip Levine: *News of the World*, Knopf, 2011 (*Cortland Review*, Winter
    2009 Feature)
Sarah Lindsay: *Twigs and Knucklebones*, Copper Canyon Press, 2008 (*Cor-
    tland Review*, Issue 42)
Thomas Lux: *God Particles*, Houghton Mifflin, 2008 (*Cortland Review*,
    Issue 42)
Anne Marie Macari: *She Heads into the Wilderness*, Autumn House Press,
    2008 (*Cortland Review*, Issue 46)
Peter Makuck: *Long Lens: New and Selected Poems*, BOA Editions Ltd., 2010
    (*Cortland Review*, Issue 48)
McFadden, Patrick, Parks, and Chang: *Hardscrabble* by Kevin McFadden,
    University of Georgia Press, 2008, *Boy* by Patrick Phillips, University
    of Georgia Press, 2008, *Field Folly Snow* by Cecily Parks, University of
    Georgia Press, 2008, *The History of Anonymity* by Jennifer Chang, Uni-
    versity of Georgia Press, 2008 (*Cortland Review*, Issue 39)
Joseph Millar: *Blue Rust*, Carnegie Mellon University Press, 2011 (*Cort-
    land Review*, Issue 54)
Mihaela Moscaliuc: *Father Dirt*, Alice James Books, 2010 (*Cortland Review*,
    Issue 50)

Gregory Orr, *The River inside the River*, W. W. Norton Co., 2013 (*Cortland Review*, Winter 2012 Feature)

Richard Rorty, *New Literary History* ("Remembering Richard Rorty," vol. 39 no. 1)

Gibbons Ruark: *Staying Blue*, Lost Hills Books, 2008 (*Cortland Review*, Issue 43)

Alan Shapiro: *Night of the Republic*, Houghton Mifflin Harcourt, 2012 (*Cortland Review*, Spring 2011 Feature)

Anis Shivani: *My Tranquil War*, NYQ Books, 2013 (*Cortland Review*, Issue 64)

Judith Skillman: *Heat Lightning: New and Selected Poems 1986- 2006*, Silverfish Press, 2006 (*Cortland Review*, Issue 41)

Gerald Stern: *Save the Last Dance*, W. W. Norton, 2008 (*Cortland Review*, Winter 2008 Feature)

Van Jordan: *Quantum Lyrics*, W. W. Norton, 2007 (*Cortland Review*, Winter 2007 Feature)

Michael Waters: *Darling Vulgarity*, BOA Editions, Ltd., 2006 (*Cortland Review*, Issue 38)

C.K. Williams: *Wait*, Farrar Straus, and Giroux, 2011 (*Cortland Review*, Winter 2011 Feature)

David Rigsbee is the author of *School of the Americas* and *The Pilot House,* both from Black Lawrence Press. He is the recipient of a two National Endowment for the Arts Fellowships in Literature and fellowships from The Djerassi Foundation, The Virginia Commission on the Arts, The National Endowment for the Humanities, and the Fine Arts Work Center in Provincetown. He is the author of critical studies of Carolyn Kizer and Joseph Brodsky and has coedited *Invited Guest: An Anthology of Twentieth Century Southern Poetry.* He is contributing editor of *The Cortland Review* and lives in Hudson, New York.